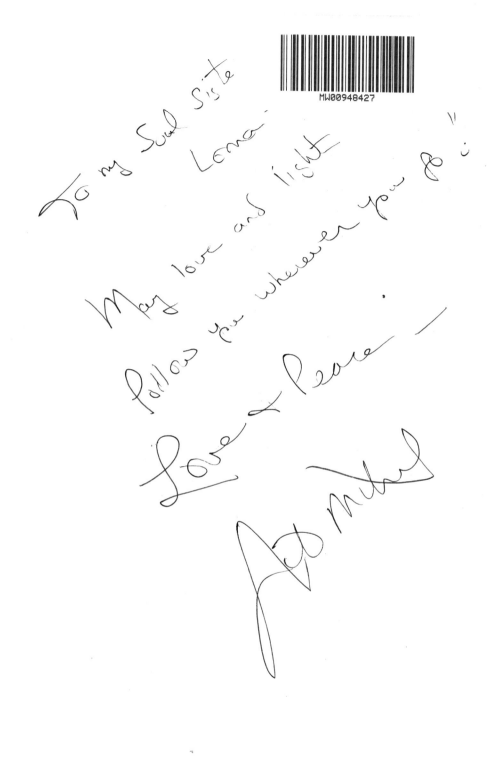

To my Soul Sister
Lena —

May love and light

follow you wherever you go

Love & Peace —

Unveiling Rosanna

Unveiling Rosanna

ISBN: 1974669343

ISBN-13: 978-1974669349

To my son Troy for your unconditional love and support.

To my sister Lisa, love of my heart,

and Debbie Fredette, a friend through eternity.
This one's for you, Deb!

Michael, thank you! I am forever grateful.

- Gail

ACKNOWLEDGEMENTS

I am grateful to my friends and family who supported me during this pivotal time in my life.

Thank you, Troy for loving me as I longed for this island in the middle of the Mediterranean. I'm happy we both saw it together for the first time so you knew why it was pulling me so. Each time I called home missing you, you were always excited that I was living my dream; you were also the voice of reason and logic on the other end of the telephone line. Today, I am proud of who you have become as a successful writer. I am inspired by you every day.

Special thanks to my editor Jennifer Agamata who often tried to reel me in from my fanciful writing. She was patient with me each time I over-wrote her edits. But I finally did listen to her guidance. I am getting better! Nonetheless, I apologize for any typos you, my readers, might find. I also thank my dear friend and Italian editor, Anna Gargiulo, and my proof-reader, Matt Warrener.

I thank Santa Maria, San Francesco and all who whispered to me and protected me along the way. Thank you, Michael for always being there. You were the force behind me who believed in me when I did not believe in myself. Each time I awoke in Capri with doubts, you sent me a message or an angel. And finally, thank you for very carefully slicing open my heart like a ripened pomegranate, all the little seeds spilling out.

To the people of Anacapri, I have used some of your names because they are so beautiful to me, and I have changed others so that your personal lives will remain just that. I have described many of you just as I remember you because I fell in love with your faces, your personalities, and who you are. For others, I have changed you or embellished your character with my imagination. All in all, it is a fabricated story that has come out of my mind and my heart.

Franco, I could not have done this without you. I thank you and your family for your love and support. Ilario Panullo, I thank you. You are sorely missed. You guided me, watched, over me, and you and your family took me into your home for memorable meals filled with love, life, laughter and amazing Italian food. Thank you, Enza and thank you Marilu and Rosa for being my long-lost Italian sisters. I cherish our love and friendship.

To Federico Salvatore and all my other friends in Anacapri—you all know who you are and what parts you played in my story. I am grateful to you for showing me loving kindness as I lived amongst you while I wrote to my heart's content.

Finally, thank you, Natale, for inspiring me to write this story.

With love and gratitude,

Gail Riena Michael

A NOTE FROM THE AUTHOR

The Birth of Roxanna -

In 1875 the Swedish doctor Axel Munthe, sailed to Capri and climbed the 770 Phoenician Steps to the little village of Anacapri. When he arrived at the top of the island, he fell to his knees intoxicated and enraptured with the village, its people, the vistas and the San Michele chapel where he would eventually build his home—the now famous Villa San Michele and Museum. He had found heaven on earth.

I share a kindred spirit with Munthe. When I first arrived in Anacapri in 2004, I too was intoxicated. I knew nothing of the island until my son and I were planning a tour through Europe, our first. Little did I know it would change my life forever. Have you ever traveled to a place that stops you in your tracks and takes your breath away? That's how Capri affected me. The allure of the mystical isle was powerful. When we returned to the States, Capri was in my every thought. It was a longing, a love affair I had to explore further. Night after night, I dreamed of the place. I had to return.

Nine months later, I left for the island for an indefinite amount of time. I had to ... I was lifeless. I could no longer find my happiness. Something had to change.

Once there, I spent the first few months at my small villa looking out over the aqua Mediterranean, Mount Vesuvius, the Bay of Naples and the islands of Ischia and Procida. Aromatic flowers covered the grounds and lined the gardens. The highlight of each day was watching the sun as it dripped diamonds onto the golden turquoise sea, then set into it. I sat for hours, memories of my life playing out before me. There was nothing to do but allow the memories of my life to come forth, accept them, heal them and finally release them. It sounds easier than it was. Someone once told me, "the mind is a dangerous place and it's best not to go there alone." Mine had traveled with me all the way from America and shared my bed with me each night, even in paradise. It was time to face myself and my ego.

Soon, we healed, both Deborah and me. I began to study the language, and soon knew enough to communicate in Italian. So, I ventured out and started to meet the locals who watched over me and told me where to go, where to shop and where to eat. The most pleasurable moments of my days were walking to town for food and supplies and stopping to say ciao and converse with them. I had never done this in America. As I look back on my life, I realize I had encased myself inside my home, my routine, and my unhappiness.

It took two months to heal all those parts of myself that I had long ago forgotten or hidden away. I was ready. I crossed the Bay to the mainland and that is when my adventures began. I took the train to Rome and then to Tuscany where I visited Pisa, Lucca, the Chianti countryside and Florence. On another trip, I took the train into Rome, met Natale and stayed for a while. Next, I traveled to Assisi and Venice.

I had been back to my villa for a few days when two friends invited me to tour the Basilicata and Campania regions with them. The trip was enchanting, sacred, heart-opening and quite comical. After all, this was the south of Italy, home of southern Italians with super-sized hearts who naturally express what they are feeling.

I eventually traveled to Greece where I visited Athens, Delos,

Mykonos and Santorini. This is where I met the pirates…

My playground was the Amalfi Coast where I roamed through Sorrento, Vietri sul Mare, Ravello, the town of Amalfi, Positano and Napoli. I visited the islands around Capri and the lost city of Pompeii.

When I decided to follow my dreams and go to Capri, I knew I would be writing a book but I did not know what it would be about until two months before I returned to the States. Roxanna did not fully form until I had healed (body, mind and spirit) and moved into a place of oneness within myself. Only then was I able to create a character such as this.

She starts out slowly but is courageous in facing her demons. I love her for her depth and strength and for never giving up. As each new day passes, she awakens more and more. She learns to trust and soon begins to follow spirit without trepidation. Only then is she able to create such magical and mystical experiences.

I have been asked, "Did you really experience all the adventures in the story? Which are real?" Good questions I can tell you that although I am divorced, my husband was not unfaithful to me like Ed was in the story. This was based on an experience from my past. However, I did go to Rome and meet Natale, and I was on the 18th century schooner with three Greek men in the Cyclades, my modern-day pirates. I was in the castle in the Chianti countryside, and I stood in front of The David in Florence when someone … never mind. You will have to read the story to find out more. I traveled to all the locations and settings that Roxanna did but I will not reveal any more secrets. I prefer to let your imagination run wild.

Everything I have written in these pages has happened somewhere inside my world—either inside my head or in my reality. Most of the events (Roxanna's adventures) that take place are "loosely" based on my own experiences. After all, I am a writer with a wild imagination, an overstuffed heart and have worn rose-colored glasses most of my life. The book is fiction.

If you are a woman searching for meaning in your life, please follow your dreams and find your own Capri. Once you discover the place that feeds your soul, it will ignite that flame within you and bring you into alignment with your passions and your purpose ... and you will have the most delicious adventure!

Unveiling Rosanna is a rewrite and revision of *The Passions of Roxanna* which was released in 2008 (no longer in print). The story has changed.

TABLE OF TRAVELS

CHAPTER 1
ISLE OF CAPRI, ITALY

"**F**aster, faster!" My heart beats wildly as the taxi driver speeds through the streets from the train station to the port. The crowded city sprawls before me, a web of ancient buildings stacked one on top of another. Traffic clogs the streets; horns honk and people everywhere speak an unfamiliar language.

"Please, faster. I can't miss the last boat."

"Signora, no go faster. Too dangerous, even for us *Napoletani*. I think you miss the last boat."

"Just try, please."

The taxi reeks of stale cigarette smoke and cheap cologne. A plastic statue of Santa Maria hangs from the mirror and sways back and forth with every turn. My stomach lurches. When did I last sleep? I flew from California to Munich ... a seven-hour layover ... the train ride from Rome to Napoli ... I'm too tired to think.

We arrive at the port.

"I hope I'm not too late." I speak my thoughts aloud, unable to keep them inside my head. I throw twenty-five euros through the window.

"*Grazie, Signora*."

Grabbing my small suitcase and laptop, I dash to buy my hydrofoil ticket to the Island of Capri.

"No, no. Gone. Last one. *Domani*, tomorrow." The seller says in his broken English as he prepares to close.

"You don't understand. I have to get there tonight."

He slams the window shut still talking to me as if I can hear him. Oh, I can't think straight ... this fog in my head. Exhaustion has taken hold of me. I walk out to the water's edge, put down my suitcase and sit on it. My eyelids shut.

"Una barca, signora?"

I look up at the silhouette of a man blocking the sun. His wife beater is stained, his hair dirty and unkempt. A gold Italian horn hangs from his neck on a thick chain.

"Yes, I need to get to Capri. Do you have a boat?"

"Si." He smiles at me.

"Quanto costa?" I'm surprised I remember any Italian at all.

"Cinquanta euro." Crusted spittle lines the corner of his mouth.

"Fifty? That's too high."

"Signora, you miss last boat." He shrugs his shoulders and cocks his head to one side.

He's right. I must get there tonight. But where will I stay? Not now ... I hand him cash and follow him to his boat where another man waits. The old fishing boat doesn't look seaworthy. A large puddle covers the floorboards and a small bucket lies on its side half-filled with water.

"I want my money back!"

"Silly American." He winks at me with his toothless grin. "Me and my brother Mario sail this boat to Capri for twenty years. You safe with us."

Stupid girl.

I say a prayer and step down into the boat. I sit and he throws me a life vest. His brother Mario is more disheveled than he is, if this is possible.

"Put on. *Calmati,* calm down."

The old boat chugs out to sea. Wait ... if he's going to Capri anyway, why is he charging me so much? Thoughts of bartering dissipate as that familiar mist of exhaustion causes a disconnect. Water laps against the old boat. The seafoam green sea before me looks like a painting, its colors shimmering in the sunlight. My mind drifts from one thought to another.

After the dream, I was searching the internet for a Los Angeles art museum when the island of Capri appeared on the screen. A sign. How could I not come?

Will I get there without this boat sinking? I'm too tired to swim so I wouldn't be able to save myself. I could end up at the bottom of the sea and no one would know. My eyes close.

How strange that I was led here. Everything happens for a reason. I remember reading that the island is only four-square miles with 12,000 inhabitants. There are two villages—Capri, a town above the port, and Anacapri, a village at the top of the island. How did I remember this? I laugh out loud and startle both men. They turn to me, wide-eyed with concern.

Anacapri calls to me. It makes no sense. My boys. Oh ... they're safe ... with their father. Now I remember. I saw them before I left and they told me to go and follow my dreams. "There's more to life than being a mother," they said. My little boys have grown up so fast. They're now sixteen and seventeen. Mothering was my biggest role and I loved it. I was so attached to them, doted on them.

"Vesuvio," Luca says as he points to the mountain in the distance. It appears to have two peaks but I know it's because of the eruption in 79 A.D. which blew its top off.

He points to a small island, "Procida." Then he points to another island and say, "Ischia." He smiles dreamily and points to the island before us, "Capri."

Luca gazes off in the distance, his eyes half-closed, his breath caught as if Capri is not an island but a woman he has known intimately. After a few moments, he recovers.

"I make delivery in Marina Piccola. Then, I take you Marina Grande." I have no idea where Marina Piccola is so I nod.

The sea is aqua, even out here in open waters. It's so calm ... smells sweet and salty ... feels like a movie ... the light ... can't keep my eyes open ...

How unfamiliar my life has become as if I'm being guided by the gods to do unthinkable things. Not long ago, I dreamt about leaving my job of five years. And now, just weeks after the dream, I resigned. My friends and co-workers thought I'd gone mad. My best friend, Gretchen told me that if I were a man, this would be called a midlife crisis.

Laughter escapes me. Mario turns quickly and yells over the sound of the motor.

"You okay?"

"Yes." I barely get the word out.

The dream ... It was always the same. I'm standing with another on the cliffs looking out to sea. I cannot see his face.

"You belong here. This is the home of your ancient ones and they are calling to you. Here, you will find what you are searching for." He places his hand on my shoulder, something my father used to do.

"But how will I get there? I have responsibilities ... my job, my boys."

"Ah, silly human. Don't you know you can have anything you desire? All you need is a dream in your heart, focus within your mind and the intention and knowingness that you already have it. This is all you need. Remember the formula. You will be on this island, your homeland, sooner than you think. Remember me, for I will come to you once you arrive."

How is it possible that I am awake, sitting in this boat, yet inside this dream ... at the same time? How can this be? The wind rises up and plays with my hair, tossing it gently, to and fro. I notice the dampness on my bare skin. The air ... so sweet ... the seawater like perfume. I smile through my fatigue.

"I will come to you on the wind," his voice echoes in my ears. The setting sun casts its orange glow across the aqua waters before me. Am I dreaming?

I'm back on the cliffs of Anacapri, the scent of flowers ... the breeze ... the sounds of the sea, a boat horn.

"Your name shall be Roxanna. You were born of the rocks and the sea. Your mother," he points to the Mediterranean Sea ... "and your father," he points toward Mount Vesuvius. "You are coming home."

I know this to be true. I can feel it. Roxanna, a name of strength, of someone who could accomplish anything ... my home, Capri ... I am no longer Deborah Allen of America.

"You mutha fucka!"

"A fung ooo! Ba Ba Ba Ba ..."

"No, you Ba Ba Ba Ba ..."

I'm suddenly pulled from my daydream. These two crazy Italians are standing toe-to-toe, fists clenched, shouting in a dialect I can barely make out.

My God, what have I done!

I'm now alert, but slow on my feet.

They could capsize the boat, or rob me and then throw me overboard! A weapon.

I rummage through my purse.

Mace!

I hold my perfume spray bottle out in front of me. Mario turns to me, teeth gnashing.

He's coming!

Everything stops. So quiet ... the mist ... angels singing ... calling me ... louder ... LOUDER ...

Mario grabs me.

CHAPTER 2

I slip through Mario's arms and fall to the floorboards like a ragdoll. I'm slumped over in the pool of water that has deepened since we left the port in Napoli. I pass out but soon awaken to the sounds of the two arguing.

"Sheet! Sheet!" (I think this means shit).

"*Mamma mia. W*hat did you do to her?" asks Luca who is docking the boat. Mario tries to pull me up, but I slip through his arms, weak and exhausted.

"*Niente!* I do nothing. She just falla' like a sack a *patate*, potatoes!"

"Not good, Mario! *Non va bene*! Now we will be arrested for bringing in illegal cheeses and *vino!*"

"We throw her into the sea and *partiamo,* leave!" I open my mouth to speak but I cannot. I still hear the singing ...

"*Basta,* stop!" A stranger hears the commotion and comes running. "What have you done to her?"

"Nothing! I swear to Santa Maria." Luca blesses himself. "We help this crazy American and she faint."

The man jumps into the boat and speaks to both men in Italian. Although I cannot move, I hear everything. Someone has bent down and is close to my face. He pries open my eyes and examines my pupil. I feel his mouth upon mine.

Ahhh ... his lips ... I'm dazed. I open my eyes. He helps me to sit up.

"Can you hear them?" I ask.

"Who?"

"Angels." But they quickly fade. I'm embarrassed.

"I don't hear anything," he responds. "You must have heard the voices of *le sirene*. That is the *Scoglio delle Sirene,* the Rock of the Sirens over there."

He points toward the large rocks jutting out of the sea, each wave crashing down upon them. He would tell me later that the three sirens would sit on these rocks at night and call to the sailors and the pirates to come to them. When they came, they would be trapped by these women of the sea, lost here forever, never to return to their homeland.

"No, it cannot be." I'm confused.

"Not everyone hears them, but you did. Are you okay?"

"Yes, yes, I'm fine. I'm sorry. I haven't slept in a few days. Long trip." He picks me up and carries me off the boat.

"Thank you."

I try to collect myself and strain to hear the voices again but Luca's and Mario's loud and angry voices drown out even the sounds of the sea.

"Piano, piano ... easy," the Swede says to them as he tries to quiet them.

Mamma mia, mamma mia!" They continue to yell. The engine races as Mario tosses my bags onto the dock. Luca throws the boat into reverse and they quickly leave.

The stranger sets me down and picks up my suitcase and backpack.

"Where are you staying, *Signora?*"

"I don't know. I don't have a room yet. Do you know where I might find one?" I'm mesmerized by him.

"Hmmm, it's Easter weekend and it seems everyone has come to the island. By the way, my name is Peter, and I have a car. Come. I will help you."

"I'm Roxanna. Thank you for your kindness." I blush. I brush wet strands of hair from my eyes and try and smooth out my wet clothing.

God, he's handsome. I could use a shower. When was my last one?

He makes a call on his cellphone. I don't understand a word since he's speaking in Swedish. I look him over. He's tall, dressed in slacks and a casual jacket, both the color of the sun. His jawline is strong and he has light-colored hair. His eyes are an iridescent green that change each time I peek at them. They stop me in my tracks and twist my mind.

He ends the call. "I have a place for you. Can you walk?"

"Yes, I'm fine now. Thank you."

He places his arm around my shoulder and guides me to his small car. The heel of my sandal catches between the cobblestones and I stumble and fall into him. He grabs hold of me with his strong arms, then stands me upright. He kneels, removes my broken sandal and stuffs it into his pocket. Then he smiles as if it was nothing. I'm too exhausted to be embarrassed.

"Okay?"

"Yes."

We reach the car. He opens the door, helps me in and fastens my seatbelt. All this closeness is making me dizzy.

"Thank you for your help, Peter. I'm so grateful you came along."

"No problem. You would have been in trouble with those two. They would have dumped you into the Mediterranean if they had a chance." He laughs.

Much time goes by while I sit quietly looking at the scenery as the little car climbs the mountainous road. The houses are whitewashed and most have open-air terraces. Later, the islanders would tell me proudly that the architecture is called Caprese style. There are no guard rails, only small plants and little rocks along the edge. The vista is magnificent even at this time of day when dusk edges its way in. We are eight hundred meters above the sea and the boats seem so small. It takes my breath away.

"Ah, *bellissima.*" He points to the marina far below. "Marina Grande, the main port. That is where you should have come in. Marina Piccola is our beach where we swim."

"What's the name of the hotel?"

I try to make conversation in the long silence that follows although I'm incapable of it, too exhausted to put words together.

"It is not a hotel. It's the San Michele Villa. I manage the museum which is on the property. I have connections. We have a room available so you may have it."

"No, no. I can't put you out like that."

"It is not a problem. Many come to the island to do work for the foundation or perform in our concerts so the rooms are there for those who need a place to stay. For now, there is room for you."

My brain misfires and I forget to ask about the foundation. Then the car bounces and Peter slams on the brakes to allow a bus to pass that has approached us from the opposite direction. I'm now alert.

"Don't be alarmed. We all know how to drive this road."

Acutely aware of how narrow the road is, I hold my breath as we hug the curves.

"It's incredible."

"Yes, when most come to visit, they never want to leave. Is this your first time on Capri?"

"Yes."

"Ah, it will work its charm on you." He smiles.

We pull into a small driveway, park the car and walk along a small street called *Traversa Capodimonte.* Peter uses an electronic card to open the gate and we enter a circular courtyard filled with color. The grounds are stunning with sculptures, flowers and tall palm trees. Even in the fading light I can see their outline and am assaulted by their scent as we move past them. I close my eyes and breathe in the perfume of night jasmine mingled with geranium and rose.

"*Fiori* … the island is known for its flowers—especially this time of year." He smiles. "This way."

He holds the door for me and we walk through a corridor and up a flight of stairs to the second level. It's quite a large villa with many hallways, terraces and stairways. We come to an apartment and Peter unlocks the door. He gestures for me to enter. There before me is a double bed dressed in Italian linens. I can already feel their touch upon my skin. He tells me where everything is in the small apartment, but nothing registers. My brain is no longer working, only misfiring from lack of sleep.

"I see you are very tired. If you need anything at all, my rooms are at the front of the villa on the left as we entered. Knock and I will come. Sleep well, Roxanna."

He smiles and leaves, closing the door behind him. I barely find my toothbrush, brush my teeth and wash my face before I fall onto the bed and into a restless sleep for the next twelve hours.

I dream all night. The spirit has taken me somewhere on the island. We come to an outlook, a portico where a great marble sphinx is perched upon a wall overlooking the sea.

"Lay your hands upon him and make a wish." The voice comes to me on the wind. I reach out and place my hand on its back.

"I wish for the answers to all that I'm searching for. I wish for freedom in my life and passion like I have never known before ... I wish for a great love." This I whisper even more quietly than the rest as if it were a secret I don't want anyone to hear but the gods themselves. Every word I speak is a surprise to me as if it's someone else is speaking them.

"As you wish, Roxanna. You will have it all and more." His laughter echoes around me. "You are in for the ride of your life. So get in, sit down and hold on. Your tiger awaits you ... or should I say, your sphinx. Ha, ha!" Then he's gone.

CHAPTER 3

I awaken disoriented and realize twelve hours have passed. It takes me a few moments to remember where I am, but when I do, I'm filled with glee.

I've made it. I'm here.

I remember pieces of the dream ... my conversation with the spirit ... the sphinx. I've never even seen a sphinx before, but remember how massive it was. I never saw its face as it was sitting on a ledge looking out over the water.

Spirit came to me again, just as he said he would. Who is he? What did I ask for? Answers ... I asked for answers ... and freedom ... passion ... and wait ... did I ask for a great love? Where did that come from? I haven't thought about love since my divorce from Ed. I will never allow myself to be hurt again. Never. But now, I feel the heat of passion burning inside me and think about making love for the first time in years. How long has it been? I can't even remember ... oh, yes ... Ed's affair and the end of my marriage. I grimace.

I'm fifty now. Life has passed so quickly. I'm no different than any other woman. Everyone I knew who had already reached fifty said it would be difficult, but I said it wouldn't be for me. I was wrong. My body had changed, my breasts had inched down my chest. My skin was a bit dryer and my face started to show my life as if it were a roadmap. I never really believed that age mattered, but as a woman walking through the doorway to fifty, it really does. I was a twenty-year-old girl as I entered the portal, or so I believed. But once I stepped through to the other side, I became a middle-aged woman.

My passions still run deep. The scent of flowers still intoxicates me. My heart flutters with each sunset, taking my breath away. And to make love again ... it makes me nervous to think of it, but I would love to. My senses are suddenly heightened and my passions course through my body. Will it ever happen?

My stomach growls.

Knock-knock.

"Roxanna, are you awake?" I grab my robe and smooth my hair which is matted and dirty, sticking out everywhere from sleep and lack of a shower.

"Yes, just a minute." I open the door and Peter's green eyes greet me.

"I have *espresso* and a *cornetto*, a croissant for you. I know you must be hungry."

"Thank you, Peter. I'm starving," I say. I open the door to let him in and grab the pastry from his hand. I quickly stuff it into my mouth.

"I'm sure you need more than this so I wanted to ask you for lunch since it's noon.

"Yes, I'd like that."

He backs out the door and says, "I can see you need a bath, so I will meet you in the garden in an hour."

I walk into the bathroom and stare at myself in the mirror.

Oh my ... Mascara streaks my face and powdered sugar coats my lips and cheek. My barrette is sitting atop my head with only a few strands in it.

I'm a wreck. How embarrassing!

We sit in the *piazza* and our food has come—*panini,* sandwiches, *espresso* and *acqua naturale* with local lemon. I try to be lady-like but I'm famished and quickly devour everything set before me.

"Any luck in finding me a place for the next two weeks? I don't want to be a burden to you."

"It's not a problem. We have two empty apartments if we should need them. I've made quite a few calls but there are no rooms available on the island for the next week."

As I eat, Peter tells me about Anacapri and how it came about that tourists started coming to the little village at the top of the island. I'm mesmerized with his story and cannot take my eyes off his, their emerald green dazzling in the sunlight. He should put those things away so I can concentrate.

"Around 1876, a young eighteen-year-old medical student named Axel Munthe was in the south of Italy and decided to visit Capri for the day. Once he arrived, he climbed the 770 stone stairs to the top and came to the little village of Anacapri. He fell in love with it and its villagers and swore he'd come back and live here. Eventually, he bought the land that now houses the San Michele Hotel, the Villa, the gardens and the foundation. There's a lot more to it and it's quite an interesting story, but you'll have to read the book to get a feel for him and the story as he tells it. When he died, he left the villa, its property and all its artifacts to the Swedish government. Other properties on the island, which he had amassed over his lifetime, were split between his family and the Italian government. I work for the foundation that was set up to manage the villa."

"Do you live here year-round?"

"Most of the time, but the tourists stop coming to the island in the autumn, so I usually go home to Sweden for a few months then. What about you, Roxanna? Where do you live and what do you do?"

"I live in a small town in southern California, Carlsbad. I have two sons who are sixteen and seventeen. And I'm divorced ... have been for years. I left my job to come here and I'm not sure what I'll do when I return to the States. Maybe a new career ... maybe I'll paint and try to make a living doing that. I don't know yet ..."

A woman with long dark hair and dark eyes walks toward us.

"*Ciao, bello.*" She bends over and kisses Peter on the lips. I know she is his lover. It's the way she holds herself and the way

21

she approaches him, that dance of romance and intimacy. It's also a look they share as if they are remembering intimate moments together.

"Rosa, this is Roxanna, a new guest at the villa. I was telling her about Anacapri."

"*Ciao, bella*; nice to meet you." She's stunning, tall with a curvaceous Italian body. Her hair is long, thick, and dark, pulled back from her face by sunglasses that rest on top of her head. Her skin is smooth and she's dressed in a tight-fitting pencil skirt and tight top. Her breasts press against the fabric, anxious to be released. At the end of her long slender legs are open-toed, high-heeled sandals. I tuck my Mephisto sandals under the table and smooth out my wild hair.

I wish I had lipstick on. I extend my hand, my bitten-down nails noticeable.

"Nice to meet you, too. Would you like to join us?"

"No, no, *grazie*. I must go." As she turns to leave, she smiles at Peter, "See you tonight, *bello. Ciao.*" She blows him a kiss and then sashays across the *piazza*. All eyes follow her. I glance at Peter and see him blush.

"She's very beautiful. Did you meet her on the island?"

"Yes, yes, I did. We have been together for about six months now. She's a school teacher here in Anacapri."

She doesn't look like a typical school teacher. I need to go shopping.

"Where were we, Roxanna?"

"I'm finished, but what about you and your life?"

"I was born in Stockholm and went to university in London."

"Were you ever married? Any children?" He is surprised by my question. "I'm sorry. Was that too personal? You don't have to answer."

"No, no problem. Yes, I was married for ten years, but people change. We decided to divorce."

"Yes, they do."

"I have a daughter. She's fourteen and lives in Stockholm with her mother and stepfather. I visit her often and she comes to the island during school holidays."

We continue to talk about our children. Eventually, I'm finished eating and Peter asks for the bill. We pay and say our goodbyes.

I walk through the small village, looking for the *seggiovia,* the chairlift to *Monte Solaro.* Peter told me I must ride it to the top of the mountain to see the best vistas on the island. I find it and jump into the chair, the safety bar quickly slamming down. I hold on tightly and focus my gaze on the sea and the village of Anacapri below.

This is the vista from my dreams. I have been here before!

The hair on my arms stands straight up and I shiver.

Once at the top, I take in the view. *Il Faraglioni,* the three famous rock formations—*Stella, Mezzo and Scopolo*—jut out of the sea in the distance. They are part of the Campanian Archipelago and it is believed that if you boat through them and make a wish, your wish will come true.

Sorrento sits in the distance with Amalfi at its backside. A small chapel sits on a far-off hillside on the other side of the mountain. Before me, seagulls are flying halfway between here and the sea far below. What a strange thing to be up so high that the birds fly beneath you. Once my feet are back on solid ground, I snap pictures from every viewpoint and then sit on the veranda sipping *acqua minerale* and contemplate my life.

I had become weary after all those years. I had always been a responsible person but felt trapped by my life and desperately needed a break. I thought that if I was the perfect wife and mother, my life would be perfect and everyone would be happy. But it wasn't like that at all. At the end of every day, I felt empty ... not with my children, but in my marriage. I barely saw Ed. These days, he'd be called an absent dad and husband. Each morning, he raced out the door without breakfast, barely acknowledging us. Then, he'd come home late every night and work on weekends, too. Sports for the boys were my responsibility. He probably attended two or three games a year.

I thought it was me ... thought it was all my fault. I didn't understand why he was hardly ever home, so I made the commitment to work harder at it. My thoughts are interrupted by a breeze, the wind blowing my plastic cup over, spilling the water I have left in it. This immediately takes me out of my melancholy daydream.

I study the tourists that have just arrived and notice they are laughing and smiling, in awe of the beauty here. The flowers are in bloom everywhere—along the paths, in the fields along the mountain, and in the distance on the ridge halfway between here and Capri. For a few moments, all sound has halted and all I hear is the solitude and a distant horn from a hydrofoil below.

My mind is not used to sitting in this silence for long, so it hurries back to the life I just left behind … my boys, Josh and Devon. They are now young men and I'm so proud of them.

I was a good mom. I loved holding them, hugging them, rubbing their hair and whispering to them that all the pain in their world would magically disappear and rainbows would appear. They felt safe with me. I still miss their childhood and having them with me every day. I wasn't ready to share them between two households.

When they got older, on those nights they were to stay with me, I found myself sitting with dinner on the table waiting for them to come home. They would bound through the door, grab something from the table and run to their rooms to change their clothes only to leave again. They were grown, no longer needing me. I had already laid the foundation for them. It was time to let them go. But it took me a long time.

So, I decided to come to Capri, this mystical isle, to find out who I am. I burst into laughter at this thought. Here I am in the middle of the Mediterranean on the other side of the world and I have a new name and a spirit who talks to me in my dreams, driving me to do strange things …

I'm crazy as a loon. I start to giggle and cannot stop myself.

"*Scusi*, what is so funny, *Signorina?*"

I'm startled out of my thoughts. He moves to my table and sits in the empty chair across from me.

"Can you share your happiness with me?"

CHAPTER 4

I hesitate. He's a stranger. But he's gorgeous to look at—a perfect nose, chiseled lips and deep-set eyes. He's tall, his hair thick, black and curly, glistening from the gel that tames the wildness. He smiles wide, his white teeth blinding against his bronzed skin that has baked in the Caprese sun.

"I was just thinking," I say. He takes my hand to shake it and introduces himself.

"I am Antonio."

"I'm Roxanna. Nice to meet you, Antonio. Do you live here on the island?"

"Yes. I am born here. I am sorry my *Inglese* is not so good."

"It's fine, Antonio. Would you like to sit?"

"Are you alone, Rosanna? That is how we say your name in Italian."

"I like the sound of it. Yes, I arrived last night." Is it safe to say so? I had heard stories about the Italian men and how they liked to pinch … and God knows what else.

"Then I will be your tour guide for the island. There are many places for you to see. I will take you to all of them. I have a scooter."

"Thanks, Antonio. I'd like that."

"Would you like to go to Capri tomorrow afternoon? I will take you to the Ruins of the Villa Jovis? Tiberius built it in 79 A.D. and lived there. Emperor Julius Caesar Augustus lived there for eleven years. You will like it."

"It sounds like fun."

"Meet me at 15:00, you know, 3:00 p.m. at the bus stop in town. Once we reach Capri, we will park the bike and walk one hour to arrive at the ruins. I will bring picnic, yes?"

I laugh because his accent is sexy and his teeth are brilliant in the sunlight.

We sit and chat for an hour, and then take the *seggiovia* back to Anacapri. I blush as he kisses my cheeks in the Italian fashion. I'm not used to this custom that seems so intimate.

As I walk back to my apartment, I wonder how old he is. Maybe thirty? Why would this handsome, young man be interested in spending time with someone almost twice his age? My thoughts are interrupted by my growling stomach.

I find a kiosk, the aroma of basil and spaghetti sauce wafting on the air. I order a *panini* sandwich with tomatoes, mozzarella and basil called a *caprese*. Is everything called *caprese* here? I'm ravenous so I devour it on the spot. When I'm finished, I think about a long, hot bath and crawling into bed with my book. I still need to recover from my jet lag.

In bed, I begin reading Dr. Axel Munthe's book, *The Story of San Michele*. I'm excited to learn more about him since we share a bond. But after only five pages, I find my eyes heavy with sleep and I am gone from this world and into the next.

After breakfast at a cafe in the *piazza*, I stroll down a small street with shops on both sides. I smile to myself, for I remember Peter telling me that the Italians call a little street *una stradina*. I love the sound of this Italian phrase.

As I window-shop and watch the locals, I hear a familiar voice.

"Roxanna." I turn and find Peter, his eyes sparkling in the sunlight, sans sunglasses.

"I'm happy to have run into you. Is everything to your liking at the apartment?"

"Yes, thank you. I love the sounds of the birds that wake me up in the morning … and the smell of the flowers. They are incredible." I'm effusive.

"Do you have plans for the day?"

"Not really. I'm just roaming the streets to see where they will take me." I don't mention my afternoon sightseeing plans.

He takes my arm in his and we walk.

"Well then, I have somewhere special I want you to see." I like the way the people here are so demonstrative and not afraid to touch each other. In America, I have never linked arms with a friend like this.

We head down the path toward the San Michele Museum and Villa which is the original house that Dr. Axel Munthe had built. In his book, *The Story of San Michele,* he writes -

> *"I built the house on my knees, like a temple to the sun,*
> *where I would seek knowledge and light from the*
> *radiant God whom I had worshipped all my life."*

Yes, he has described this place perfectly—a temple to the sun. The villa is white with columns and porticos everywhere. So many photographs to take … so many sacred spots to remember. We enter the villa and walk through each room. As we move through the master bedroom, I notice Kouros, the statue that represents Greek youth, standing next to his bed. How strange that I have one in my bedroom as well. Ah, a bond between us. I was meant to come here.

We leave the house and enter the arched Sculpture Loggia—an open portico to the gardens filled with Munthe's art collection. The flooring is inlaid marble and a Cosmati table lies in the center of the room. Its top is a mosaic of intricately inlaid colored marble and gold. A life-size reproduction of *Mercury Resting*, a gift from the city of Naples, sits at the far end. Other sculptures line the loggia—a Helmeted Ulysses, a bust of the Emperor Tiberius, a life-size bronze of Artemis, the bust of Athena and many others. The loggia overlooks a courtyard where a replica of Verrocchio's fountain—*Boy with a Dolphin* sits in its center reminding me of children laughing and playing.

We move through the grounds, the gardens, an open gallery and then come upon the pergola supported by thirty-seven columns that Munthe designed himself. I know he must have spent many hours out here for I suddenly feel raised gooseflesh on my arms and his spirit all around me. It's as if he never left.

Peter tells me that Munthe wanted to build a house *"open to the sun and the wind and voices of the sea, like a Greek temple, with light, light everywhere."* And he has done so.

"It's beautiful, *paradiso*."

"I knew you'd like it."

We walk to the end of the pergola where we stop and gaze at the Marina Grande port far below.

"There," he points, "are the seven hundred and seventy-seven Phoenician Steps that Munthe climbed when he arrived in Anacapri that first day."

"So many steps ..." They descend, winding round and round until they reach the bottom of the island. It's picturesque. My desire to paint awakens and my body tingles all over as if my blood were made of little champagne bubbles. I've never seen anything, felt anything like this before. To live here forever ... wake up here ... walk here ... to bid good night to the stars and the sea before I retire ...

Be still, my heart.

This is how Munthe must have felt. I feel his soul upon this land, his breath whispering in my ear, "Take care of this place for me."

We walk up stone steps that lead to another portico.

"Wait until you see the chapel and the 3,200-year-old Egyptian sphinx."

My breath stops.

"A sphinx?"

The dream ... my feet are still moving one in front of the other although I'm frozen in time. There, sitting up on a ledge with its back to me, is the same grand sphinx as the one in my dream. It's framed by an arched window, a view of the sea behind it. Peter is speaking but I hear none of it.

"... They say if you have a wish, stroke its back and it will come true." His hand is upon mine as I reach for the sphinx's left hind quarter and rest it there.

I wish to feel passion every single day that I'm here, I whisper inside my own mind so that only the gods can hear. My heart beats wildly and I'm finally forced to take a breath.

"Are you okay, Roxanna?"

He notices the shock and wonderment on my face.

"I dreamt about this sphinx."

"Then it was your destiny to stay at the Villa."

I pull my hand from his, self-conscious that we are sharing this intimacy.

"Munthe also dreamt about the sphinx. In his dream, a spirit came to him and told him that one day, he would find it under the sea. And years later, when it was time, he had a second dream. This time, the spirit told him where it would be. So, he took his boat, sailed exactly to where he was told to go, found it, pulled it out of the water and brought it back here."

Did I hear correctly? A spirit also came to Munthe in a dream? And am I really standing on the same spot as he did, with a 3,200-year-old sphinx that I dreamt about?

"Come ... one more important place for you to see."

We arrive at the entrance of the San Michele Chapel and Peter steps back as if he is delivering me to San Michele, Archangel Michael himself.

Breathe ... don't forget to breathe, Roxanna. Tears escape me. Peter is talking to me but my emotions have carried me away.

"The little chapel was built during the Middle Ages, dedicated to Michael; everything inside is from the 13th to the 17th centuries."

He points to sacred artifacts that are about the room. The first is a wooden statue of San Michele, his carved eyes still shining with love if that's possible. Statues of Joseph and Mary sit on the right wall and a baptismal font on the left. A 15th century crucifix and a 3,000-year-old statue of Horus, the Egyptian God, are also in the room. The floor is the same beautifully inlaid multicolored marble as the Sculpture Loggia. The room is roped off to keep the tourists out but Peter has stepped forward to unlink the chain for me. He motions for me to enter. My heart races, then slows as I adjust to the sacred energies around me.

"When Mr. Munthe came here and saw this chapel, he fell to his knees and knew he had to build his home here on this very spot. He restored this place after it was burned by Corsairs in 1535 led by the infamous Barbarossa. You know, the pirate? That's his castle up on top of that mountain."

He points upward. But I can no longer see or hear him speak for I have been transported to another time inside this holy place.

"I have found heaven," I say out loud. He steps closer to me.

"I knew you would like it. It's spectacular."

We linger for a while before leaving and I hope Peter does not speak so I can recover. If he does and I need to respond, I will weep instead.

Eventually we walk through the gardens, past the fountain of the boy with the dolphins and out the gate. By the time we reach the exit, I have recovered.

"Well, I need to get to the office. We're having a concert here in the chapel on Friday night and I have much work to do to prepare."

He takes my hand as if he is going to shake it but kisses both my cheeks instead. I barely thank him because I feel too delicious. I come to my senses and remember I must meet Antonio in the *piazza* in one hour.

CHAPTER 5

"**C**iao, bella."

That smile ...

"I have my scooter; is good?"

That thick Napoletano accent ... the smell of heavy cologne ...

"Yes, but I have never been on a bike before."

What am I getting myself into?

There are no cars on the streets in Anacapri, except the main road that connects Anacapri to Capri below. So, we walk to a parking lot across from the bus station and find his scooter. He places a helmet on my head and clasps it for me. We ride off into the crowds on this gloriously beautiful island that smells like sage and fiori. Within minutes I'm riding along the cliffs, holding on tightly to this dark-haired, dark-eyed Italiano with chiseled features while my skirt blows in the wind baring my legs.

At this, I laugh out loud and Antonio says, "What makes you laugh, Rosanna?"

"Nothing, I just can't believe I'm doing this!"

"Hold me tight, Rosanna, *capisci*?"

"Si, *capisco*, Antonio. I understand." I smile big.

"I maka' you happy today. I show you a good time."

I lean into him and grab his waist tightly as we maneuver a corner. Is this a dream?

"Hold me tighta', my angel. Both hands! Don't fall off. You can squeeza' me as hard as you like." The wind and the roar of his scooter drowns out our voices as we shout each sentence.

"I will show you more of this, my sweetie."

This is something to write home about. I'm titillated but want to weep at the same time ... must be my hormones ...

"Look at the sea, Antonio, and the sun ... like little jewels on the water." How romantic. I've died and heaven has dropped me here.

"*Si, la luce del sole*, the light of the sun. And we are 750 meters uppa.' Hold me tight, *bella*." The scooter bends dangerously to the left and I realize there are no guardrails.

"Ahhhh! Antonio, we're going to die!"

Who back home would ever believe I'd be having this wild adventure, on the back of a scooter with a 26-year-old (he told me his age) Roman God who wants to show me everything Italian!

Oh no, a major hot flash. Not now.

I unwrap my pashmina from my neck ... oops! It soars like a bird, the wind carrying it upward, then down onto the cliffs.

"Oh, dear. I just bought that yesterday."

"*Dimmi*. Tell me; I did not hear you."

"Nothing."

We arrive at our destination where Antonio parks his scooter and pulls out a sack filled with our lunch. The walk is long, an hour to get to the Villa Jovais, home of the emperors. As we hike along the path, I can't help but stop and smell the flowers, the fiori that Capri is so well known for. Since it's April, all are in full bloom. I dance around them filled with glee. I can't control myself. I try to bend down close enough to smell each one, become one with their intoxicating nectar. They're everywhere.

Antonio stoops to pluck one from the earth.

"No! It will die. You should leave it there," I tell him.

"Oh, no, *bella*. They would be honored for you to hold them until they take their last breath. They have grown beautiful just for you."

I swoon. Then I begin to giggle for I'm deliriously happy. I haven't giggled in years. Here I am in the south of Italy and this young, Italian guy is picking wildflowers for me.

When we reach the ruins, Antonio has gathered a large bouquet and tied it with a small rope made from grass and stems. I accept it graciously.

We walk to a ten-foot-tall monument, a black patina of the crowned Madonna and Child. Antonio blesses himself and says a prayer.

"I love Santa Maria," he says.

I love the way Italian men love Santa Maria. I say a prayer and bless myself, too.

He opens the sack filled with salad, bread, cheeses and limoncello.

"I have never had this before. What is it?"

"It is limoncello. My grandmother makes it. She takes eight lemons and then removes the skin. She uses only the skins. This is very important. She adds alcohol and then puts it in the freezer for twenty-eight days. This is very important too, Rosanna ... no less and no more." He is adamant that her recipe is the best and that her limoncello is far better than any other in all of Italy. This makes me smile.

"After twenty-eight days, she takes it out and pours it through, you know, the cloth with the holes in it? Then she boils the water and *zucchero*, sugar. Then she puts the sugar and the alcohol in a jar in the freezer for twenty-eight more days. Only then is it ready to drink. That's how you make limoncello."

He pours and hands me a cup and I taste it. The liquid burns a little as it goes down.

"It's good, but be very careful, Rosanna. It will make you do crazy things; is powerful so you cannot drink too much." He treats me as if I'm a school-girl he's trying to protect. I slowly take another sip and eat the sandwich he has made. He pours me another cup and I drink it all.

Then suddenly, wham! It hits me. I feel as if I've fallen backwards into the arms of my own grandmother's featherbed ... all soft and warm. Antonio smiles at me, enamored that I'm giggly.

"Nowa I have to take care of you ... you drink too fast."

"Must be the limoncello, hiccup."

"No more for you." He smiles playfully. I'm still laughing and try to stand, but quickly lose my footing. He jumps to my rescue, grabs me and sits me down next to our picnic lunch. He reaches for my face and tries to kiss me.

"No! I'm old enough to be your mother... or your grandmother."

"But you are young to me ... *bellissima*, and your skin is like *porcellana*." Suddenly sober, I move away from him quickly and start to pack our lunch.

"*Mi dispiace*, I am sorry," he says. "Come; I take you somewhere else."

After walking for thirty minutes, I am no longer intoxicated. We are standing at the Natural Arch and the *Grotta di Matermania*, a naturally formed arch made of rock that has been hewn out by the wind and the sea. I think it should have been listed as one of the Seven Wonders of the World. Okay, maybe I'm still feeling the effects of the limoncello.

Antonio tells me that during the Imperial Age, cult rituals were performed as an offering to Cibele, the goddess of fertility, here in the cave. I imagine the orgies and try to visualize what that might have looked like.

We sit and watch the sun as it descends into the sea. I feel myself soften and my passions begin to rise. Could it be the limoncello? Or is it the smell of Antonio's heavy cologne and his bright, white smile? I suppose it could be my thoughts of the orgiastic rituals that took place here.

Once we arrive in Anacapri, Antonio walks me back to my apartment and asks me to dinner the next night. He was a perfect gentleman, after I put him in his place, so I say yes. He moves toward me to kiss my cheeks but surprises me and pulls my face toward his. He kisses my lips. Startled, I pull away.

"It's just a kiss." He shrugs his shoulders and shows his pearly whites, winks and says, "*Ciao*."

I turn and walk through the gardens toward my room, still thinking about the kiss. We need to have a talk.

I fall asleep restlessly contemplating passion which has seeped into my dreams. Each time I awaken, it comes to me in whispers ... not a peaceful night's sleep, but one instead filled with my own heightened senses.

It's a new morning and while exploring the island, I stop for espresso and sit on a beautifully painted tile bench. It's still quiet as the local shop-keepers await the buses that will bring the tourists. Their days are long, lasting until the dinner-hour. How hard they work. Nonetheless, they are always smiling.

As I walk by, I often hear them singing as they move through the streets or work in their gardens. They talk with their hands and use their whole bodies to express themselves—from speaking with their children, telling them they love them, praising the cooks in restaurants or talking with friends. As I watch them now, I realize that they aren't trying to express what they think but instead, what they feel.

My thoughts are interrupted. "*Ciao, bella. Come va?*"

He is handsome. I have seen him often in the *piazza*.

"*Ciao*," I say shyly.

"My name is Bruno. *Come ti chiami*, what is your name?" His eyes are an opalescent pale green, his hair cut short like Caesar's and he has a perfect and well-toned physique. He bows down and takes my hand to kiss it.

"My name is Roxanna. Nice to meet you, Bruno."

"Rosanna, I welcome you to this island."

"Grazie, thank you."

He entertains me with his stories of growing up on the island, many of them quite funny. His mother and father were born in Anacapri and he shares his memories of helping his grandfather in the gardens that overlook the sea.

"It is a beautiful place, Rosanna. The sun is always shining, the birds are always singing and the tourists always come." He stands. "I must go, but we will see each other again." He kisses my face.

"*Ciao*, Bruno."

An hour has passed and I realize I have been sitting here with this silly grin. I can't help it. This place has somehow softened me. I am no longer in my head but in my heart, a place I have not visited in a while.

The heat has reached its peak for the day as locals stroll about the *piazza*. One man holds his three-year-old son in his arms as he hugs and kisses him. A little boy of about eight stoops down to look closely at a flower that has grown out of a crack in the cement. "*Bello,*" he says and smiles. Do they come out of the womb romancing life?

A man sits with his little girl of about five. She sits in his lap and continually reaches up to rub his balding head and pat the side of his face with her little palm, all the while sweetly calling him Papa. He lovingly kisses her hair and her cheek. Then, she falls asleep in his arms as he continues to hold her and caress her. It's as if I'm being shown a new way to communicate. When I was a child, I was often ridiculed for talking with my hands or expressing my emotions so I learned to suppress them. But here, it's normal behavior.

I think about my passions that I have stuffed inside me and left unexpressed and the ones I have not yet realized. Is passion noticing the beauty of life around you? Is it expressing how you feel with your fingers, your lips, your heart? Is this what romancing your life is? Each day that passes here, I can hardly contain these new feelings that are building up inside me. At some point, I'm afraid I'll blow wide open.

The next night, I talk with Antonio and clear the air. I tell him we are friends and only friends. He apologizes and seems sincere so we have a nice dinner. Afterwards, he takes me to a villa on a far-off side of the island—the Villa Fersen—a place where Marie Antoinette's lover, Jacque d'Adelsward Fersen lived for a time. It's magnificent and opulent with an opium den on the bottom level. The views of the sea are incredible as is the entire villa and gardens. I could live here I think.

Over the next few weeks in between my sight-seeing with Antonio, I continue to walk through the village each day meeting and greeting the locals and getting to know each of them as they welcome me with open arms. I also see Bruno, most days, sitting on the bench. We have espresso together and sometimes he brings me a cornetto. We have become good friends and he makes me smile when we are together.

The narrow walkways weave intricately through the village, often causing me to lose my way. But all is perfect since I find hidden villas and lovely gardens. I notice the rock walls that have been meticulously cemented together bordering the properties.

I pass by this day and watch the owner building a wall. I know he works in the village because I have seen him there. But still, he is out here each morning and evening, breaking rocks, laying them and setting them in place. Others do the same. They take such pride in these walls as if they represent the strength of their families and the strength of the island. It's all about the sea, the sky, the sun and the rocks, for Capri is an island built out of rock. I remember that the shores here are not covered with sand, only rocks and smooth stones.

Roxanna ... I mouth my name. How appropriate that I find myself here and have been blessed with this name, a name of strength.

Each day, I watch the men and women tending their gardens filled with grapevines and fruit trees—apple, peach, kiwi, plum, apricot and lemon. There are raspberries, strawberries, fava beans, artichokes, tomatoes and basil and other herbs in the gardens. Each day they water and prune, and speak to the earth that birthed them. They touch the fruits and vegetables lovingly as if they are their children. Their yards are impeccable; and if they work in the shops in town during the day, they are hard at work in their gardens at first light and late into the night singing as they work.

In America, I had forgotten to step outside my home, forgotten that the night air soothed the soul and that the stars and the moon infused energy into the body. I had forgotten that the earth calmed my nervousness. But here in Capri, these people have always known and never forgotten.

The streets are quiet here since everyone walks or uses a scooter. Only a few taxis and buses travel about the island carrying the tourists back and forth. Otherwise, a tranquility blankets the place and you can hear your own thoughts.

The women are strong as they care for their families. Each day, they walk to the market to purchase whatever is needed carrying their heavy bags the distance. I notice how the men treat their mothers, wives and daughters with reverence. They love them, placing them on pedestals as if they are all Santa Maria. It's their culture, passed down from father to son. Even as young boys, they know their mother is special, hence all women are sacred.

Every day, I continue to meet new friends. There is Nuncio and his sons at the family *ceramica* shop, and Ciro, the man in the kiosk on *la stradina*, the little street from the main *piazza* to the San Michele Villa. Federico Salvatore, my friend, the great painter of the island plays his guitar for me when I stop by his studio. Alessandra works at the Profumeria, Franco and Vinnie own Barbarossa Pizzeria, Danielle and Maria are at Il Martino, and Carlo works at the limoncello factory. I'm falling in love with each of them as if I'm having a love affair. I'm giddy with anticipation each morning when I awaken, excited at the thought of walking into town to see each of their faces and share kisses with them.

CHAPTER 6

Today Antonio and I are sightseeing. We have arrived at Marina Piccola, the place I landed when I first came to the island. I thought for sure that if I returned, I would hear the sirens again. But I do not.

This day, the sunlight is in that perfect place in the sky. The *Scoglio delle Sirene*, the Rock of the Sirens lies before us in the sea. The water is like a vast aquamarine pool covered with liquid gold that the sun has dropped. Since there is no sand on Capri, the water's edge is strewn with bits of colored rocks and stones that have been polished by the salty sea. Mixed in with them are bits and pieces of colored glass and painted tiles. I imagine these are centuries old, from a time when pirates threw their bottles and emptied wine jugs overboard after nights of intoxication.

Besides occupying my time, I find that Antonio is also occupying my mind. He is a passionate Italian and I'm often caught off guard when he reaches for my hand or holds me close as we walk the island. He is too territorial and protective of me when other men are around, as if I belong to him. Such odd behavior.

Note to self: spend less time with Antonio. You are becoming a little too attached, my friend. It's time for you to find a young girl your own age.

I remember a recent conversation.

"You know, you must have been so beautiful when you were younger, Rosanna; do you know what I mean?"

"Thanks Antonio. I feel ancient now."

"No, no ... you are still beautiful now, but I can imagine what you were like when you were my age."

After being here for a few weeks, I realize I'd like to stay on Capri longer. I call my boys and my ex-husband and tell them. Ed says, "Stay. We're pretty busy here. The boys are still finishing up school and we've got some small trips planned. I'm afraid if you return now, you will not be seeing much of them."

I suddenly feel crestfallen ... lonely.

I walk through the village and to the cliffs that overlook the sea where I sit and contemplate my life. Memories I had forgotten and buried now come forth. When I married Ed, I was so in love with him. I was so happy to be his wife and give birth to two beautiful babies. I managed the house, the family and Ed. I was the one who held it all together. I was the rock.

My marriage passes before me in movie-like clips.

Ed was rarely home. First there was school, then the law firm. He wanted to make partner so he worked 24/7. I always accepted that he was a hard worker supporting his family and that he was so tired when he came home, the last thing he wanted was a needy wife. I never complained and I never cried in front of him. I had no voice. I was the perfect wife ... his words, not mine.

Then the boys grew and no longer needed me. There were sports, scouts, friends and sleep-overs. Then long phone calls with girls. But I couldn't let them go. I remained an overprotective mother.

I flash back ten years to my 40th birthday. Ed was busy for months because he had finally made partner at the firm. He often worked until midnight. I bottled up all my feeling including my fears of turning forty. I couldn't talk to Ed but I did talk to my friend, Gretchen. She patted my hand and told me I would be fine, but what did she know? After all, she was seven years younger than I was.

I talked to my mother and she smiled and said, "Dear, nothing will change. You will pass into your forties and it won't matter a bit." So, I stuffed my fears and my longings deep down inside me.

I signed up for jazzercise classes and went religiously. I tried desperately to lose the ten pounds I had gained over the years. Within two months, I had lost six ... only four more to go. But food was my savior when I was lonely ... all those nights alone in the house ... all those times I went to bed sex-starved, Ed snoring beside me. I cried myself to sleep, wondering what it would be like to make love to someone else. Was this normal? Of course, I never talked to anyone about it.

The water of the Mediterranean shimmers before me like a sea of diamonds. But the image is soon blurred by more memories.

The night of my fortieth birthday plays out before me. I had to remind Ed, at least four times, that it was an important birthday for me. We had dinner plans at my favorite restaurant with two other couples—a romantic Italian place on the water. It was pricey but it was a special occasion.

As usual, I had to call the office to see if Ed had left. He had not. He'd forgotten. He apologized and raced home. He also apologized for not getting a birthday gift and said he'd make it up to me. I now realize he had forgotten most of my birthdays ... no gifts ... no cards. I never cried or complained ... just accepted it.

That night, I was embarrassed that we were an hour late, everyone there at the table waiting for us. As soon as we walked in, I saw pity on their faces. I wonder how much they knew?

That day, I had my hair cut and colored, had a manicure and a pedicure and even purchased sexy lingerie I thought Ed would love. The kids were with my parents for the night so I had planned champagne, soft music and a few sexy moves I had read about. When we arrived home, I put soft jazz on and went into the bathroom to change while Ed was undressing. After cleaning up a bit and splashing on his favorite perfume, Oscar de la Renta, I danced seductively as I made my way into the bedroom. He never saw me because he had fallen asleep. I jumped on the bed; I tried to awaken him, but he never moved. Then, I lost it and started crying which soon became louder and louder. He opened his eyes wide with surprise.

"What are you doing?" he asked.

I was seething with anger and hurt as I stood over the bed, tears streaming down my face.

"It's my birthday! You're already asleep. I wanted to surprise you ..." I couldn't stop.

"Aw, I'm sorry, Deb. I'm tired." He tried to sit up. "You look good but isn't that a little tight?" He pointed to my lingerie. "I thought you were taking exercise classes?"

I could no longer see through my tears. All the hurt and pain I had felt throughout my marriage had bubbled up and I suddenly realized I meant nothing to him! I had enabled him and let him walk all over me. It was my fault.

I pull napkins from my overstuffed bag and wipe my face and blow my nose.

"Rosanna, why are you sad?" Bruno has come up behind me and pulls me to him. I fall into his arms and start to sob. He holds me until the tears are gone. I don't tell him everything but I do tell him it's personal. I have recovered now.

"I will keep you company," he says.

We sit quietly looking at the colors of the sea. This safe place with him soothes me. I don't feel invisible or less than with him. I feel important enough because he seems to care about me, whether I'm happy or sad. I smile and squeeze his hand.

"Thank you, Bruno. It means a lot to me."

"We are friends. I will always be here for you if you need me."

He walks me to my apartment and kisses my cheeks at the door. He hands me a piece of paper with his phone number written on it.

"If you are sad or need someone to talk to, call me and I will come to you."

But I make it through the night, alone with my memories.

For days, I have stayed in the gardens until my self-loathing has finally dissipated. Spirit visiting me in my dreams twice this week has also helped. In both, he reassured me that this was all part of my process—the memories and feelings coming to the surface so I could heal them. I had been unconscious in my marriage, just as Ed had. We were both to blame.

Spirit said that each time memories come up, let them and practice the Ho'oponopono Prayer. "I'm sorry, Ed. Please forgive me. I love you; I thank you." Then say, "I'm sorry, Roxanna. Please forgive me. I love you; I thank you. Now I am complete."

So, I do. I feel like I'm a mesh screen that everything comes into and moves through. I have processed rejection, grief, sorrow, sadness, self-loathing and anger. I think I've finally healed everything. I hope ...

I have taken myself to dinner at the Capri Palace, a 5-Star hotel in Anacapri where the rich and famous come to be pampered in seclusion. I have dressed in a pretty skirt and top and painted my lips. I also purchased a new pair of strappy sandals from one of the local shops where the owner and his family have made these shoes for four generations. I keep telling myself I am beautiful and I am at peace. My daily mantra. If I say this enough throughout the day, I start to believe it. This learning to value myself and love myself enough is all part of my healing process ... even taking myself to this fabulous restaurant for dinner.

I pretend I'm someone famous and they treat me as if I am. Of course, I'm paying through the nose for it ... because I'm worth every penny. Seriously, I have three waiters who are constantly at my table for all my needs—the *aperitivo*, a glass of sparkling prosecco; a canapé—a bruschetta style toast covered in tiny vegetables and dressed in pesto; Sicilian olives and Marcona almonds; the *antipasto*—a prawn cocktail; the *primo piattio*—a light minestrone soup; the *secondo piattio*—baked sea bass encrusted in sea salt. My *contorno*—a side dish of fresh spinach bathed in butter and garlic. I have no room for *insalata* but I do save room for *dolce*, sweets—a delicious tiramisu. The waiters, one female and two males, remove my used silverware and clear my table of crumbs. They replace my linen napkin between each course and they constantly ask me if I'm pleased. I smile each time and thank them. I am Roxanna, no signs of Deborah and her broken pieces this night.

I move into the lounge where a piano player sings Josh Groban and Vittorio songs in Italian. I listen with my eyes closed, enjoying my glass of their best *vino*—Ciabot Mentin Ginestra Barolo from the Domenico Clerico vineyards. Then, I happily make my way back to my villa apartment.

I'm making love in my dream this night. Although I cannot see the face of the man, it's erotic and I'm so well taken care of that upon awakening, I'm still breathing hard. It has opened up that part of me and unleashed passions I have never known before.

CHAPTER 7

My body is damp when I awaken, memories of the dream still with me. I realize how lonely I am and finally admit it to myself. I need to walk, to move, to dissipate some of this energy I'm feeling. I decide to go to Marina Piccola to watch the water and walk amongst the smooth stones that cover the shoreline. With sketchbook in hand, I spend half the day there then visit the restaurant that overlooks the *Il Faraglioni*, the famous rocks. I am preoccupied with my sketches so once again, I become centered.

Eventually, I make my way back to Anancapri and the bench in the main *piazza*. As I enjoy the sun, thoughts of Ed and my marriage surface. I remember all the times I felt invisible. There were long stretches where we did not make love for one or two months at a time. Then I would become hysterical and he would have sex with me. It wasn't normal. He just wasn't that into me ... said he was tired from working so much.

When I was pregnant, as soon as we found out, our infrequent sexual encounters stopped completely. Maybe it was me ... maybe it was my fault. It must have been my fault. God, it WAS my fault. All of it.

I cannot stop the tears and bury my face in my hands.

"Oh, *bella*." Bruno approaches. He kneels before me and wipes my tears. I cry harder.

"Please tell me what is wrong. *Un minuto*; I be right back." He leaves. I digress.

Yes, I was lonely, and wanted Ed to make love to me like I had seen in movies. I dreamt of it. But it never happened. Now, here I am, a fifty-year-old woman with the feelings of a young girl, the fire inside me smoldering like Mount Vesuvius.

God, help me.

Bruno appears, a big grin on his face, two small glasses of yellow liquid in is hands.

"Nectar of Nona. It heals everything—headache, sickness, heartbreak. My mamma put it on my gums when I was teething."

His smile is contagious and his story makes me laugh. Eventually, my tears stop and he hands me the cup of limoncello.

"But I confess. It is not my grandmother's. Hers is the best on the island." He takes a sip. "Do you know this drink?"

"Yes," I laugh.

"This is to heal your tears. It is medicine." His eyes tell me it's true.

"*Per amore!*" he says. We clink our glasses and toast.

"*Alla vita,* to life," I say in return. I taste the golden liquor and savor it in my mouth. Instantly, I become warm inside as if my own grandmother is next to me, consoling me. My stomach muscles relax and I begin to breathe easily again. He drinks his quickly and smiles into the sunlight while I sigh, happy that he has interrupted my self-loathing. We sit quietly for a few minutes.

"You are a beautiful woman, Rosanna." He takes my hand in his and brings it to his lips. He kisses me there and I can feel the moisture of his breath that is left upon it.

"You know we are the best of friends now."

"Yes, for the last few weeks."

"We see each other almost every day, here, on this bench. We have spent much time together."

"Yes, we do."

"What, you are not laughing? I make a joke."

At this, I do laugh.

"I am serious now," he says. "I am here for you. And I am happy my jokes are funny and you are no longer crying."

"Thank you for that."

We sit quietly enjoying the sun like two cats. He goes off for one more limoncello for each of us and returns. As we sip the golden liquor, he tells me funny stories about what it's like to be Italian. By the end of the second glass, we are laughing out loud and holding hands.

"Rosanna, I'd like to take you to one of the ruins on the island that not many know about. Would you like to come with me?" He whispers in my ear.

He still has my hand in his and is rubbing my palm seductively with his index finger. He must know this is a turn-on, or maybe it's just me. I pull my hand away.

"I am sorry. I hope you are not afraid of me. You know I will never hurt you."

"I know what you want." I'm so nervous I think of vomiting. He squeezes my hand and studies me.

"You are my beautiful friend and you are special to me. I would like to be with you, hold you, comfort you, make love to you. I want to show you that you are not alone."

"I can't. It's not right."

"Not right for who, Rosanna? For you? For me? We are two *solo* people. We have no one, no lover or husband or wife. We can do whatever we want with each other." He reaches for my hand again and I let him take it.

"I promise to keep you safe. I will never hurt you."

He stands, steps back and places his hands in his pocket, waiting while I think about his offer.

I sit quietly, wondering if it's the right thing to do ... if it would be bad ... or good ... or spectacular ...

"Bruno, could we please have another limoncello?" I smile nervously.

He leaves and comes back with a small paper bag which holds two paper cups and a small bottle of the nectar.

"Come. I have a scooter."

Oh, no. Not another scooter ...

We ride to the other side of the island and the *fortino*, the fort—a thousand-year-old ruin, one thousand meters above the sea. The view of the Mediterranean and Mount Vesuvius is spectacular. He parks the bike and hand in hand, we carefully walk the tiny path. We arrive at the fort and he pours the limoncello. We toast.

"To you and to Santa Maria," he says.

The drink opens me up like a flower blooming in the warm sunlight ... since this is my third.

It is silent here, except for the muted sounds below. Time stands still as I'm transported back to a delicious time of youth when I anticipated love. I feel the butterflies in my belly. We stand together and I rest my fears in this safe place next with him. Of course, the limoncello has helped.

Bruno is behind me, his strong arms wrapped about my waist, holding me in place. He slowly kisses my neck and breathes into my hair, then moves his fingers down along my bare arm, tracing my skin as he goes. He turns me around to face him. His breathing is heavy with anticipation, his eyes wide-open and fixed upon my face.

He covers my mouth with his as if he is savoring a juicy plum that is over-ripened. I think I hear music ...

My passions bubble up inside me as he presses himself into me. I feel all of him through his linen slacks and shirt, his perfect physical definition ... his waist indented where his abdomen starts ... his well-defined and muscular chest. His hands are on the back of my neck as he holds me in place, all the while speaking to me in Italian in between his kisses. He's doing many things to me at the same time ... breathing me in as he kisses me, speaking to me and holding me tightly.

We continue to kiss as we become one, and merge with each other, the sea, the sky and the ancient rocks. It's as if I'm outside my body, hovering above watching, but inside it at the same time, if this is at all possible.

It's as if I'm in a dream and time is standing still. He lays me down on the rock wall, ever so gently. I have lost my mind, all thoughts and judgments gone. I have also lost my clothes ... when did they come off? I don't remember.

All my fears and my years melt into the old fort as I allow myself to be held and loved. He reaches for my breasts, his lips making a beeline to them. I do not remember what happens in the next moment. But I do allow him to have his way with me and I do the same with him. I have no inhibitions and am no longer the timid woman I have always been.

He whispers in my ear and into my mouth in between his own breathlessness. I hear the faint sound of motor boats in the distance and a bird that passes by, but then, there is only silence. The wind caresses my body everywhere that his hands are not, and that is not too many places.

"*Tu sei così bella. E' dal primo giorno che ti ho incontrata che aspetto questo momento.* Since the first day I met you, I have been waiting for this moment. *Tu sei la piu bella donna di Capri,* you are the most beautiful woman of Capri."

I must be dreaming … here, high above the Mediterranean under the bluest of skies, on the wall of a thousand-year-old ancient ruin with my lover. In this moment, I am a goddess.

"*Bellissima, bella.* Oh, Rosanna … *ah, mio bella donna. Lo le so che tu sei una donna di passione …* beautiful Rosanna."

Lost inside this magical world of letting go into bliss and romance, I do things that would make me blush any other time but this. I'm no longer self-conscious of my aging body. I'm Aphrodite, and he, Apollo. This is not the love-making of two humans, but that of the gods. I wonder if they are looking down upon us with smiles upon their faces, clapping their hands ecstatically as they shout, "Yes! They have found freedom and ecstasy at last!"

He continues to kiss me all over and whispers sweet words to me.

"*Amore mio,* my love, you are far more beautiful than any twenty-year-old. You have such *passione.*"

I'm confident and let the breeze have its way with me now that he's finished. He tells me I am lovely and I know I am. I am beautiful … loved … satiated.

After we both return to earth, Bruno sits up and pulls a small velvet pouch from his pants which had been tossed aside.

"I have been carrying this with me since the first day I met you. It told me it was for you." His accent is thick and his eyelashes dust his cheeks as he speaks the words. "You have given me the gift of you, and for that I want to give you something to remember me by." He opens the pouch and shows me a gold cross, lined with emerald stones.

"I thought of you when I saw this. It was meant for you. It told me. It is a gift from me, Bruno of Capri and this island, to protect you and give you strength."

He places it around my neck and clasps it. I am speechless. Then he kisses me in that place where it falls between my breasts. When he raises his eyes to meet mine, they are filled with tears.

"Oh, Bruno. Thank you." Now, I'm crying. I throw my arms around him and fall into him, but I have knocked him off balance. We topple to the ground in a heap and laugh.

"Oh ..." I try to move from him but the limoncello and all the physical activity in the sun have turned my arms and legs into Play-doh and the love-making has made me useless. We wrestle, trying to remove ourselves from one another. He tries to lift me but we're laughing uncontrollably and cannot become untangled. He reaches for my face and a wisp of hair that has fallen.

"Rosanna, I like that you make me laugh. You have healed me."

I reach for him and kiss him.

"No, I'm the one who is healed." He smiles. "Thank you for keeping me safe and making love to me, Bruno. I will never forget you or this day."

We continue kissing as we again become one with the sea, the sky and the ancient rocks. Our laughter has been replaced with desire and we fall into love-making again. My God, please don't stop ... ever.

Afterwards, we doze for we have found an opening in the universe and slip through it into this sacred place where love softly rests. And as the sun starts to move toward the earth, we open our eyes and realize how hungry we are. I dress myself while he kisses me all over, and again, I am giggling. So many giggles have spilled out of me ... little jewels of happiness.

"Thank you, Rosanna, for giving yourself to me."

I know he's a gift to me and that I'm the lucky one for I no longer feel the heaviness I felt earlier today. I've been transformed by him and this experience and I feel light, alive and young again. I did it! I have made love!

We walk back up the path to the scooter, and as I wrap my arms around him, he clasps my hand tenderly. I've had more intimacy this day then I had during my entire marriage.

We stop for pasta at a little family restaurant near *Il Faro,* the lighthouse. We are their only patrons and the owner and his wife serve us. Bruno orders dinner and chianti and we settle in. We are giddy with laughter and still glowing after making love in the sunlight on the fort high above the sea. But suddenly, he becomes serious.

"Rosanna, you have shared your story with me. Now I must confess mine to you."

I listen intently, not sure what he will say.

"It has been four years since I have made love." He looks down at his hands and is silent for a few moments. Then, he continues.

"I was in love once. My girl, Ilaria, I met her when I was twenty-one. I went down to Capri to buy fish from the *pescheria,* the fish market. The daily catch is brought to this market and they have the best. She worked there and waited on me that day. When she smiled at me, my heart started to go crazy and I could not speak. She was beautiful. Her eyes sparkled like stars and her smile, *bella ragazza.*" He disappears for a minute so we sit in silence.

"I went back to the fish market every few days. So much fish for my family. My mother laughed every time I bring the fish home. My father told me to ask her for dinner. So, one day I did and she said yes. We fell in love and saw each other every day. She was the one for me."

"What happened? Where is she now?"

Tears well up in his eyes and I reach for his hand.

"We were to be married. But she died." He lowers his head as the tears slide down his cheeks.

"I am so sorry, Bruno." It takes him some time to compose himself.

"A car accident in Napoli. She was with her brother and someone hit them at night. He lived but she did not."

51

"I cannot imagine how difficult this has been for you. You're too young for such a loss."

He continues to cry. The food comes, but I wave the husband and wife away. After some time, he stops and I hand him a tissue from my bag. He blows his nose. I pick up my wine glass.

"Bruno, let's toast, to Ilaria who is in heaven with Santa Maria and the angels." We clink our glasses.

"*Salute.*"

"*Salute*," he repeats. He gulps down the full glass quickly as if it will heal him, then places it on the table.

"It has been four years. Rosanna, I have never looked at another woman or let anyone in until I saw you sitting in the *piazza*. I knew you were special. I knew your heart. You made me laugh. Then you told me about your marriage and your husband. You have also suffered for love. I knew you were sent to me to heal my heart."

I'm crying now, because he has healed me.

"I am sorry for making you cry." He reaches for my hand.

"No, Bruno. You have healed me. I'm no longer afraid of love. Our time together was very healing and you were such a gentle and kind lover. You were safe. You protected me; I thank you for that."

"We were destined to meet." He pours more wine into our glasses and we toast again. The husband and wife are relieved that we are smiling and finally bring us our food. As a matter of fact, they do not charge us for the meal and when we thank them, we both cry, so they do, too. We are all crying like a happy ending in a movie.

We ride back to town and Bruno walks me to my apartment. We linger at the gate and hold each other tightly, not wanting this day to end. Then we kiss. We're both crying, but it's not because of the grief anymore. It's because of the joy and this tenderness we have shared.

"Thank you, Rosanna. Thank you for sharing yourself with me today. Thank you for melting away my grief. I will never forget you."

"Is this goodbye?" I laugh.

"No, no ... we will see each other again."

"It's okay, Bruno. We will share limoncello again in the *piazza*. You know you deserve someone your own age. You will fall in love again and have babies. It's your destiny."

He smiles big.

"*Arrivederci*," he says. And we hug one more time.

I roll over in bed and review my time with Bruno. It doesn't seem real. My body and soul have burst wide-open and a new woman has been birthed. I have lost all the grief and pain and the fears of being with another man. Bruno held my hand the entire time and kept me safe as I rekindled my passions. I now remember what it feels like to be a woman.

But the most magical thing was that we helped heal each other.

CHAPTER 8

The Caesar Augustus Hotel is perched high atop the cliffs of Anacapri and overlooks the sea and the port town of Marina Grande far below. This property is known for its vistas of the islands of Ischia and Procida, and the Bay of Naples with Mount Vesuvius and Sorrento in the distance. The Farouk Suite sits on the top floor which is the best suite in this elegant hotel.

It's a new day and I decide to treat myself to something decadent and delicious because I'm worth it. Wow ... I never would have done anything like this before. I've always been so frugal. And now, I know I'm worth it ... and I can!

Checked into my room, I stand with my back to the door, astonished. There before me is a massive bed which looks out toward the balcony and a view of the Mediterranean and Mount Vesuvius. The bathroom holds an immense tub surrounded by windowed-walls to the sea below. Tapered-candles are set all around ... need I say more?

I walk to a painting set in an opulent, scrolled gold frame on the wall that has caught my eye. But once in front of it, I realize it's a very large picture-window to the sea. I'm breathless. Then, I step out onto the balcony.

"It's not a dream. I'm really here."

My heart has been sliced open like a ripened pomegranate, all the little seeds spilling out. Overcome with emotion, passion grows inside my breast igniting my soul, pushing the tears upward and out through my eyes.

"Where have you been, my soul? I thought I was dying."

I return to my room and fall back on the bed with the fluffy pillows and Italian linens. I'm so happy.

The light in the sky has shifted. This is the time of day when the sea reflects shades of lavender and blue with aqua trim at its shoreline far below. I pull myself from this spot and move inside to the marble tub where I run the water and light the candles and incense. Then I step in ... one delicious inch at a time. As I close my eyes, I dream of living this way, every day of my life, filled with gratitude and love. I realize I can create this if I want to. So, I set my intent and make a commitment to myself that I will live a life filled with all of this. I don't know how, but I know in my heart that it will be so.

Throughout the night, I walk from my bed, out through the open doors to the *terrazza* and back again. I have the need to gaze at the sky and the sea every twenty minutes, for I don't want to miss a thing. The vista changes each time the light does so it's new in every moment. First, it's by starlight, then moonlight as the moon moves upward into the sky. Just before dawn it's a soft, golden light. My breath catches each time I gaze at the magnificence of this place where heaven and earth have merged.

At one point, I'm dreaming and standing on the balcony, the spirit beside me. Together, we gaze at the Mediterranean and Marina Grande below. Music plays in the distance.

"Come, I want to show you where you will live."

In an instant, we are somewhere else in Anacapri looking out to sea and the vista of the sea here is as beautiful as the one from the hotel. Gardens surround the villa and statues line the walkway that runs the length of the property. There are also two terraces with hand-painted mosaic-tiled floors and a table with chairs on each.

"Keep looking and you will find this place, Roxanna; here, you will be inspired to paint!" He lovingly touches my arm.

"How will I find it? And who are you?" Before I finish my questions, he's gone and I'm alone. I will myself to remember each word and each picture in my mind, for I don't want to forget a thing he has said or the vision of where I will live. I want to know it as soon as I come upon it. How silly of me ... how could I ever forget?

Bang! Bang! Bang!

What! I bolt upright in fright and fall off the bed, my hair covering my face.

"Ouch ..." I try to find my robe.

Click. The door unlocks and in enter two men.

"Wait! Stop! I'm not dressed."

I am naked so I hold the sheet up to cover myself and back away, tripping over the blanket, its corner tucked into the bed. A short man of about 70, 4' 10," light hair and powder-blue eyes, enters in a white dinner jacket as if he is on his way to a dinner party. He rushes toward me and lifts me off the floor. His eyes are wide as he observes my nakedness so it takes him a bit to collects himself. He sets me on the bed, his eyes still riveted on me.

"Who are you? What are you doing here?" I ask, still shaken and a little embarrassed.

"I am sorry, *Signora* Allen. I am Enrico. I work in the hotel. We think there is a problem! It's 11:00 a.m. and you do not come down. I knock and knock but you do not answer. You must come down for breakfast because the kitchen is closing."

"I was sleeping and I'm not hungry."

"We apologize for the misunderstanding. But you must understand that when a woman comes to our hotel *solo,* sometimes they are love-sick or something. We must watch them so they do not harm themselves for love. Are you love-sick? Excuse me for asking such a personal question." He bows down reverently.

"No, I'm fine. Could you please go?" I'm mortified.

"*Signora*, I apologize again. I will bring you *espresso* and *cornetto.*" He bows from the waist as he backs out the door with the other young man who is as embarrassed as I am.

I finally collect myself.

No man has seen me naked in ages and within a few days here, there have been two. I can't stop laughing. *So much for modesty.*

Twenty minutes later, I'm fully clothed when I hear a knock on the door.

"Come in, Enrico." He has my breakfast on a tray and sets it on the *terrazza*.

"Again, *Signora* Allen ..."

"Please call me Roxanna."

"Roxanna, a strong name." He has sparkling blue eyes and a nice smile. "I wish to apologize to you again. Is there anything else you would like?"

"No, *grazie.*"

"Well if there is anything at all, do not hesitate to call me and ask." He hands me a business card with his name on it.

"Wait, Enrico, there might be one thing. I'm on the island looking for a place to stay and everywhere is booked. Do you know where I might find a rental for the month?"

"I own a few properties; let me see what I can do. I will let you know."

"Thank you, I really appreciate it."

He leaves.

CHAPTER 9

The next few days are busy ones as I work with my new friend Enrico to find a place to stay. The island is booked solid; the *fiori* are in full bloom, their scent drawing everyone here. Enrico has a small stone house on his property and offers it to me for a fair price. So, I prepare to move.

It's my last day at the San Michele Villa, so I stop at Peter's door to thank him and say goodbye. He greets me with a smile.

"How are you, Roxanna? You have been busy?"

"Yes, I've been meeting so many new friends and seeing all of Capri's secret and beautiful spots. How have you been?"

"Good. Rosa and I have been good. We took a holiday to Firenze last week. She wanted to show me the museums. It was nice to get away before the summer season is upon us."

"Florence is on my list. Maybe I'll make it there before I return to the States."

"What are your plans?"

"I'm staying on the island for another month. I can't seem to leave this place."

"Yes, it seduces everyone who comes."

"Peter, thank you for your hospitality and the gift of the apartment. I will never forget what you have done for me." I hand him a bottle of wine. "This is for you."

"It is not necessary." He turns it over in his hand and reads the label. His eyes grow wide with delight. "A '97 Brunello di Montalcino from Toscana. How did you know this is my favorite? This is considered one of the best wines in Italy. Thank you, Roxanna." He is clearly excited.

"It's the least I can do. Thank you so much for helping me and saving me from those two crazy guys that first day."

"Yes, it was quite an adventure for you. I cannot believe you hired them ... and that boat."

"I know. If you had not come along, they surely would have thrown me into the sea." We both laugh.

"I must go. I'm meeting Enrico in the *piazza*. He is taking me to a small house on his property."

"I know him well. He is a good man. Enjoy your stay. Maybe we will see each other again."

"That would be nice." I kiss both his cheeks—right cheek first, as is the custom. "*Ciao*, and *molto grazie*."

"*Prego,* you are welcome."

I meet Enrico. He hands me a key and gives me directions. The walk to my new home is about a mile outside the little village so I move through the small maze of tiny lanes, luggage in tow. As I enter through the gate to the little stone cottage, again, my breath is taken from me. The view of the sea and the bay is lovely.

I walk the long path through the gardens. Grapevines and lavender wisteria hang overhead. Flowers and statues are scattered throughout. I recognize *The David*, Dionysus and Venus. At the edge of the property facing the Mediterranean stands a sculpture of a sphinx. It seems he's watching over me. I take this as a good omen.

The building appears to be at least one hundred years old. It has glass walls and doors open to the sea with one small bed, a writing table and a small kitchenette. Although it is sparse, it's incredibly romantic, an artist's retreat. I can see myself painting here.

The landscape and gardens are lush. A small pathway lined with little potted plants runs from the cottage to the cliffs overlooking the sea and a *terrazzo* with hand-painted tile flooring sits off to the side. Three bas-reliefs, each one a Roman god, are cemented to the front wall of the cottage by the door. A stone bench and table made of inlaid tiles sit nearby. Bistro tables with slatted chairs rest lazily in the sun.

Enrico has instructed me to eat anything that grows here. There are lemon, kiwi, peach, pear, mandarin orange, and apple trees. The gardens are filled with tomatoes, beans, lettuce, broccoli, artichokes, fresh *basilico* and other herbs and vegetables. I praise the gods for such gifts as these, including the gift of him.

After giving thanks, I open my suitcase stuffed with the extra clothing I had purchased to accommodate my longer stay. I have a new light-weight black leather Italian jacket I had purchased to keep warm on those scooter rides with Antonio. There is only one pashmina scarf, the other, caught on the wind falling to the cliffs below. I laugh out loud at the memory.

I admire my new Italian jeans that have replaced the ones I brought from America after losing my middle-age spread. This, I attribute to my new diet of *olio d'olivia*, olive oil, salad and pasta. I eat lighter these days, my choices consisting of organic produce grown on the island.

After unpacking, I decide to explore the property and take pictures with my camera. I don't want to forget anything about it, this *paradiso* I have fallen so gently into the lap of. My desires accelerate like the rising tide of the ocean. I want to paint. Soon … I will know when … For now, I am enjoying the rapture of being here. I sit on the *terrazzo* while little lizards lie about me basking in the sun and white butterflies flit about my head. Feels like a fairy tale…

The sea beckons me as the late afternoon sun spills its diamonds upon its waters. I close my eyes and feel the love of this island. The memories … Antonio teasing me, his beautiful and seductive smile against his darkened skin … Bruno and the gold and emerald cross I still wear … the view from the *terrazza* of the Farouk Suite at the Caesar Augustus Hotel … I am lost in these precious moments of the heart and the sounds of the birds chirping in the trees fall away.

Memories of my suffering and depression in America have faded away. What a gift. Life is strange sometimes and makes you do strange things. But this holiday is beyond my wildest dreams.

I don't know how I want my life to be but I do know that in this moment, I can create anything I want. I cannot see where I'm going, but I know how I want to be each step of the way. I don't ever want to forget the smell of the *fiori* or the aroma of an Italian cooked meal. I never want to be so busy that I don't hear the birds singing or the sounds of the night, or the wind as it moves through the trees.

I want to laugh and make love again like I did with Bruno ... kiss, hug, hold hands, dance, paint and ride on the back of scooters. I want to feel all of life and enjoy every moment.

The cells in my body are colliding. I take a breath and try to control them. This is what I want to create ... a life filled with passion. I close my eyes. In these moments, my old life and all my fears, my anxiety, my pain, my jealousy, my tears, my sadness, my grief and my loss ... gone.

Praise God!

Hours pass. Finally, the sun sets into the sea and the music of my life quiets inside my head and my heart. I rise from my seat and go in to make something to eat.

CHAPTER 10

I have traveled halfway across the world and all I want to do is sit and gaze at the sea. It soothes my mind and spirit, the same feeling I felt when making love with Bruno. I often wonder if I imagined our mystical liaison. But I have proof; I'm still wearing the cross. I suddenly realize I've not seen him for a week. I wonder what he's up to ...

The town of Capri is a thousand years old with ancient archways, cobblestone streets and little *piazze*. Big villas sit in the hills and apartments line the streets overlooking the shops and boutiques below. The rich and famous come to the town of Capri while those who come to Anacapri are looking for quiet and privacy, away from the paparazzi.

The 5-star luxury Grand Hotel Quisisana stands before me. It's quite impressive and well-known for its famous patrons. Since I haven't been out much these days, I've decided to treat myself to a 5-star dinner. I am seated at a table with a view of the Mediterranean when the waiter, Raffaello, comes to me.

"Buona sera, Signorina."

"Buona sera." I'm old enough to be called *Signora*, so naturally I'm flattered.

His hair is dark with bits of silver running through it. His nose is strong and creases run down the sides of his mouth. Although there are many patrons here, they all melt away as he tends to me. We are alone and time has stopped, just for the two of us.

What is happening to me?

"Menu?"

"*Grazie.*" I try and focus but cannot seem to.

"A drink?"

"*Si*, chianti."

He brings me a glass and sets the bottle on the table. "Do you have any questions?"

"I'm not sure. What do you recommend?" His eyes have such depth that my pulse quickens.

"May I order for you? You will not be disappointed."

"That would be lovely." He gazes at me as if he is covering me with kisses ... or is it my imagination?

I feel like the only one dining this night. I sit for hours as he brings me plate after plate—risotto smothered with medallions of the sea, seared fish that smells fresh like the Mediterranean, one course after another, smile after smile. Each time he attends to my needs, his jacket sleeve brushes my arm and its hairs stand at attention. His hand touches mine as he refills my glass. Our eyes meet and lock.

"Roxanna, are you sure we have not met?" He smiles nervously.

"I have never been to Italy before. This is my first time. Have you ever been to California?"

"No."

"Then we have never met before today."

He is familiar to me, as if I have lain in his arms before and loved him deeply.

"Roxanna, do you believe in past lives?" he whispers. "I am sorry. You must think me foolish." His hands shake as he scrapes the crumbs from my table.

"No, I don't think you're foolish at all. And yes, I do believe in past lives. Why?"

"I feel like you have been my wife before. Silly of me, yes?" He glances off into the distance.

"You seem familiar to me as well, Raffaello."

He moves to another table but soon brings *espresso*, then *i dolce*, an array of sweet desserts—little pastries, cakes, cookies and chocolates—then limoncello. It's all far too much.

Although I have enjoyed my time with him and do not want to

leave, I must. My body cannot ingest any more food and I cannot sit any longer.

"Please, no more food or drink."

"Are you sure?"

"Yes, I have to leave to catch the last bus to Anacapri."

"One more *espresso* … or limoncello …"

"I feel like a big stuffed *cornetto*!" We both laugh.

"When will I see you again?"

"I will come again. I promise." He takes my hand and kisses it as if it were the bare skin of my breast … I shiver.

"I will wait for you, Roxanna, every day … until you come again."

To take my finger and caress the crease that runs along his mouth would be like making love to someone's face … a secret touch that arouses the senses … but this is too intimate a gesture, for he is a married man.

He shudders as if he has read my thoughts.

"*Ti amo tesoro mio*, my treasure," he says.

On my walk back to the *autobus*, I blush at my behavior. I don't recognize myself. All these breathless moments around beautiful men. This coquettishness is not who I am. Is it wrong to engage in these types of conversations? Was I outwardly flirtatious? He couldn't possibly hear my thoughts …

My mind tries to understand what has taken place this night. Then, I realize my soul is now driving me and the rewards have been the love I have been shown in so many forms. Maybe my encounters with Bruno and Raffaello were unconventional, but they were profound. Maybe in this lifetime, they have come to show me how to love myself more.

I am deeply and forever changed. Making love to Bruno gave me courage and the permission I needed to open myself up and unleash my passions. Connecting with Raffaello tonight has opened my heart. I no longer feel lonely. I feel his love for me. I'm happy with my life and no matter where I am in this world, I will always know there is someone out there who cares for me. My heartache is gone. My grief is over. Tonight, it has blown apart into a million little pieces and dissolved forever.

CHAPTER 11

Dawn comes early this morning. I lie in bed and listen to the sounds of the June bugs buzzing in the flowers outside my cottage. I scan the room and observe the bookcase filled with old books, their titles in English, Italian and German. A simple chair sits in a corner and lace curtains dress the glass doors. A thin lace fabric is fastened to the ceiling over the bed. It drops into three sections reminding me of a material hanging on a clothesline as it billows in the breeze. My bed linens are beautiful yet simple—soft, white and Italian. Sunlight streams in through the windows and doors adding a golden glow to the space.

After an hour or so, I remember that Antonio has promised to take me fishing today. He said we would go somewhere in Anacapri and not down to the sea in Marina Grande or Marina Piccola. How can we fish from the cliffs, I wonder? I guess I'll find out.

After walking the mile to town, I meet him at Monument Square in front of *Il Martino*, the newspaper stand and internet point I visit daily.

"*Journo*, my sweetie."

"*Ciao*, Antonio." He smells of heavy cologne and his black hair glistens in the sunlight from the gel he dresses it with. I laugh as I imagine he has splashed himself with it for the fish.

"Come. We will be there soon."

He hands me the helmet and helps me fasten it and we ride the scooter to the farthest point on the island. We arrive at one of the old ancient forts (not to be mistaken for the one Bruno and I visited). This fort is smaller. The sun blazes brightly as we climb over the rocks high atop the island.

"Rosanna, you stay and sit in the sun. It is not safe for a woman down below. I bring you fish." He walks carefully along the uneven volcanic rocks with their sharp tips and jagged edges, slowly placing one foot in front of the other.

"Rosanna!" He is half way down to the sea and I can barely hear him. "You can take your clothes off, you know. No one comes here. *Ciao.*" His teeth sparkle in the sunlight even from this distance.

Naked ... I couldn't. Suppose someone comes ... I remember seeing women bathing topless at the little beach near Marina Grande. No one seemed to pay much notice to them.

Go ahead, Rosanna. Don't be shy, I tell myself. Although my encounter with Bruno has opened me up, I'm still self-conscious of my body. That's why I have come to the island with a one-piece black bathing suit which covers all my parts I think should stay hidden from the world.

I lie on my towel and bask like a lizard in the 100° heat. It's so hot that little pools of moisture have collected beneath my suit. What was I thinking! My justifying mind reminds me that women wear black so they appear thinner than they are.

I am thin and beautiful. Why do I still wear this?

"Ha," I laugh big and bold into the wind.

"Roxanna, I do believe no one in southern California has made love like you, the goddess Aphrodite herself, high atop the cliffs on a romantic isle in the middle of the sea on the other side of the world."

I stand, the rivulets of sweat slithering down my face, my neck and between my breasts like little snakes. I scan the rocks and notice Antonio far below. He blows me a kiss then turns back to the fish. I pull my swimsuit down beneath my breasts exposing them and quickly lie back down. The cool Mediterranean breeze brushes seductively across my nipples and the dampness on my body. I gasp before quickly falling into a delicious nap.

A bird awakens me and I notice the sun has moved to that

place in the sky telling me it's about 4:00 p.m. The rocks beneath me are hard so I try to reposition myself many times. But my body is finished with lying down and my skin has had enough of the sun. I pull my top up just in time. Antonio walks toward me with a string of ten fish.

"Are you okay, sweetie?" he asks.

"Yes, but I'm tired of the sun. Can we go?"

"*Si, si* … I am finished. Look. Now I make you dinner, sweetie." He smiles proudly.

"That's a lot of fish, Antonio."

"I know! *Aspetta,* wait until you taste them; they are the best you will ever have and you will never forget me after I cook them for you."

He comes to my villa and cooks a meal for me that is far more impressive than one prepared in any five-star restaurant. I will always remember the smells and the taste of these little silver fish that are meaty and sweet. Antonio fries them in olive oil, herbs, and salt and pepper until their skin is seared and crispy. I realize the fish smells like the sea as if we were on it. I will remember his recipe so I can recreate it myself but know I will never taste fish this fresh again unless I catch them here on Capri and cook them the same day.

"So, what do you think, my sweetie?"

I'm speechless and cannot find the words to explain my delight.

"I've never tasted fish like this before," is all I can say.

"*Si,* I am the best cook." He smiles proudly and thumps his chest with his thumb.

"Yes, you are a good cook, but the fish … it smells and tastes like the sea and is so sweet." I realize he probably doesn't understand. After all, he has lived on this island his entire life and has eaten this fish many times. How could he possibly know what I'm talking about?

"Yes. The fish on Capri is the best! But I am the best cook, too." Seated across from me at the small inlaid tile table, he takes a drag of his cigarette.

"Do you like my grandmother's *vino*? She makes it every year. I help her. You know, Rosanna, she lives with us. She makes the wine and the limoncello. She also prepares the tomatoes for the winter and makes olives and jams. I love my *nonna*. She is very strong."

"Yes, the wine is good. Where is your grandfather? Is he still alive?"

"No, he died ten years ago, and my grandmother came to live with us. My father goes to their villa and takes care of the grapes and the gardens every morning and every day after work." I knew his father was a shopkeeper in the village.

Antonio pulls out a sack holding a bottle of limoncello. He pours each of us a cup and we continue to talk about our lives.

"And what about your family, Rosanna?"

"My father and mother live in San Diego and I visit them almost every week. My ex-husband lives there, too. We share custody of our two boys."

"Why did you divorce, Rosanna?" He moves closer, intently waiting for my response.

"We married young and I supported him through law school. He was never home. Then I had the boys. He spent long hours studying; there was school and then he worked hard for ten years hoping to be a partner in the law firm. It finally paid off, but I still never saw him."

He pours me another limoncello although I am already feeling the effects of it and the wine.

"That's what wives do. The men work hard here, too and the women take care of the home and the children."

I glare at Antonio. Old hurt and anger start to bubble up inside me, fueled by the wine, the limoncello and Antonio's remark.

"I was the perfect wife and the perfect mother. I did it all myself—homework, scouts, sporting events. I never complained. I thought it was a perfect marriage and this is what a perfect wife does." I begin to pace back and forth. "I cooked his favorite dishes every night. I was a gourmet chef, for Christ's sake."

My wounded inner child is shouting to be heard, my heart beating wildly. I'm pacing faster and faster ... back and forth.

"But he was always working late. '*Sorry, Cookie,*' he'd say."

68

"Cookie?" Antonio asks quizzically.

"Yah, my cute little pet name. He called me that because he thought I was so damned funny. That was when he loved only me!" I'm seething now.

Antonio nervously lights another cigarette.

"I was always so damned lonely. So, I tried to do better ... to do more. So, one day I bought sexy lingerie, took a bottle of his favorite Chateau Latour from the wine cellar, packed a picnic lunch and stopped for Kung Pao Chicken."

"What is Kung Po ...?" Antonio asks. But I can no longer hear him.

"I drove to his work. His office was the only one with lights because all good husbands had gone by then! It was 9:00 p.m. But not him ..." I begin to wail.

"I heard strange sounds ... sounds I didn't like. I opened the door and saw them—her bent over the desk and him having sex with her."

I laugh maniacally.

"I screamed. Ed jumped back, surprised. She fell off the desk onto the floor and I threw the bag of Chinese food at them. What a sight, Ed with all that Kung Pao and noodles hanging off his ... you know." I'm sobbing.

Antonio starts to laugh and I glare at him. I grab my limoncello and guzzle it down then slam the glass on the table in front of him. He fills it obediently.

"All those years ... my life ... wasted. *'I want a divorce, Deborah. I don't love you anymore. It's not you; it's me.'*"

I turn to Antonio.

"Can you believe that shit?"

Antonio is bugged-eyed, his mouth agape.

"We were high school sweethearts. He was my only love, the only man I ever made love to. I knew everything about him—how he liked his hard-boiled eggs cooked for twelve minutes and thirty seconds ... perfect ... how he liked me to press the creases in his slacks after they came back from the dry cleaners."

I'm getting angrier by the second, if this is at all possible. I slug back my drink as Antonio nervously smokes one cigarette after another. He's quiet, not daring to interrupt me.

"Yeah ... I had perfected the Stepford wife role. I created a new recipe for him for dinner at least twice a week. I made lunch for him every day and always stuck a love note inside. I even kissed them with lipstick and splashed them with perfume. I was his cheerleader, for Christ's sake! What about me? All those years."

Antonio blesses himself.

"Oh yeah, I was amazing." Antonio starts to say something but I interrupt him.

"We rarely had sex. Most times, it was so quick I had to fake an orgasm." Which I am now reenacting for Antonio. I continue to ramble.

"He never had a fucking clue. Yeah, I was a model wife. It was all about Ed. He never thought about me!"

I'm now hysterical, talking gibberish, seething with anger and hurt. I start throwing our dinner plates against the wall of the villa, my wine glass, and anything else I can get my hands on. I grab the ashtray.

Antonio jumps up and grabs me, holding me tightly in his arms.

"Rosanna, no worry. Calm down. He's not here."

"You don't understand. You're just a baby, a little boy. You have no idea how scary it is out there ... can't trust anyone ... *sob* ... anyone ... *sob* ... with your heart.

"Why didn't you fight for him? There must be something you could have done better."

I pull away from him.

"Wrong thing to say. I did EVERYTHING for him! And what does he do to me? He has a fucking affair with his secretary. He told me he wanted to marry her. And he did!"

I begin to howl, all my pain flooding out of me like a raging river.

"But is okay in Italy. Men have affairs."

"You are such a jerk, you know that?" I turn and walk toward the villa. "LEAVE, Antonio. You're dead to me! Just like Ed!"

He stares, confusion on his face.

"What did I do?"

"GO!" I turn and stub my toe on the little slatted chair near the door. Owwww ... that hurts."

He shrinks away from me and scurries out through the gate as I limp toward the villa. Once inside, I throw myself across the bed, my head spinning from the wine and the limoncello … every scene replaying itself like old reruns.

"Do you love her?" He stares at me blankly. "DO YOU LOVE HER? Answer me!"

"Yes, I love her. I'm sorry, Deb."

Then six months later, as soon as the divorce was final, "Deb, I'm getting married. I hope you're okay with this. The kids like her. She's a nice woman. She loves the boys and will be a good stepmom."

I close my eyes and remember my world blowing apart. I was still grieving the loss of my perfect life, my husband, my family while he had already moved on.

I remember the sleeping pills that night. I almost succeeded.

I cry myself to sleep. But it's fitful, filled with reruns. And in between each one, I'm vomiting the limoncello, the fish, the wine and all the old emotions that have been stuffed down inside me for so long.

I walk outside into the darkness, only the stars to light the moonless sky. I'm anxious and grieving at the same time because my former life has invaded my new life and the newfound happiness and solitude I've worked so hard for.

I had locked the hurt and memories away for years. It was safer that way. But now …

I don't want to lose myself to the madness of his betrayal again.

You are stronger now, Roxanna. It won't happen.

I try and take a breath but can't.

Your old life is gone. You have complete control over your own happiness now.

I finally breathe. I will move on from this and promise to honor those pieces of myself that I've found on this island.

At four in the morning, I crawl into bed and fall into a deep sleep. The spirit comes to me and we are standing before the sphinx on the edge of the property.

"Your heartache is in the past, Roxanna. Leave it there. If you were meant to be together still in this lifetime, you would be. But you are meant for greater things. Your soul is free, and you are here in *paradiso* on a great adventure. Enjoy it. This night, you have healed all of it and you will now move forward."

He touches my heart then disappears.

I awaken late morning enveloped in a soft and sheer mist of tranquility. It's as if all the heartache, the memories and emotions of the night before were nothing but a dream. Then, I remember Antonio saying, "There must have been something you could have done better."

Thank you, Antonio.

CHAPTER 12

For the next week, I sleep long hours and rarely move from the villa. The memories of Ed's betrayal that I relived that night with Antonio have finally receded into the mists of the past. My heart has healed.

Each day, I watch the sky and the sea as their colors change. Then, I watch the flowers bloom finding each new one that has come out to dance in the sunlight. White butterflies and lizards with long tails and bright green stripes painted down their backs lazily move about. Sometimes, I hold my breath in hopes they might come closer but if I breathe at all or move an inch, they scurry away.

Eventually, I'm ready to leave *Mio Paradiso* and visit the town of Capri. This day, the *autobus* is filled with tourists, everyone lined up holding on for dear life as the driver rounds the deadly curves of the road leaving them gasping at each hairpin turn. I too am standing and holding onto the handrails as we edge the cliffs. Many riders are excited and sometimes horrified as the driver maneuvers his way around the other buses and taxis as they climb the mountainous road heading toward us, only inches between both vehicles. With no guard rails to stop the bus from plummeting over the side, our breath catches as we hug the cliffs overlooking the port 600 to 1,000 meters below (depending on which stretch of the road we are on).

Once we arrive in Capri, I walk to the Gardens of Augustus

where ancient statues of the gods sit amongst the flowers ... another inspiring place to paint.

A group of twenty school children have come to the gardens for an outing and their teacher has asked me to take a photograph of them. As soon as the children see this, six of them come running with their own cameras. Laughter fills the garden as the children jockey for position in the front row for the photos, and the ones that speak English are calling to me.

"*Signora, come ti chiami*? Your name?"

"Roxanna," I reply. But for some reason, they cannot get their tongues around it and proceed to call me "Caterina." How Caterina has come from Roxanna, I do not know. No mind. I'm enjoying them. The name sticks and for the next fifteen minutes, I'm known to everyone as Caterina. They all shout "*Grazie*" and "*Ciao, Caterina*," as they leave.

Walking down the wisteria-lined path, I meander slowly, taking everything in for I don't want to miss a thing or hurry to get anywhere. My thoughts are interrupted by a sign that reads *Toilettes*. I need to visit one, so I walk up a short path where an elderly gentleman, about eight-five, is tending to the restrooms. He doesn't speak a word of English, but somehow manages to invite me in for a cup of *espresso*.

"*Espresso?*" He's short with a beret cocked to one side of his head and a twinkle in his eye. His hair is thick and white. He points to himself and says, "Alberto."

"*Si, si.*" Why not? He seems like a lovely man. Another new friend. I smile and he winks at me. "I am Roxanna."

We sit and try to communicate through sign language and with what little Italian I know. The conversation is not a long one, for we both have grown weary of the words, *si, capisci* and *no capisco*. But I linger for a bit after I finish my coffee.

"*Grazie*," I say as I prepare to leave. He comes to me for the customary kissing of the cheeks but to my surprise, he grabs my face tightly and kisses me hard on the lips.

I slap his face!

He slaps me back!

I slap him again ... just to finish it!

Then I walk as fast as I can, leaving him standing there holding his cheeks, mumbling, *"Mamma mia."*

Still shaking, I walk the path to the gardens and then stop.

Roxanna, it's just a kiss! Get over yourself!

I begin to laugh and can't seem to stop. People passing stop to look.

"I'll never get used to this 'Love Italian Style!'" I say out loud.

Every woman who is having any self-doubt about her beauty or her age should come here for an ego boost. Lost in this thought, I enter *Umberto Piazza* and hear my new name.

"Caterina! Caterina! *Buona sera!*" All the school children, my new friends, are walking through the square excitedly waving at me with smiles on their faces.

"Ciao ... ciao!" Nothing like children to take you out of yourself.

I continue to walk and explore the village of Capri this night, enjoying the sights and sounds. The sun is setting so I stand in the *Piazza Umberto* looking toward the horizon and suddenly hear music as the wind carries it upward from the port.

Most days at the villa, I lounge on the chaise enjoying the sounds of the June bugs and watching the black and yellow hummingbirds that resemble bumble bees.

Enrico comes by twice daily to water the gardens and to prune the plants. He always has a pair of cutting shears in his hands. Oftentimes when we walk, he clips branches and flowers sculpting as he goes. It is the most beautiful garden I have ever seen—bushes, flowers and trees everywhere with rocks strategically placed that create little paths with vines and wisteria hanging overhead.

Oftentimes, he will have a cup of the wonderful tea I've brought from the States, a mixture of black teas with jasmine and rose. It soothes my soul when I drink it, reminding me of home.

"Roxanna, I am moving you to a bed-and-breakfast for a week and then I will find something more permanent for you. I am sorry you have to move again but I have negotiated a very good rate."

"No problem, Enrico. I appreciate everything you have done for me. Where will I go?"

"It is called *Maruzzella*. Do you know the steps you walk to get here?" By now, I'm used to getting these types of directions.

"Yes."

"Good. Go down to the trash cans. Do you know where they are?"

"Yes, I remember." I have passed them every day on my way to and from town, the row with three small green bins where the townspeople carry their small bags of trash each day to be collected.

"You go down those steps and it is right there on your left. You cannot miss it. Take your things there tomorrow."

"What does *maruzzella* mean?" I'm learning new Italian words daily but this one seems strange to me. It's pronounced "**mar**-roo-zella."

"It is the name of the little thing inside the round shells ... like this." He draws a picture of a snail in the dirt.

"That's a snail." I wrinkle my nose and Enrico laughs.

"I don't know why, silly, eh? It means little snail."

Although I'm not looking forward to leaving my little villa, I know I will be well taken care of, as I have been since I came to the island. I came here with nowhere to sleep, met Peter and stayed at the San Michele Villa. Then I met Enrico who put me up here. I trust him for my next place.

The sun blazes high above me as I carry my overstuffed suitcase and backpack to Maruzzella. I walk the long distance towing my luggage behind me and realize I will miss the little cottage.

A large and colorful bougainvillea grows over the rounded wrought iron gate. A hand-painted ceramic tile reads, "Casetta Bettina" and the building is a bright white. I ring the bell at the gate and a woman appears. She takes me to my room where everything is white—the walls the floors and the bedding and towels. It is blindingly beautiful and delicate. How fresh. I am elated with the place.

Unlike the cottage, my room is enclosed with screens, a luxury many don't have on the island. The bathroom has a modern enclosed shower and everything is white, bright and clean, "fresh" as the Italians say. That is the English word they use to describe it.

A writing table and chair sit facing the window and a large closet covers one wall. I unpack as if I will be staying forever, for this makes it feel like home eventhough my stay will be temporary.

Maruzzella sits in the middle of a vineyard and the grapes are starting to take form. Many hidden terraces are scattered about the property, so many places to sit in the shade and sketch. My favorite is at the edge of the property where I have a view of the sea so I sit and draw for hours. My notebook has become filled with drawings of places I have visited and scenes I have been inspired by. It also contains snippets from my heart that have spilled out onto the paper ... poetry, now an expression of my passions.

> *The wind and the sea whispers to me –*
> *"Come!"*
> *"I have love for you – as wet as my waters –*
> *as vast as my seas;*
> *and I will wrap you up*
> *inside my blue skies and soft breezes."*
>
> *My soul cries out.*
> *"I am coming."*

I have settled into my peaceful surroundings. A tabby cat lazily follows me from place to place. We try to outsmart the sun as it moves across the sky. It is hot this day, so hot that my arms are moist and little beads of sweat run down the nape of my neck. Thankfully, at 7.00 p.m. a breeze arrives and cools the air.

I listen to the wind blowing gently through the vineyards. It's a sound I have never heard before so it's hard to describe. It's louder than the wind blowing through the trees in a mountain forest and sounds like a crowd in an auditorium, all clapping their hands at the same time. It is music to my ears stopping me in my tracks.

Inspired, I sketch and write poetry until the sun is ready to set. It beckons me as it has every evening since I arrived. I chase it until I find an opening to the sea and the sky—a *terrazzo* at the edge of the vineyard in the middle of a little garden, a small settee canopied with overhanging grape leaves. From here, I watch the isle of Ischia and the sun above it as it starts its evening descent. Once again, that familiar elixir called passion rises inside me.

CHAPTER 13

It was far too beautiful this morning to stay in bed so I decided to take a long early morning walk about Anacapri. The island is quiet, everyone just awakening. Some are out watering their lemon trees or tending their gardens. Even the sea below is soft and quiet. I could stay lost in this sound forever.

After *espresso* and a *cornetto*, I stop by *Carthusia, I Profumi di* Capri where they sell parfums said to be made by Carthusian monks. The scents are rapturous, the effect, I imagine, due to their chanting over them as they blend them.

"Alessandra, *ciao. Come va?*"

"*Bene, bene* ... and you, Roxanna? Where have you been? We have not seen you for some time."

She's a pretty woman, about forty and has light brown hair pulled back in a barrette. This day is humid but she is fresh and unbothered by the heat and the dampness in the air.

"I am well. I have been busy."

I try to think of what has taken up my time but nothing comes to mind. We make small talk as the tourists stroll in and out of the shops looking for treasures to remind them of paradise. We try to guess which countries they come from, a game we have played before. Then the conversation turns to men and which nationalities make better husbands.

"American men make the best husbands. That's what I'm waiting for ... a handsome American man to come into my shop and take me home with him!" She smiles dreamily. I do not want to cloud her dreams with my memories so I leave them buried.

"No, Italian men are the best," I say. "They love their women as if they are the Madonna herself."

I remember Mother's Day on the island. I watched all the families strolling through the streets. The fathers were holding their babies and the hands of their wives. And if there were no babies, they walked with their arms around their women holding them close as they swelled with pride. I think of Enrico and how he had spoken about his wife, and Mario about his. Mario is a friend of Enrico's who checks on me occasionally, bringing me vegetables and sometimes home-cooked meals that he and his wife make.

"I never think of the Italian men that way." Alessandra wrinkles her nose. "They like to have lovers on the side. This is not good." She has lowered her eyes and is frowning as she adamantly shakes her head from one side to the other.

"But it's because they love all women so much, they don't know what to do with them and want them all. They are like little boys in a candy store." We both laugh. Eventually, the store swells with tourists and we say goodbye.

I come upon Federico's studio. When I first met him, I introduced myself as Roxanna. He said, "Ah, Roxanna is English. In Italian, we say Rosanna. But I will call you by your English name. Yes?" I liked him immediately. And besides, I am used to both.

Each morning at 5:00 a.m. he goes for a swim somewhere on the island and sketches the scene before him. He has become my mentor, oftentimes, sharing his creations with me and explaining how the light was at that time of day and how he has captured it. We talk about technique and sometimes I sit quietly beside him as he sketches the street scene before us.

Federico and a woman sit on stools outside, waiting for the tourists. He looks fresh and cool in his pale-blue linen shirt and pants and strapped sandals. Although he's in his late seventies, he seems much younger. He's a passionate man, always humming a tune or singing when he is not talking.

"Roxanna, I want to see you paint. You must paint. Let your *passione* fly free! You are keeping them all bottled up inside … *Mamma mia.*" Federico brings his hands to his head as if he has a headache. "You are wasting your life away not painting. It is a gift from God!" He begs me, his hands clasped together as if in prayer.

"Soon ... soon Federico ... I've been busy." It's an excuse, I know. But, I'm afraid. What if I can no longer paint? No longer have the talent? Or worse, what will I unleash inside me? And will I be able to live with all the emotions it will stir up?

"When you are ready then." He turns and moves inside to the settee in his studio. I follow him.

"Would you like me to sing for you, *bella*?" Federico has already picked up his guitar and is tossing the strap over his shoulder. He strums the strings and they create a flamenco-like melody.

"*Si,*" I respond, even though he has already started. He ends the melody and starts an American tune, "Love Me Tender." Eerily, he sounds like Elvis himself. He often plays classical music or flamenco ... so much talent in one man.

"Federico, it's time to go. I must leave."

We have been sitting for an hour. We both rise and move to the door. He hugs me and kisses both cheeks.

"Where are you going?" He asks.

"I'm on my way to the San Michele."

"Ah, *si, si.* I understand. It's calling you, eh?" He smiles. "When you come again, we will have champagne, yes? *Ciao, ciao.*"

"*Ciao,* Federico."

I love the way the islanders say *ciao* twice. I feel special because it's so intimate and only for the closest of friends.

As I continue down the street toward the San Michele Villa, I run into my friend, Donata, her arms laden with groceries. Donata is the daughter of Mario who tends the gardens at my villa. The first time I met her, her three-year-old boy, Luca played at her feet while we chatted. His father is *Napoletano*, so baby Luca is very expressive like the *Napoletani*. He scrunches his face up when he's curious and he talks with his hands. To me, the *Napoletani* know life, feel it and express it passionately. Donata said that her son had come out of the womb that way. I fell in love with him instantly.

Donata, her name meaning "Gift from God," was born in Anacapri. Her hair is blonde, accenting her eyes which are deep brown pools you can become lost in. Her heavy bags have pulled her cotton dress up a bit so she tries to smooth it under the weight. I take them from her.

"Donata, *ciao. Come stai?*"

"Roxanna, *ciao, ciao ... bene, bene*. And you?"

"I'm good. Where are you going?" I ask.

"I have been for a long walk and to the market. And you, Roxanna?"

"Just walking the town. Where's Luca?"

"He's with my mother. He is a crazy boy, full of energy. I cannot take him to the market when I shop." We both laugh for we know how Luca can be. "Roxanna, please come to dinner? We would love to see you."

"I would love to."

"Good. What about Wednesday, in two days?"

"Yes, I will come."

"Come at 19:00, you know, 7:00 p.m." My friends always note the time in both ways, just in case I can't figure it out.

"Do you remember how to get there or should I send my husband to meet you?" Their house is at the end of the island and the winding path that takes you there is edged with flowers that intoxicate you with each step.

"I remember. I will call you if I get lost. Can I walk you home with your groceries? I can help."

"No, no, I can do this, but thank you." She smiles at me. "I will see you on Wednesday. *Ciao, ciao*, Roxanna." We hug and kiss goodbye.

I had dined with Donata and her family when we first met. She taught me about the Italian culture, their traditions, and also helped me with the language. She is my Italian sister and best friend.

As I walk on, I remember my first dinner with her family. Her husband Marcello was the first *Napoletano* I had met. He was of strong build and had a presence about him. He hugged me hard and kissed my cheeks as if we had been friends forever. It was then that I understood why Luca was so demonstrative; it is the *Napletano* way.

Mario, Donata's father is also an expressive man. He's well-known and loved by all on the island. If anyone needs anything, Mario is there for them. His thick brown hair falls over his forehead in a cowlick, making him seem like a teenager instead of his sixty-five years. And the sleeveless tee-shirt he always wears adds to the illusion.

That first night, Marcello and Mario cooked pasta and fish as we women—Donata, her mother Lousia and I, sat at the outdoor table on the patio and laughed and talked as the men poured us homemade sparkling wine. They kept refilling our glasses, enjoying the fact that we were giggling and having so much fun.

Louisa is only a few years older than me, a petite woman and strong like most of the women in Capri. I have seen her carry not only Luca but also sacks of groceries from the market to their home. Her hair is short and dark and she has dark eyes and a beauty mark on her face reminding me of Sophia Loren. We had such fun that night and I was treated as if I were a member of the family.

The gates of the San Michele are before me, bringing me back to the present. I pay and walk through the *porta*, through the *museo* and into the villa. I never tire of this tour through each room for it's as if I'm coming home to my own place and I'm simply walking through noticing everything that's dear to me.

I have enjoyed reading Munthe's book and am in awe of this man who has had a very big life. I walk the grounds and envision him as he strolled through this garden with his dogs and his pet monkey. He would walk to the edge of the *pergola* each night and light his pipe in anticipation of the sunset. I can feel his spirit all around me and in each room inside the villa. I envision him at his writing table, a bas relief of Apollo hanging above his head as a life-size statue of Kouros stands guard across the room.

His description of how he felt the first time he came to the island, walking up the 770 stone steps that Tiberius had built, captivates me. As the story goes, he was delirious by the time he made it to the top, the locals feeding him food and wine for strength. I, too wanted to get down on my knees and kiss the ground when I arrived in Marina Piccola but I was busy swooning from the songs of the sirens, Peter's kiss and my lack of sleep.

So, there is a bond between us, Munthe and I. It was my destiny to come here just as it was his. *"The light, the light ... everywhere ..."* I remember his words.

I walk the gardens and gaze at the flowers and the lush, green trees that he planted so long ago. When I return to the States, I will create a garden such as this.

I near the sphinx and place my hand upon its backside but realize I have no wish. So, I linger standing beside him looking out over the sea, amazed at its beauty. My thoughts are soon interrupted by a familiar hand on my shoulder.

"Roxanna, this is your life. You are who you will always be now that you have found yourself. And you may go wherever your soul leads you. Whatever you wish for is yours!"

I'm startled. Then suddenly, he's gone. I laugh at my own insanity and my tears begin to flow. I weep with joy for I have so much to be thankful for.

It's been four days since I arrived at *Maruzzella* and this morning I awaken feeling blue. My sons have filled my dreams and I miss them terribly. I lie in bed until noon, the darkness inside my mind keeping me company throughout the morning. They day is long and finally, it's 6:00 p.m. I call them. I try to sound cheerful but they sense my truth.

"Mom, is everything okay? You sound funny." Hearing Josh's voice, I start to weep.

"I'm fine. I just miss you both." I try to make light of it.

"We're fine. We miss you, too but everything's good here. I have a new girlfriend." I hear the excitement in his voice.

"It's Mom." I hear Devon asking Josh who's on phone.

"What's her name? Where did you meet her?" I pull him back to me.

Her name's Amber and she has blonde hair. She's pretty, Mom. I met her outside the movie theater."

"Mom!" Devon is on the other line. "How's it going? Got any stories?" He always loved my stories. It was a game we played when he was a little boy.

"Devon, I miss you both so much." I start to cry again.

"Mom, stop. We're fine. We're just chillin' with Dad tonight, watching a movie. Cynthia had to go to work."

Although my sons have turned into men overnight, their voices deepened, I only hear them as my little boys.

"What have you been doing?" Devon asks. I tell them about the island and my new friends and about how I spend my days. Devon has asked for a story, so I weave one about Axel Munthe and the San Michele Villa while Josh listens on the other line. We talk about the photos I've sent them and Josh's girlfriend. Devon hands the phone to their father and when I hear his voice, I break down and cry.

"Cookie ... sorry. Deb ... I mean Roxanna ..." He laughs. "I'm sorry, still getting used to all this. They're fine. They're happy here with us. Stop worrying. They miss you but they've been busy. It's their time away from you now. They need to be dating and spending time with friends. Let them go."

"Maybe I should come home, Ed ..." He cuts me off.

"No, absolutely not! You need to stay through the summer. Enjoy yourself. Figure out what you want to do. I'm envious. Look at you. I wish I was there instead of you, so don't do anything you'll regret. Stay until September. It's not like you have anything pressing to come back to."

I think of my sons, but Ed interrupts my thoughts.

"Right now, I'm getting to know my boys and frankly, I like it. I'm not quite ready to give them back. I wish I hadn't missed so much of their childhood." He's reflective.

Josh is back on the other line.

"Mom, stay for the summer. Dad and Cynthia are taking us to Yosemite so we won't be here if you come home. Be strong, Mom. Love you."

Josh hands the phone to Devon.

"Mom, stay for the summer. We want you to meet someone, maybe get married again." He laughs and I begin to smile.

"Are you both okay with this?" I need reassurance.

"Yes, we are. But you need to send more pictures. We love you Mom." They both talk in unison.

"Bye."

"Bye."

"I love you both."

"I mean it; stay," Ed says firmly. "And if you need someone to talk to, call me. I'll straighten you out."

"Thanks, Ed."

I hang up the phone and think of my ex and how our relationship has grown stronger. Who would have thought that a cheating husband and a bad divorce would turn into something good? He listens to me more now than he did when we were married.

I think about how much Ed has changed since that night I found him with Cynthia. I'm not sure he ever thought about getting caught. He was in the moment, thinking only about himself and her. Their relationship has lasted and they are still happily married. I guess it was meant to be. But did they have to marry so quickly after our divorce was final? That, too sent me over the edge. I never thought I'd recover, my depression so deep.

In the end, he realized the effect his affair had on me when he saw me disappearing inside myself, withdrawing from life. I was no longer the vibrant, strong woman who was always in control of everything. I was unresponsive for months ... incapacitated. A few weeks after their marriage, I was at the bottom. I had the pills out and started taking them. He came to the house just in time, said he had to pick up paperwork. Then I was admitted for evaluation. They said it was a suicide attempt. That wasn't my intention. I just wanted the pain to stop.

It was a time and place I never want to go back to. I was in therapy and heavily medicated for months. Ed came daily and I think he realized then, how impactful his betrayal was on me. He had been the love of my life. I met him in college, the tall, dark and handsome intellectual. That rainy night we met, he offered to walk me back to my dorm and shared his umbrella with me. I decided then that he was the one I would spend the rest of my life with.

Finding him and Cynthia having sex was like ripping my heart out of my chest and stealing my life from me. He never understood how much he had hurt me until my therapist explained what happens when a loved one cheats and the other sees it firsthand. It took me a long time to forgive him. But over the last few years, we have softened toward each other and I like him better now than when I was married to him.

My depression and suicide attempt got his attention and he began to look at his life. He finally went for counseling and recognized he had been absent from our family. He started to pick up the slack with the boys, and was there for them during my recovery. If I was too emotional or too depressed to have them, he would come to my rescue immediately. I know it might seem strange to some, but he was my rock.

That night when Antonio made dinner and I unleashed all my anger and pain was the night I finally forgave Ed. I still don't know what happened except that I spewed out everything that had been stuffed inside me.

CHAPTER 14
SORRENTO, ITALY

Many travel to Sorrento and the Amalfi Coast for their honeymoon. They say it's one of the most romantic place in the south of Italy so I had to come and see for myself.

I disembark from the hydrofoil and ride the bus up the hill and into town where the flowers and lemon trees come into sight. Sorrento is quaint and beautiful as it overlooks the Bay of Naples, Mount Vesuvius and the island of Capri. The architecture is grand and the *Duomo*, the cathedral, is in the center of the city on the Corso Italia, the main street that runs through the city. Although it appears to be a simple church from the outside, once you step inside, your breath will leave you.

It was built in the 11th century and rebuilt in the 16th century in Romanesque style. The nave is filled with sculpted arches held up by marble columns. Beautiful paintings and ancient frescoes dress the ceilings and walls. I kneel in a pew and say a prayer of gratitude for my good fortune these days.

After giving thanks, I walk through the town and follow a narrow street that leads me through a maze of alleyways into the old town of Sorrento. It's a hidden area filled with boutiques, coffee shops, cafes, wine bars, restaurants and markets that sell lace, linens, handmade clothing, Limoncello and wine, and specialty foods that Sorrento is known for. The largest lemons I have ever seen lay in carts for sale.

I am reminded of love and romance as I note the couples milling about. Two lovers pass by and I know they are newly-wed. I can tell by the way they hold on to each other. Each time she stops to gaze in a shop window, his eyes are fixed on her and not on what she is looking at. I realize that even here, I'm the only *solo* person. But I'm quickly distracted by the man selling flowers.

"*Molto bella.*" He smiles and winks at me as I pass by. I turn my head to see if he's speaking to someone behind me, but there is no one.

"*Grazie,*" I respond.

The clouds dance across the sky giving the streets a much-needed break from the sweltering sun and the damp humidity. A young man holding a menu stands in front of a *trattoria*, a towel draped over one arm. The tables behind him are dressed in red and white checkered cloths. Little vases filled with geraniums decorate each one.

"*Buon giorno, bella. Vieni a mangiare,* come to eat and drink." He smiles at me with shy eyes.

"*Si, grazie.*" He takes me to an outer table where I can see the tourists as they pass by.

"*Prego,* you are welcome."

I am seated and watch as people eat gelato or enjoy their *espresso*. Flowers are everywhere and the fragrance of geraniums is soothing. I sip my *vino bianco* and breathe in their sweetness and the aromas of Sorrento. Then I close my eyes and savor the moment.

"Go to Rome, Roxanna ..."

I bolt upright in my chair and look around. Then I realize it's the voice of the spirit. Rome ... I have always wanted to visit there, visit the Sistine Chapel, the Vatican, the Coliseum, and Palatine Hill. Why not?

Over lunch, I dream of Rome and how I will conquer it. These thoughts keep me company all the way back to Capri.

Back at the villa, I change my clothes and leave for the bus to Capri and the bookstore to purchase a tour book of Rome. Then I take myself to the Hotel la Palma for a light dinner. As I read my travel guide, I decide I will stay in the opera district because the woman in the bookstore recommended a boutique hotel there. She said it's quaint and close to the train station.

The first day, I'll visit the Borghese Villa, its museum and then the famous Tivoli Fountain and the Spanish Steps. The next day, I'll visit the Vatican and the Sistine Chapel ... and the Coliseum and Palatine Hill ... well, maybe I'll see these on the third day. I'll stay until I have seen everything in the city. I cannot contain my excitement. They probably look at me here and say, "There she is again, that giggling American woman.

Another adventure. What a life I'm leading.

I think back to the emails I've sent from *Il Matino*, the internet cafe. I have a network of six girlfriends who live vicariously through me so I email them every few days to tell them what I'm doing. They live for those emails as they work their jobs and care for their families. A few even wish they were here with me living the dream while the others just want to hear my stories. What new adventure will I find in Rome to tell them about?

I'm pulled out of my daydream as a crowd gathers on the small street before me in front of Armani. Many have their cell phones or cameras out and are trying to snap photos of whoever is inside.

"Would you like anything else, *Signora*?" The waiter has come.

"No, *grazie*. Who are they waiting for?" I ask.

"Sophia Loren. She is very beautiful."

Donata said she had seen her shopping in Anacapri two days before and that she was a small woman, still as beautiful as she was forty years ago.

"She has a villa on the other side of the island, above Marina Piccola," says the waiter. "It is the big compound at the top of the mountain."

I pay him and walk out to the street to wait with everyone else to catch a glimpse of this famous beauty. The stores across from the La Palma are the high-end shops—Georgio Armani; MASA, a male and female clothing store; and Snobberie with its sexy Italian lingerie and undergarments, lacey G-strings and matching bras which adorn the windows. All, cater to the wealthy. Movie stars shop here and try to hide from the world when they come. But they cannot escape, even here. The only saving grace is that this is *paradiso* and the crowds are a lot smaller.

I study the gorgeous Italian women as they walk by, amazed by their beauty. They are adorned in beaded halter-tops and have heavy necklaces of gold and gemstones draped around their necks. They either wear long flowing skirts, very short tight ones, or Capri pants of white linen, the fabric of choice here on the island because of the sweltering heat.

I watch them with their long hair. Most wear it pulled back tightly in a ponytail, or pulled up in the Romanesque style with a clip or barrette gathering the top half only at the back of the head, the rest falling loosely around their shoulders.

Capri is a magnet for the rich and famous, unlike Anacapri which is more of a hidden treasure. If you don't know where to go, then you might not find it as interesting or as exciting as Capri. But I now consider myself a local because I know where the best restaurants, the best shopping and the best hikes are off the beaten path. It's a village untouched by time, the people precious to me.

Paparazzi are lined up and Ms. Loren walks out onto the street. She is radiant and petite in a floral dress that reaches mid-calf with spiked, strappy sandals on her feet. I'm not sure how but she manages to walk gracefully on the uneven stone streets. Her skirt moves with each step, flowing as if it has been orchestrated. Her breasts peek out of her top, and a sizable collar of gold leaves is draped around her neck reminding me of something that Cleopatra would wear for Caesar.

She stops for a few moments and smiles at the crowd allowing her fans to snap photos. As she turns to leave, I hear the men both young and old say, "*Bella, che bella ...*"

"*Grazie, grazie mille ... arrivederci!*" She raises her hand over her head signaling her departure and smiles wide. Yes, she is small, but oh, she is larger than life.

CHAPTER 15
ROME, ITALY

The walk to my hotel in the Opera district is only four blocks from the train and my backpack on wheels is light. With the heat, I only needed to pack a few things—three thin skirts and tops, two dresses, a nightgown and my swimsuit. My toiletries and hairdryer are the heaviest, but a necessity. Where would a girl be without them? I also have my sketchbook with me, for I know I will be inspired after visiting the museums. The uneven Roman stones on the sidewalk echo rat-a-tat-tat underneath the plastic wheels.

The smell of tomatoes, basil and garlic blended with geranium floats through the air invading my senses ... the perfume of Italia. I hear the musical sound of the language being spoken all around me along with the soft vroom of scooters as they move through the busy city. Little cafes and shops are tucked in between the hotels. As I walk by one of them, I hear that familiar phrase.

"*Molto bella* ..." The Romans are very expressive and vocal about what or who is beautiful to them, just as they are in the south. I wonder if all of Italy is like this?

My hotel is easy to find and directly across from the Opera House. I check in and am in my room within thirty minutes of leaving the train. I immediately throw open the shutters and take in the view. Children chase pigeons in the *piazza* while their mother smile into the sun, happy with life.

Ancient buildings line the streets. Their windows are large, many of them open so I have a view inside. I spot a man walking around in his room bare-chested. He's on the telephone talking with his free hand, moving it with each word as if it helps him make a point to the person on the other end of the line.

A pretty, dark-haired woman in the building directly across from me is bending over the windowsill hanging clothes on a line.

"*Aspetta, aspetta,* wait, wait." Frustrated, she calls to her little ones who are asking for her attention, although I cannot see them. A sudden breeze comes out of nowhere, unusual with the heat, and picks up the edge of the linen sheet she is hanging, carrying it upward on the air.

I'm in Rome! I hug myself. I had begged Ed to take me, but he was always too busy. Who would have guessed I'd come here alone? I move from the window and start to ready myself for my trip to the Vatican.

It's noon and the sun beats down on the city as if it were punishing it. It's a sweltering heat with much dampness and not even the tiniest of breezes so it takes getting used to. I'm able to stay cool by moving slowly and dressing in lightweight linen.

I arrive in Vatican City where thousands of people are milling about. Hundreds stand in the scorching sun waiting to get into the museums. A thousand or so walking about the *Piazza della San Pietro,* Saint Peter's Square. The two fountains, designed and created by Maderno and Bernini, are impressive, but what steals my breath is the 83-foot red granite Egyptian Obelisk sitting on bronze lions. Once I recover, my eyes move to Saint Peter's Cathedral. It is massive. I read it holds up to 60,000 people making it one of the largest churches in the world. It took over 100 years to build and was designed by the best—Bramante, Michelangelo, Maderno and Bernini.

I move toward the colonnade for some shade. It seems to reach upward toward the sky, its roof lined with, I think, 140 statues of saints. I'm amazed at the magnitude and beauty of this sacred place.

I am quiet for a long time with no thoughts, only emotions. I know I have been here before. When? Another lifetime perhaps? I envision myself walking underneath this portico with a large book clutched tightly to my breast. I'm dressed in a habit, the clothing of a nun, and devotion swells within my heart. I cannot see anymore and the vision is lost, the sounds of children's laughter beckoning me back to the present. I rise and move out toward the fountains where I dip my fingers into the water and bring them to my lips. I want to fall into it, be blessed by it, but I know it is forbidden.

After a time, I enter the enormous Basilica and wait for my eyes to adjust to the dim light. The smell of incense intoxicates me. Bernini's *Balducchino*, his sculptured bronze tabernacle containing St. Peter's throne and tomb sits in the distance. Its gigantic hood and four colossal spiraling columns are decorated with olive branches and vines. A great sculpture sits in every corner. Each time I think one great work of art is superior, I find another that rivals the first.

I pull myself away to move toward the first chapel where I find Michelangelo's *Pieta*. It takes my breath away and tears flow freely down my cheeks. I weep openly as everyone else does around me. He was only twenty-four when he sculpted this. His depiction of the Madonna is soft and delicate, and although she is grieving, her face is serene as if somehow, she has found peace with the death of her son. Michelangelo must have had great love for her to have created such beauty with his fingers and the palms of his hands as he smoothed her skin and sculpted her delicate features. He has captured not only her youth and her sweetness, but also her strength.

Her gown is splendidly sculpted. It almost appears to have movement as it drapes over her body and falls to the floor. Mary's eyes make apparent her love and compassion for her son. The body of Christ, his skin clinging to his ribs ... his lifeless limbs, one arm resting on her lap ... I am overcome. I must pull myself away.

I sit on a wooden bench in quiet contemplation. I have the need to pray after seeing the *Pieta*, even though I have not been a practicing Catholic since I was twenty. Since I've come to Italy, I have found Santa Maria everywhere. If there is a grotto in the rocks or on a mountainside, it becomes a home to a Madonna statue. She is displayed and adorned with fresh flowers and candles at the entrance to every villa. I pray to her, thanking her for the gifts and miracles I have received since arriving in Italy. I tell her I love her and honor her for her life, her strength and her undying love. Then I linger for a bit.

I eventually move and come upon four huge pilasters containing four colossal statues, each representing the crucial moments of *Christ's Passion*—St. Longinus, St. Helen, St. Veronica and St. Andrew—all sculpted by Bernini. I study their fine lines and detail and am mesmerized by their size. I move from one room to another, taking everything in so that it is etched upon my heart. When I'm finished, I walk outside into the sunlight.

The Vatican Museums are next and I walk in without standing in line. Another miracle. I move through each gallery, each room, each hall and make note of everything I see. In the *Pinacoteca*, the picture gallery, paintings and portraits line the walls. In Room VIII, I find Raphael's *Trasfigurazione* painted in oil on wood. I feel the reverence he was trying to convey. In this same room is his *Madonna of Foligno* ... the colors of the paint, the context, the emotion ...

In Room XII, I stop before Caravaggio's *Deposition*, a startling portrayal of emotion. It's brilliant. Then, I come upon the entrance to *Capella Sistina,* the Sistine Chapel. As I enter the portal, my eyes scan every inch of every wall, the floor, the table, the ceiling. Each is frescoed, painted, sculpted or inlaid with ornate tile. Every inch of the room is a work of art in and of itself. Housed here are works by Pinturicchio, Botticelli, Rosselli, and Ghirlandaio who was Michelangelo's master. Then of course, there is Raphael and Michelangelo, two of my greatest mentors. I move closer to observe the heavy layering of the paint ... such time and effort, such attention to detail. Upon the air, I trace the lines of each painting with my fingers, the need to paint begging me for release.

"I can do this, too. I know I can."

Then the Chapel ceiling ... I had seen pictures, but this ... this, I have no words for. I know it had taken Michelangelo almost five years to finish. He has sculpted or painted every square inch but I am not prepared for what is before me.

Keep breathing, Roxanna. I am overwhelming … my senses on overload … immense … the masterpiece of the world … scene after scene across the entire dome. I cannot tell which is painted tromp l'oeil, architectural columns or scroll work. It's all so perfect.

All nine panels depicting the *Episodes from Genesis* are here: *Separation of Light and Dark; Creation of the Sun and Moon; Creation of Trees and Plants; Creation of Adam; Creation of Eve; Fall Follow; Noah's Sacrifice; the Flood;* and *The Drunkenness of Noah.* Then, there are the Prophets and the Sybils, Jesus' Forefathers and *Episodes from the Old Testament.*

I hold my breath as I study the scenes of *The Fall*—Adam and Eve as they are being forced out of the garden; the serpent as his body wraps around the tree of knowledge; Sybil, her beauty captured, her pose; the *Creation of Adam;* the finger of God reaching out to touch Adam's, and the look in Adam's eye. I had seen the likeness many times before but now that I see the original before me, I realize the power of it.

The *Last Judgment* hangs on the wall above the altar. For more than an hour, I take in all I can. I breathe it in, live it and love them all, every blessed scene. It's as if Michelangelo has only left moments before my arrival, for I can feel his heart, his soul and his energy.

Walking the streets back to my hotel, I realize how inspired I am. But I am also overcome with emotion because of the beauty I have seen and felt. I must lie down to quiet my mind and my heart. I realize that although I came for adventure, what I have found instead is my passion for history and the arts.

To live in a city such as this, I would surely spend every moment with these masters and their creations. I know why Rome is called the eternal city, for today, I have been touched by these great masters and felt their souls whispering to mine.

CHAPTER 16

After being on sensory overload all day, I take a two-hour nap. This and a bath help wash away the excess energy that is left over from the day. I dress in my thin, black, flowered Italian dress with bits of lace at the hem which I purchased for this trip. I had seen it on a mannequin and fallen in love with it because it reminded me of promises of love in Italia.

"You're silly, Roxanna," I say to myself.

My reflection in the mirror is that of a woman who is thin and sexy. I have lost much weight.

"Per l'olio d'oliva. To olive oil!" I shout aloud in the empty room.

I roam the streets, the sights and smells intoxicating. The waiters stand before each cafe, smiles on their faces and menus in their hands. Italian Music plays everywhere creating an ambiance in this city of romance.

A handsome middle-aged woman strolls toward me with an equally handsome man. Their arms are intertwined and he holds onto her as if she is his greatest gift. Both have dark hair and chiseled Romanesque features. She wears a light flowered summer dress, he a light-colored suit, like many of the men wear in the city this time of year. I wonder if he's sweating from the heat. But they never are; they are all so cool and unaffected by the humidity. They both smile at me as they pass. I watch her walk, sauntering beside him. She has his full attention; he only has eyes for her. He smiles as she speaks to him, both flirting with each other as lovers do.

Three elderly men sit at a table in a cafe. Two of them have hats, the kind that breathe with the heat. They are swapping stories but stop to gaze at the beautiful woman. "*Molto bella,*" I hear one say. And all sit in silence until she turns the corner. Then they begin again.

I walk to the fountain near the train station and then to the church, but it's closed for the night. I make a mental note to return when it's open.

I head back toward the opera district but via a different street. On the corner, I find an old building that's part of the original wall that had once protected the city of Rome in ancient times. It must be a thousand years old. I touch the brick with the palm of my hand and rest it there in hopes of communicating with the past. If these walls could talk, what stories would they tell?

I enter *Il Forte Ristorante.* A young Roman takes me to the rooftop where there are six tables, tapered candles at their center. A decorative wrought iron fence with potted plants borders the room. Bougainvillea has grown up the sides and covers any view of the street, the effect picturesque. A young man with a beard and long hair plays Italian folk music on an acoustic guitar.

I'm seated at a table and given a menu.

"*Sera, bella.*"

"*Sera, grazie.*"

"My name is Natale." He sounds it out for me, "Nah-**tah**-lay. He's tall and dressed in a white dinner jacket, his eyes deep and brown, his nose prominent. I mistake him for being French but his accent tells me he is Italian.

"I am Roxanna. Nice to meet you, Natale." He studies me as if he is searching for something.

"I will take good care of you tonight, Rosanna. I be back *un minuto.*" He smiles and bows before backing away.

"*Amo l'Italia,* I love Italy," I whisper to myself so only I can hear.

The room is filled with laughter and singing which makes me forget I'm alone. Natale soon returns with a carafe of *chianti.*

"For you, *bella.*" He pours and I taste and it.

"*Molto bene ... perfetto, grazie.*" I smile.

"May I recommend the *pesce*? It is sautéed with Italian herbs and *limone*."

"*Si*, I would like the fish."

"I will bring you *insalata e pasta*. Yes?" His eyes penetrate me with each word.

After he leaves me, I catch my breath and realize that to go to a restaurant in Italy, to be waited on, to order food and then to eat is like making love with the food and the waiter. It's haunting the way he studies me. I sip my *chianti* and giggle.

I sit for hours as I'm entertained by Raphael the guitar player. Two women and a man are sitting at the table next to me, both laughing and singing along with him. They turn to me and invite me to their table to join them where I learn they are from Germany and in Rome on holiday. We enjoy each other and share stories through dessert. The music stops and Raphael says "*arrivederci.*" I cannot believe it's midnight. Where has time gone?

"*Bella*, stay and have drink. Please wait for me."

Natale has brought over a bottle of limoncello and glasses for all of us. Remembering how potent the elixir is, I sip it slowly. It reminds me of the controversial Absinthe—the emerald green liqueur I had heard so much about, that is now banned everywhere except the Czech Republic, for it makes you do strange things.

Natale returns to the table.

"You will stay for me, yes?"

"No, no; *sono stanca*, I'm sleepy, Natale."

"No, *bella*. Please. I have scooter. I show you Roma by night. I will not disappoint you." Lost in his eyes, the limoncello and the magic of Roma, I cannot resist.

"I'll wait for you, but could I please have an *espresso*?" He grins, happy that I have asked.

"Si. I hurry, *ritorno al piú presto.*" He's gone.

"We're leaving now, Roxanna. It was nice to meet you. Enjoy Rome." My new friends kiss my cheeks and I watch as they depart. I sit alone sipping my *espresso* but don't have long to wait.

"*Ho finito*, Rosanna; I am finished. I have many places to take you. Have you visited Roma before?" He is excited.

I wonder how many times he takes female patrons on this "Rome by Night" tour on the back of his scooter ...

"This is my first time," I answer.

We arrive at his bike and he fastens my helmet. I get on and wrap my arms around his waist.

"Hold me tight, *bella*. I will show you things you will never forget. You will always remember me this night."

I'm sure I will.

He pulls my hands together at his waist and drives off. I love scooters ... I love the light bur-r-r-r of the engine. It soothes me and lulls me into a soft and safe peacefulness. I close my eyes, enjoy the ride and listen to the sounds of the eternal city.

We arrive at the Trevi Fountain. I've officially died and gone to heaven. Before me lies the most famous fountain in the world. It's massive and spectacular.

"*Fontana di Trevi.*" He stops the scooter and pulls me by the hand. "Here, you stand. I take *foto*."

Natale positions me then snaps a photo with my camera. Then he shows it to me. The photo is dark as night but he thinks it beautiful still.

"*Molto bene*, Rosanna." He rolls my name around in his mouth like a sweet, hard candy.

Natale turns his back on the fountain and pulls two coins from his pants pocket. He hands one to me.

"We throw coins. Is good luck. Wish for something good to your heart, Rosanna."

I smile, my eyes closed and my back to the fountain. I remember my wish for love, passion and romance and I ask for it before tossing the coin over my head. All I hear are the sounds of the water rushing over the statues and back into itself, and the sound of a mandolin playing a romantic tune close by.

"Come."

He takes my hand, guides me to the scooter and we ride off into the night. I cannot remove the smile on my face. And I don't want to.

"*Vaticano,*" he tells me.

We have arrived at the Vatican and walk into the *piazza*. I remember it from daylight but it's so much more romantic at night. All the statues of the saints atop the colonnade are lit like beacons of light. Natale holds my hand and tells me that this is his sacred place, the place he comes to when he is troubled. We walk to the fountain on the left and dip our fingers into the water. He blesses himself and then he blesses me.

"You are beautiful, Rosanna." He bends into me and kisses me on the lips. It's a gentle kiss, a long kiss, his lips pressing into mine with firm sweetness. It's a purposeful kiss as our bodies pull at each other like two magnets. We connect. He takes both my hands and clasps them so they are inside his as if for safe keeping.

"*Amore mio* ... you make Roma magic." I am speechless.

We leave and ride over the *Ponte Sant'Angelo*. Ten sculpted angels lining the bridge guide us along the way. Sitting atop of *Castel Sant'Angelo*, the Castle of the Angels is a statue of Archangel Michael. The structure is bathed in golden light and it dreamily reflects upon the water. Here, we sit for a while to catch our breath.

Next, we drive to the Forum, Palatine Hill and the Coliseum, all spectacular at night. Then, we drive to the Victor Emmanuel Monument which seems massive in the dark. I vow to come back during the day to explore it. This entire night, Natale walks beside me, so close that I hear his every breath. I feel safe with him. But all good things come to an end. It's 3:00 a.m. when we arrive at my hotel.

"I have enjoyed you, Rosanna. Thank you for showing me Roma by night. I'm happy to see it through your eyes. You have beautiful eyes, you know."

I swoon over his sweetness, his words and the dimples in his face. I hadn't noticed them in the restaurant as if he had been saving them for this moment. I gaze at him and my breath catches. He kisses me long and hard but with such tenderness, all the while holding my face in both his hands as he lovingly plays with my lips. His tongue moves all over them and he licks my mouth inside and out. It is the steamiest of kisses. I gasp for a moment from the heat of it and pull my head back a bit.

"Please come home with me tonight, Rosanna. I want to make love to you."

God, he's direct!

"Natale, we hardly know each other."

"My heart feels sorrow here." He takes my hand and places it on his heart.

"I will see you, maybe tomorrow?" I'm shocked at my response.

"*Allora, domani.* I will count the hours until I see you again." He pulls out a pen and a card and writes his number on it for me. "Call if you change your mind tonight. If not, *domani* under the stars *a mezzanotte*, at midnight after work. Wait for me in front of the *ristorante,* Rosanna." With that, he smiles and blows me a kiss goodnight.

Fantastico.

I dream Natale and I are together, sitting on a grassy Roman hill, my body draped across his lap. He brushes my hair with his fingers while he whispers words of love to me. I'm a young girl and my passions rumble inside me still upon awakening.

The next day, I tour around Rome visiting the ruins of the Roman Forum and Palatine Hill. I envision Nero standing on the portico of his house and Caesar walking the streets, his white toga flowing in the breeze, his diadem—the wreath of laurel upon his head.

I can almost see the vestal virgins in the atrium of the temple and I remember reading that before Caesar was assassinated, he had delivered his last will and testament to the Temple of the Vestal Virgins for safekeeping. I envision Marc Antony stealing it away to deliver it to Caesar's wife Cleopatra after his death, and her running to the forum to see her husband lying on the steps on the Ides of March, that last day in his history ... the last time she would lay eyes upon the man she loved.

When Augustus was emperor, he made his imperial residence here as well as Tiberius, Caligula, Flavius and others. Octavian,

Caesar's successor walked here and young Caesarion, the son of Cleopatra, came here as a young teenager in disguise after his father's death. He wanted to learn about his heritage but could not be found out or he, too would be assassinated. I can feel their spirits in this Eternal City.

After hours of walking through the ruins, then resting beneath the shade of the arch, I walk to the Coliseum. In the tour guide, I learn it took eight years to build this arena. Gladiators were trained to fight to the death here against other men and wild beasts, and Christians were fed to the lions for all to watch. Although I'm in awe of its size, I become sick in my stomach and leave. I've never understood all the fighting and the violence throughout the course of history.

Instead of pondering it too much, I leave and walk to the Victor Emmanuel II Monument, the massive monument from the night before. It seems to spread out over city blocks and is so majestic that I cannot capture it in one photo. It will have to shoot many and place them side-by-side to see it in its entirety.

The king sits upon a steed at the entrance to the monument with massive steps behind him leading up to the colonnade. Colossal Winged Victories with carved wings stand guard at each end. The building is of bright, white marble and the structure is covered with bas-reliefs too numerous to count. Before its steps lies the *Altar of the Fatherland* which holds the *Tomb of the Unknown Soldier.* I walk the long flight of stairs to the colonnade and through the halls viewing the frescoes on the ceiling ... another overwhelmingly incredible wonder of Rome.

As the day comes to an end, I make my way back to the hotel to bathe and rest before dinner and the midnight hour. I'm anxious to see Natale and his dimpled, smiling face.

At 10:00 p.m. the streets are filled with people coming and going to and from dinner. They eat late in Italy and life does not stop at midnight, but instead comes alive and continues into the wee hours of the morning. The cafes are filled with patrons and music floats through the air. Again, the scents of Rome intoxicate me—the smells of tomatoes, basil and garlic, night jasmine and geranium.

I step inside Natalie's restaurant and wait to be seated. His dimpled face greets me and tells me he is surprised to see me.

"I am so happy you come again." He takes me to the rooftop.

"You no order. I bring you specialty of the house." He leaves quickly, only to return minutes later with *vino* and sparkling water.

"Enjoy, Rosanna."

The restaurant is full and Raphael is performing and singing once again. Natale walks toward him and whisper in his ear. Raphael nods and smiles at me.

"*Per* Rosanna."

Natale has requested a song for me. He beams and steals glances my way as Raphael sings. I'm delighted. No one has ever done this for me before.

Soon, Natale delivers a pasta dish with *frutti di mare* laid upon it. As the music plays in the background, he winks at me.

"*Dolce,* dessert, Rosanna? I make special for you."

"No, no ... I'm full. I can't eat anymore."

"Okay. *Allora, aspetta,* sit and listen to the music."

Soon, it's midnight and the patrons have left the restaurant. I sip limoncello while Natale finishes his shift.

CHAPTER 17

"**I** show you special place, Rosanna."

I'm sure you will. I smile wide.

I sit on the back of his scooter, my arms wrapped around his waist. We ride quickly through Rome and out to the edge of the city where we climb a hill. We park the scooter and walk to a belvedere where busts of great heroes sitting upon Roman columns line its edge. I'm amazed at the panorama. Stretched out before me lies the city of Rome dressed in white lights that sparkle in the moonlight. He tells me the name of the park but then he kisses me and I choose to remember the kiss instead.

His fingers move across my face as if he is reading Braille. He traces my neck and every inch of my skin there, and slowly, his hands move down my back to that place where it curves into my lower spine, then down to my bottom.

He pulls me into him and his chest touches mine. I hold my breath. The blackness of passion in the night has veiled me like a welcome mist removing all thoughts. He continues to kiss me tenderly. It's a dance of sorts, he masterfully making me want him more. I try and speak but he kisses my open mouth. I buckle.

I reach for him but he steps back from me. I take a deep breath to steady myself. Minutes later, he takes my face in his hands. Our foreheads touch and he gazes into my eyes.

"*Amore mio* ... You come all the way from America for me." Every cell in my body tingles. He grabs my hand and gently pulls me.

"Come, I take *foto*." He positions me next to the bust of Caesar with the lights of Rome in the background.

"Smile, *Bella*."

We sit on a bench afterward, his arm draped over my shoulder, the other resting in my lap. It feels so natural to be together with him.

"I come here often to see the night. *E molto bello*. Roma is a romantic place, you know."

"Yes," is all I can say. My body perspires with the heat of the Roman night and Natale.

"Come."

He takes me to the bridge of Sant'Angelo which connects the castle to Vatican City. I have been here three times in two days, surely a sign. I think the angles are trying to tell me something. The night slowly unfolds as we walk, talk, laugh and kiss. Natale speaks Italian to me, then translates it into English so I can understand ... ah, the romance ...

At 3:00 a.m. we reach the hotel, same as last night. He lifts me off the scooter and kisses me. Only this time it's different, for this is the kiss that never ends. It is long, so long that I forget my name. I also forget his name as well ... just for a moment. The only thing I remember is how he feels and how he makes me feel.

Somehow, we make it to my room although later when I try to remember, I cannot recall much except that I was lost in the abyss of his kisses. A kiss is so important. It's like drinking nectar or a delicate wine. Once it touches your lips, you become intoxicated, losing your senses and your sight. It stops your breath and brings a smile to your heart. I have digressed again.

Once in the room, he throws open the shutters and the sounds of Rome enter ... the last thing I remember.

He is a thoughtful man and asks if I will allow him to use a condom. I had not planned this and had not thought of it. I remember that Bruno used condoms as well. Of course, I say yes.

We make love, he the sculptor, his bare hands and fingers the tools. He is a skillful lover and together, we travel to that sacred place where two souls merge. This time is different from my time with Bruno. With him, it was about me healing myself and satiating my desires that had been pent up for a lifetime. With Natale, it's all about passion and desire.

I will not explain the events that took place this night for I cannot put them into words. But I can tell you that it was a sacred time. And when we were finally replete, the night had turned into dawn. The sun was rising and the swallows had come out to feed. The city was still soft without sound except for their cries which lulled us to sleep.

It's midmorning and I'm on my back, a sheet draped over my breasts and torso, my leg resting languidly on top of the thin material. Natale awakens and kisses me.

"I don't know the words to describe you, Rosanna. You make me feel like I am in church and forgiven for my *peccati* ... how you say in *Inglese*?

"Sins." I roll over and kiss his cheek and touch his dimple. "You make me smile, Natale. You are sweet ... *sei molto dolce.*"

At that, he rolls over and starts kissing me all over again, first my face then my neck. I squirm.

"No!" I squeal.

He speaks in Italian which I don't understand but I love it nonetheless. I try to get away from him but he continues to pursue me, covering me with kisses, trying to get to my breasts, my sacred Venus. Oh, how I love this cat and mouse game. I finally relent and for the fourth time, we make love. I am powerless with his passions but I don't care.

Hours later, I open my eyes and see him watching me.

"I thought last night was a dream and you were not real, but you are." He kisses the palm of my hand and each finger as if he is blessing them.

"Rosanna, what you do to me, I love this. I have not felt this way for many times."

"You mean for a long time?" I laugh.

"Sorry, sometimes I forget the words."

"Natale, don't apologize. I love the way you communicate with me. I'll teach you English and you can help me with my Italian."

"I am so hungry, *Bella*, I could eat all of you." He comes at me and tries to bite me.

"No!" I shriek playfully pushing him away. "I need to eat real food or I'll faint. I'm famished!"

"Me, too. Food for our, how you say ... *forza*?" I try to understand what he means but don't have a clue until he is kneeling over me flexing the muscles in his arms.

"You mean strength." I laugh because it's so comical.

He pulls me close to him once again and kisses me gently before we both rise from the bed.

We spend this day together and the one after this, and the next one as well. For three days, Natale calls work requesting the day off to be with me. Time is lost for us and we don't care to keep track. Only the light of day and the coming of each night remind us that we have lost more time courting love. Did I say love? I think this is it ... although I've never experienced this before.

Is it too soon to think so?

I keep my room at the hotel, but spend all my time, day and night, at his apartment. We sleep together, make love together, eat together and even sit quietly together. We watch the sun as it sets over Rome, its glorious colors kissing the horizon. And we make a wish and kiss each other as it lowers itself behind the city. He reads the newspaper to me in Italian and tells me stories. I am enjoying this quiet, soft, safe place with him.

Some days, we ride his scooter to the ruins, the museums and the basilicas. I have never smiled and laughed as much as I have with Natale. He takes me to the Santa Maria Maggiorie Basilica where I have a religious experience. The Mother comes to me and I am in bliss. Natale understands because he, too loves Santa Maria.

We visit Saint Peter in Chains, its belfry the tallest in Rome. It holds Fuga's *Great Canopy;* Michelangelo's exquisite sculpture *Moses;* and Sangallo's golden gilded ceiling containing scenes from the Old Testament. Everything is decorated in gold and marble.

We visit Bernini's *Fountain of the Tritons* and then head to the oldest street in Rome, the *Appian Way* where tombs and catacombs of the patrician families of Rome are buried. Next is the Baths of Caracalla, one of largest public Roman baths built in the second century A.D. Then, we travel to the *Borghese Villa and Gallery* where masterpieces by Bernini, Caravaggio, Domenichino, Rubens, Raphael, Canova, Messina, and Leonardo da Vinci are housed. I think that everyone who ever painted or sculpted might be here and I fall in love with the grounds and the art. The city is very romantic and having Natale as my guide makes it even more so. He is so loving and tender with me that I no longer feel invisible ... an old feeling that haunted me when I was married to Ed.

So, this is what it feels like to be seen and loved ...

At the Villa, we see *Prometheus Bound* and *Leda and the Swan*, then Bernini's *Apollo and Daphne*. I'm overcome by Canova's Statue of Paolina Borghese in the pose of *Venus Victrix* resting lazily on a chaise, her head resting on one arm, the other on her hip and her long slender legs out before her. When we leave the museum, we walk across the lawns to the lake and come to a marble bench. Here, he asks me to sit and pose like Paolina.

"I take *foto*."

His eyes sparkle. I have never been looked at like this before. My heart and my lightness of being are telling me that I'm falling in love with him.

I pose once again for another photo and this time, I am a *regina*, a queen, for this is how I feel with him. If we shared a future together, would it be like this forever? Or would the newness eventually fade like a dull coin?

They all do ... just like my marriage.

Most days, we wander around Rome and discover its hidden places. We visit ruins that aren't on any map, and churches I have never heard of, all of them decorated with ancient frescoes and paintings.

Eventually, I check out of the hotel and move into his apartment on the third floor near the Trevi Fountain. We cook every meal together and eat by candlelight. Natale says it's the only way to eat when you are in love.

Each day before breakfast, Natale walks to the little bakery down the street and brings back *cornetti* and oftentimes, flowers for me. Oh, how I love them. He awakens me by kissing my hands, then looks in my eyes and tells me I am beautiful.

CHAPTER 18

A month has passed and I am still in Rome. This morning, I awaken from a dream where I am standing in the Forum, an easel before me and a brush in my hand. On the canvas, I have captured the light of the fading day as it washes over the city. I can see it clearly, smell the oils and feel the brush between my fingers.

Natale is still asleep beside me. I realize I have fallen in love with his face and want to paint him, although I am nervous at the thought of it. I'm not sure if I remember how. To paint a portrait might be too much after all these years.

I quietly leave the bed to bathe.

I sink down into the tub, close my eyes and reflect on how my life has changed. I have grown, all the darkness, heaviness and sadness now gone. I have found a happiness I never had in my marriage and I'm feeling love for the first time in a very long time. It feels good.

I gaze about the tiled bathroom. The walls are bright yellow. White towels hang on their hooks from the night before. The only decorative thing in the room is an old Murano glass mirror embellished with tiny glass flowers, a few broken.

It's sparse but neat and clean. I like the way Natale lives—cleanly and simply. Everything has its place and it feels safe. And his cooking ... who would have thought Italian men could cook like this? I love his pasta and the fish he fries for me, squeezing the lemon over it at the very last moment, a ritual he talks me through every time, all the while, telling me how important timing is for the lemon.

"*Amore mio*, why are you awake so soon? I miss you. When I wake up, I think you have gone."

I'm startled and jump, splashing water everywhere. He sits on the edge of the tub, his well-defined chest and the hair that covers it at eye-level. I reach out to touch it.

"Now, you get me wet!" Before I can blink, he steps into the bathtub and kneels over me.

"No!" I shriek. It's a tight fit for two but he manages to maneuver himself into position and is now on the bottom as I lie across him.

"I'm cold now, Natale."

"I warm you … mmmmmmm, *amore mio*."

He playfully cups his hands filling them with water and pours it over me. His arms embrace me and he wraps his legs around mine. It never ceases to amaze me that with each touch, I become aroused. But this time, I fight him off.

"Not now, Natale. I have more pressing business to discuss with you."

"*Che*, what? What is more important than love, *amore mio*?"

"Can you take me to buy paints today? I want to start painting."

He's surprised.

"You paint? I did not know this. What do you paint, sweetheart?"

"I used to paint scenery and landscapes and sometimes portraits, although it was a long time ago … years in fact."

I remember the last portrait I had done of the boys when they were younger. It still hangs in my living room.

"I want to paint you, Natale." I take my finger and outline his cheekbones and his dimples that indent the moment he begins to smile. "I want to capture these."

He grabs my face with both hands and covers my mouth with his. I melt.

"Rosanna, I love you. Will you marry me?" I nervously touch him.

"Natale, I've only known you for a month." I try and make light of it.

"*Sono innamorato di te,* I am in love with you."

I step out of the tub.

"Come. The water is cold. I will make you breakfast. It's my turn today."

He senses my distance and quickly follows me into the bedroom, water dripping onto the floor.

"Rosanna, what is wrong?"

I'm not sure how to answer.

"We barely know each other. It's too soon to even think of this." I anxiously move around the room picking up clothing from the floor. I quickly make the bed.

"When I saw you, I knew you were the one for me," he says.

"That's so silly. I'm too old for you to think we could have a life together. You should get married and have children."

"Why? You cannot have more children?" He is surprised.

"No, I cannot. I'm too old. Didn't you realize that?"

"No. you are young to me. But if you cannot have children, it is okay. I still love you and want to marry you."

Natale! Stop! This is crazy! I have so much going on in my life right now. We just met. I belong in America with my boys. I came to Italy following a stupid dream!"

My chest suddenly tightens and I can't breathe. I kneel on the floor. Alarmed, Natale moves closer as I lay down and close my eyes. My heart pounds. He rushes to the bathroom and wets a towel which he places on my forehead. By now, I'm crying.

"Rosanna, I love you. I want to take care of you. I know we are meant to be together. We have been together for four weeks and we are like music together. I knew when I saw you. I felt it in my heart ... right here." He places my palm on his chest. "When it is right, it feels like this."

We stay quiet for a while, me on the floor and him sitting beside me.

I finally recover and sit up. "Come, I take you to buy paints," Natale says. Neither of us speak of marriage for the rest of the day.

He takes me to an art store near the Spanish Steps where I choose two soft-haired sable brushes for detail work, a palette, a knife and oils in eight different colors. Then there is the stretched canvas, the thinner and primer. My mood lightens at the thought of painting. Natale smiles when he sees how relaxed and happy I have become. He shyly kisses my cheek and I kiss him back. I think we have both recovered.

We ride the scooter back to the apartment and I try to hold on to my bags filled with supplies and the small canvas. We move through the busy city streets trying to dodge the moving cars and pedestrians, leaning to the left and then the right. The air is thick with humidity but I welcome it. I love the feel of this city. Would I love it if it were not for Natale, I wonder? Maybe it would be a little less romantic but I would love it anyway.

The light in the airy apartment is bright, the windows facing the south west. Natale is happy to sit for me as I sketch him. He is willing to do whatever it takes to make me happy right now. Eventually, we move to the balcony. He gazes out to the street and watches people as they pass by and I sketch away. I must practice so I can capture each detail of his face before I even touch the canvas. We sit for hours and I trace his nose, the curve of his lips, his eyelashes.

"*Ho bisogno di mangiare*, I need food to eat, Rosanna. Can we rest now?" He takes my sketch pad and studies his image.

"This is me?" He seems surprised. "Is this my nose? I like to see it. It is nice." He grins and his dimples pop out.

I have an idea.

"Natale, I want you to smile so I can paint you with those dimples."

"I cannot do this forever, sweetheart."

I decide to snap pictures with my digital camera and use them to sketch from. I don't usually like to paint from photos but I want more than anything to capture his expression, his dimples and his eyes. I want to remember him always, with this face that shines with such purity and happiness.

"*Aspetta*." I laugh proudly each time I'm able to squeeze my favorite words into a conversation. I love the way it sounds coming from my mouth. I leave briefly and come back with my camera, already snapping photos of him as I step onto the balcony.

"You make me smile, Rosanna. You are ... comical." I giggle at his use of this word. He comes toward me and I keep backing away, a game between us. He chases me through the apartment and I continue to dodge him, moving carefully between each piece of furniture and through each doorway. We end up in the bedroom and I fall onto the bed laughing, my sides aching from it. He comes to me and pins my hands over my head and starts to growl like a dog.

I become excited and from my excitement he becomes aroused. I tear at his thin tee-shirt to get to his skin and the hair on his chest. Our love-making is heated and passionate; thoughts of food are long forgotten.

"Do you think we will last forever like this, *amore mio?*" We lie together, his arms embracing me as he studies my face. I cannot escape him.

"I don't know, Natale." I tell myself it's time to be honest with him. I'm struggling to find the words and afraid I will hurt him but I start anyway.

"Natale, I went to Capri in search of something. I was unhappy in my life. I didn't know what I was looking for or what I would find there, but I knew I had to go. My boys are in America. You know, we talked about them."

He kisses my forehead.

"I know you miss them."

"Yes, I do, and I miss Capri. But I love Rome ... and I've fallen in love with you."

There. I said it. He kisses my lips gently and I see the pleasure and relief in his eyes so I continue.

"I'm confused, Natale. I came to Italy to heal myself ... and my life. I never expected this. I never expected you."

He holds me tightly and his chest swells against mine. He pulls me into him and kisses my hair, and in this moment, I want to stay here in his arms forever, protected and loved by him. It feels so right. I have found my sacred place in this world.

I melt into that meditative state after you are satiated from making love and begin to fall asleep. The sounds of the city blow in through the open window, background noise for the emptiness in my head and the joy in my heart. It creates a fairytale dream where I'm walking the streets of Rome in my new life. I'm alone and carrying a flower-filled basket. My heart is full and I love Natale and my life.

Another week passes and there has been no more talk of marriage. We are sitting on the balcony when the telephone rings. Natale answers it. When he turns back to face me, he tells me he has been called into work.

"They need me, sweetheart. You be okay alone?"

"Yes, I'll sketch."

Although I'll miss him, it will be nice to have this break from him. We've been together day and night for five weeks. I can no longer hear my own thoughts and feel like I'm slipping away from myself again. Is this a requirement of being in love?

Natale leaves and I pull out my laptop to transfer the latest photos from my camera. Then, I pull them up to view them and choose the ones I will use. This leads to sketching and I become lost in Natale's face. After a few hours, I stop to watch the colors of the city change as the sun is setting. I want to paint the hues of this glorious sky as well. I feel like the painter I used to be ... seeing everything through an artist's eye. I'm so filled with passion for the brush, the smell of the oils. Natale flashes into my mind and once again, confusion twists my thoughts. Not sure if it's the wine, the smell of the oils or fear, I grow dizzy and must lie down.

In the dream, I'm standing at the Forum, the spirit beside me. "Roxanna, you cannot linger here too long. You are not finished yet. You have so much more to do."

"I think I love him. Am I crazy?"

"No, sweet woman. You are intoxicated with life and love and all that it offers you." He laughs and lovingly pats my shoulder.

"You have only touched the tip of this. Welcome to your new life!"

I'm stunned and speechless.

"Stay as long as you like, but at some point, you must leave."

He disappears and I awaken. I want to debate with him as to why I should stay … or leave. Would Natale wait for me if I left tomorrow? Does he love me enough? Do I love him enough? If I'm gone for months or a year, would our love withstand time?

For God sakes! I've known him for six weeks! This is crazy. Maybe it's the sex … or the magic of Rome.

I pace the floor. My stomach turns. I barely make it to the bathroom and retch. All thoughts leave me, except my anxiety. I feel crazed and out of control emotionally. I haven't felt like this since…

"STOP! I can't do this!" I order in the empty room.

I go to bed, hoping I'll be asleep when Natale returns but sleep does not come. After an hour of tossing and turning and the craziness in my head, I move to the balcony with my sketchpad and soon, I am lost in sketching.

The door open.

"Sweetheart, you wait for me." He has returned. He kisses me and sits.

"Was it a good night?" I ask without looking up.

"Si, but it is better now that I am here."

"You have to work while I'm here. How will you eat?" I try to make light of it, but my mood is dark.

"I don't need food when I am with you."

I pull away from him.

"What is it, Rosanna?"

"I don't want to talk about any of this. I'm sleepy."

"Then we will go to sleep. Come."

I'm afraid he might want to make love and I'd be lost inside him and this fairytale, held captive by my own heart.

"No, I'd like to sit for a bit. You go. I'll come to bed soon."

"I sit with you and have a drink of limoncello."

He moves to the freezer and pulls the bottle with two little glasses. The alcohol and the coolness of it soothes my throat.

"Che cosa, what's wrong, Rosanna?" His eyes are serious, as if ready for a deep conversation; I'm uncomfortable with the moment but know I must speak up.

"Natale, my time here in Rome has been wonderful. But ..."

His eyes are wide, waiting for me to finish. He holds my hands, kneels before me and gently brushes my wild hair from my face. Then he rubs my cheek from top to bottom with the side of his thumb.

I continue. "I'm afraid of the power of this and how I feel about you. It's all so cloudy. I don't know what's real and what isn't. I don't know how I feel. I'm confused and feel pressured to commit to you and I'm not ready to do that. I only recently left my boys to visit Capri and I love it there. The timing is not right for me to be in love ... I'm not sure about what I want. I'm not sure about anything." My sobs come from deep within me and Natale tries to console me.

"Here drink; drink all now." He hands me a full glass of the thick lemon drink. I gulp it down and the heat of it stops me from crying because I need to breathe. He pulls his chair over, sits and reaches for my hands.

"*Amore mio,* you don't have to make any decisions about us now. I am sorry to pressure you. I know you were not looking for love when you came to *Roma.* Santa Maria knew it was time for us. She sent you to me ... *la forza dell' amore,* the power of love."

He smiles weakly and I know he's hurt. He continues. "I won't pressure you again. I will be here for you. I will support you. We will find the answers together, *mio amato.*" He casts his eyes downward, his lashes wet with tears. He kisses each of my hands.

I should leave, but I'm afraid ... afraid that part of me will be left behind in this relationship and I don't know if I can survive that again. I don't know if I'd be strong enough a second time.

The silence between us is broken.

"Sweetheart, you take the time you need. I will wait for you. I have never found someone like you. You are the one for me." Tears flow freely down his face.

"I love you," I say.

We reach for one another and embrace but the chairs create distance between us. We rise and move to the balcony and sit to watch the lights of the city. No more words are spoken this night, for there is no need of them. Everything has been said. We do not make love, but instead, fall asleep in each other's arms.

We move through the next day, parts of us left behind in the conversation from the night before. My insides churn as I continue to contemplate whether to stay or leave.

My world has turned upside down in the eternal city.

CHAPTER 19

This week, I finish my sketch on the canvas and it's a perfect likeness of Natale.

"*Magnifico.* I love my face. I have never seen it like this." He hugs me tightly. "*Il mio artista,* I am proud of you."

But I cannot bring myself to start painting, for I know if I do, I will have to stay until it's finished. The longer I stay, the more confused I'll become. A dark cloud has settled over me.

We are sitting on the patio and Natale has been unusually quiet. He stares at the sky, lost in thought.

"Natale, are you okay?"

"No, you turn me inside out." He begins to weep. "I know you think this is just a fling, some Italian guy with a pretty American *turista*. How can I prove to you that I am serious about us spending our life together? Rosanna, please stay with me. My heart will break if you leave me."

I feel like a caged animal.

"Can't you see I'm broken? You don't want me! I couldn't make my marriage work, couldn't keep my husband interested in me. He left me for another woman! I was a perfect wife and I was still not good enough. Then I had a nervous breakdown. I tried to end my life, Natale. I'm damaged!"

I'm horrified that I've let slip my deepest fears and darkest secrets. I'm inconsolably, now sobbing loudly.

Natale moves closer and reaches for me.

"It hurts me to know you have suffered these things. I cannot fix your past. But I can change your future if you stay with me, *amore mio.* I will never hurt you. I will never cause you pain. I am not perfect, but I am a good man." He kisses my tears away. "You don't have to make any decisions now. I will wait for you."

He pulls me to him, both of us weeping. His arms are strong as they hold me; his heart is soft, his tears wetting my hair and face. After a while, I speak.

"I have to leave. You know I do. I don't want to, but I must. I promise I'll be back. I just don't know when right now."

He cries harder.

"I'll write you, call you. I promise. I love you."

He's filled with despair and cannot speak. He pulls me to him and holds my face for a long time. Then, he kisses me. With Natale, each kiss is different, especially this one. This one means it's the last kiss … it's a desperate kiss.

I pull him slowly to the bedroom and together, we make sweet love to each other. He is slow and gentle and for the first time, I am the aggressor. I don't want it to end. I caress him and touch him with my fingertips … every inch of him so that I will remember this moment and never forget it. I want it to be seared into my soul as if it had been burnt with a branding iron, the scar always there to remind me of how deeply I felt this love.

I keep my eyes open so that nothing escapes me … so that I will remember the expression on his face when he loses his mind with pleasure, shuddering into that abyss of passion. I hold him tightly and I enter through that precious gateway with him, digging my nails into his back, leaving my mark. If it's painful, maybe it will be felt more deeply, more intensely and maybe it will mean more to both of us. He doesn't seem to mind.

We crawl inside each other in these moments, not wanting the other to escape or to be left behind. And then we fall asleep, intertwined as if we are one. There is no ending to me nor beginning to him.

Natale awakens to a soft breeze blowing through the thin curtains. It's that special time when the sun is spent after making love to the earth all day … just as we have done. It isn't quite sunset but an hour away. His gaze upon me is filled with both love and pain. He knows I might not come back to him.

"*Mi sono innamorato di questa donna,* I have fallen in love with this woman," he says. He lingers over the bed as he reaches for my cheek and caresses it. "I know you are different than other women. You go. Do what you need. Please, come back to me …"

He kisses me goodbye and leaves the apartment for work. He never asks if I will be here when he returns and for this, I am relieved.

I lie in bed and weep for hours. Crazy thoughts whirl through my mind like a hurricane. I have fallen in love with him and he loves me. So why must I leave him? The other me, the voice of reason that I hate to listen to, speaks.

"Roxanna, you need to go now. Move forward. Return to Capri and finish what you came for. Once you know what you are looking for and have put all the pieces together then you can come back to him."

I weep uncontrollably. But finally, I stop. I pack my things and leave a note for him scented with my perfume of geranium, rose and patchouli. I don't want him to forget me. On the paper, I write:

Natale,

Please understand. I will see you again soon.
Time will move as swiftly as the blink of an eye.
You forever have my heart.

Ti amo, amore mio,

Roxanna

CHAPTER 20
ASSISI, ITALY

It's after midnight and the train station is empty adding to my loss. I'm not sure where I'm going so I scan the board and see Assisi. I think of San Francesco, my old childhood friend and pray he will be there to greet me.

○

Natale returns to the empty apartment after work and knows immediately that she has left. He finds the note on his pillow and sits on the edge of the bed. He reads it and tries to take a deep breath but the lump of grief that sits in the middle of his chest lets little air through.

He's devastated ... hurt. His heart is broken. He lies on the bed, fully clothed and awake until morning.

○

I am sure Natale has found the letter on his pillow. I envision him reading it as he sits on the bed, his head in his hands weeping onto the paper. My soul hears him cry out, "Rosanna ..." but his voice is lost in the sounds of the train station.

Alone in my seat, I finally let the tears fall. Now I know why Italian women dress in black, pound on their chests and wail. It's because they have been loved by an Italian man. The love is deep. It enshrouds you like a sheer mist that never leaves you, no matter where you are.

What am I to do? No answer comes.

Eventually, my eyes are swollen and half-closed; my tears have stopped. What have I done ... allowing myself to fall in love ... allowing myself to hurt him? God help me. I'm angry with that part of me that told me to leave him. I want to go back to Rome, to be in his arms. But I cannot. Not yet. What about Capri? I no longer feel its pull. I must be crazy. There is no escape from thoughts of Natale until somewhere near the town of Terni where I finally fall asleep.

The spirit and I are standing on the cliffs of *Monte Solaro* in Anacapri.

"Roxanna, why be so hard on yourself? He has called you forth just as you have called him. You are not responsible for his broken heart or this sadness you think you have created. This is a beautiful thing and both of you agreed to come together and let your souls drive as you both enjoy the ride. Forgive yourself. This love will not die. Hearts don't break ... only egos do. You will never forget this great love you shared. Why don't you sit back and see where you are guided to next?"

Before I can open my mouth to express my anger or ask a question, he's gone. Then from this reality, I hear "Foligno," the stop for Assisi. I need to change trains.

It's 6:30 a.m. when I arrive in Assisi. By now, I'm numb. I'm spent and I barely have the energy to find a taxi but know I must. I pray the driver can find me a room with little effort.

Sleep. I need sleep.

"*Tassi.*" As soon as I raise my arm he pulls to the curb and I get in without looking at him.

"*Buon giorno, Signora.*"

"*Buon giorno.* I have no reservation, but need a place to stay. Do you know of somewhere?" I raise my eyes for a moment and notice he's a large man, barely fitting into his seat. His eyes are kind.

"*Si.* I take you to San Francesco." He doesn't make small talk with me and for that, I am grateful.

Soon, we arrive at a *pensione* next to the *Basilica di San Francesco* and luck is on my side as they have a room available and allow me to check in at this ungodly hour. I'm thankful to San Francesco.

I fall into a restless sleep where my dreams are filled with Natale begging me to come back to him. When I awaken, it's early afternoon. I bathe, not wanting to leave the tub and its water, but the need to eat compels me.

A small cafe is attached to my *pensione* which looks out over the Umbrian Valley. The scenery before me is lush and green as wispy clouds move lazily across the sky leaving their shadowy imprint upon the land as they go. It's peaceful here, the perfect place to heal. The memories are starting to fade and my wounded heart has stopped bleeding.

Food is necessary for my body although I cannot eat much. I have toast and tea, but leave most of it behind. But the little I do eat soothes my stomach and nurtures me. I reminisce about the last meal Natale cooked for me and my eyes begin to well up again. I blink the tears away.

San Francesco, I ask for the strength to get through this and for my pain to be taken away. I think this quick prayer.

I walk to the Basilica of Saint Frances that was built into a hillside. Construction began in 1228 and it was finally finished in 1253. It's unusual because it consists of two churches—the Upper Church and the Lower Church. I had read that after San Francesco's death, his followers continued building it as if it would bring him back to life.

I sit quietly in a pew and am enveloped by the silence. Since I was four, I had the ability to communicate with saints and angels as if the veils of time had dissolved between us. I knew I could not share this with anyone or they would think me mad. When I was younger, Francesco would come to comfort me when I was confused or troubled. I loved him as if he were a friend or a father. As a teenager, I read everything I could find on his life in hopes it would bring him to visit me more often. He was born in a stable somewhere in the early 1100s, just as Jesus had been. And throughout his life, he had been so in love with God that he denounced all earthly possessions to imitate Christ and travel with only his message, "that all men are brothers no matter what walk of life they came from."

The incense has thickened the air and it brings me out of my daydream. My heart is filled with love and my mind is clear. I now see before me the great gift that I've been given. Rome was no mistake. It was meant to be. I realize how funny life is, to travel to the other side of the world and walk into a restaurant and meet the man of your dreams ... the man you might spend the rest of your life with ... if I choose to.

I don't have to figure it out right now. If he waits for me and I choose to go to him then so be it. It was meant for us to be together. If he does not wait or I change my mind about my feelings for him, that will be perfect, too. I'm mystified as I sit here. Nothing matters. In these moments, I am no longer in pain. All I feel is the deepest love and a knowingness that all is as it should be.

"Shall I call you Roxanna now, woman of many names?" Francesco is beside me in his brown robe, a rope belted about his waist. It's good we are alone in the church. They might think me mad as I laugh out loud.

Yes, Roxanna, the name I shall take to my grave this time.

"Then Roxanna it is. It has been a long time since we last spoke like this. Were you twelve then?"

I think back. I had started to question my ability to see and hear spirit and told my best friend at the time. She laughed at me, called me crazy and told others. The children were cruel, often ridiculing me. It was painful for a twelve-year-old. So, I denied it and lost the ability to see them and communicate with them.

Yes, twelve. I lower my head and am filled with sadness at the memory.

"It's all perfect and as it should be. It happens to all of us. But you are here with me now."

I nod.

"Then we shall sit together." We are silent for a few moments. "Roxanna, enjoy your life. You still have much living to do. Go and fly free like the birds that I love so much. Bathe in the sea of time

126

and drench yourself in all that is for it will be over in a flash. Live, laugh, love. Be happy. Give of yourself. Teach love and compassion by being you … teach others to have it all by being you. You be the example and your gift will be your fulfilled life! You have not lost anything; it will come back to you. Do you understand?"

My heart is full and I weep.

"*Capisci*?" I laugh at his Italian as a tear slides down my cheek giving me away.

Si, capisco.

"Good then. You know you are loved. Life is perfect for you in every way. You have so much love to give that it would be wrong for you not to share it. You are on the right path. I remember you and I hold you deeply in my heart. Go with my love."

I don't want him to leave.

Will you come to me again? I plead.

"There is no mistake you came to Capri. It is a sacred place where we spent much time together. Go to the *Piazza Umberto* and I will come to you again."

He's gone, his voice fading in the echoes of the *basilica.* All I hear are the voices of the pilgrims that are filing into the structure. I linger, bathed in his love, my heart wide open.

Eventually, I take my leave and as I do, I notice the door to the other level. I enter and am now inside the room that holds his tomb. I walk past piles of sacred candles that are there for a small donation, and pick up two. I come upon what is left of him physical form, now encased and shrouded with flowers. I have no tears, only a smile for he is still alive to me. I have just spoken with him.

A woman prostrates herself across his casket collapsing on it, sweeping most of the flowers to the floor. She's sobbing, uncontrollably. I feel her grief and want to tell her he stands behind her, his hand upon her shoulder but I do not. Instead, I move out into the Umbrian sunlight.

Once again, I am transformed. How many more changes will I go through?

Life is never as it seems. Once you think you've climbed to the top of the mountain and looked out over the horizon, a thousand more peaks stand before you waiting to be climbed. The art of climbing is in mastering each step. I had journeyed well with Natale and now, I feel a deeper love and understanding in place of the pain.

I sit on the grass and close my eyes, the heat of the sun hot upon my face. And I remember the word *sun-kissed*.

So, this is what it feels like to be kissed by the sun.

I make a promise to myself that I will journey on until I know I'm finished, and then return to Natale, whether it be forever, or just to walk with him again one last time. This pledge to my heart will hold me together through my travels, knowing he will be there at the end.

Tonight, I dine next to the *basilica* at a little restaurant. Instead of a meal, I order an hors d'oeuvre of shrimp in lemon with a light sauce of mayonnaise, parsley, pepper, celery, lemon bits and other spices; the local bread; and a salad of fennel, greens, and tomatoes with little tiny slivers of lemon and lemon zest. I also enjoy a glass of the local Umbrian wine. And as I look out over the massive but simplistic church, I realize I have found my center.

After dinner, I walk through the ancient town which is enclosed by a ring of old walls that protected the city during the Middle Ages. Once I reach the end, I arrive at Saint Claire's Basilica. There is such a holiness about this place—as if the saints are here to soothe the souls of weary travelers who have come to be consoled.

When I return to my room, I see it through new eyes. It is sparse but warm and comforting. The single bed is covered with simple white Italian linens. There is a closet, a writing table and a chair but no television or telephone or anything else in the room for that matter. The building is so old and medieval that the windows are round portals in both the bath and the bedroom, and adorned with simple white linen curtain panels. The walls and the floors of both rooms are completely tiled.

I climb into bed and sink into it. I have received what I came here for and now it's time to leave. Where will I go next?

Venice ... I nod off, dreaming of a gondola slicing through the waters of a canal beneath a moonlit sky.

I awaken to a soft breeze wafting through the open window and listen to the sweet sound of hundreds of tiny voices—little birds chirping across the Umbrian countryside. I jump from my bed and stand on the tips of my toes to look out the small window. There in the distance is a lush, green panorama, trees hither and yon, and the sunrise in the sky dripping shades of gold and salmon at its edge. Cast over it all is a sheer veil of mist adding to the glorious vista before me. I'm enraptured. What a magnificent way to be called awake.

"Thank you, Francesco."

CHAPTER 21
VENICE, ITALY

The train ride from Assisi to Venice is uneventful. I arrive at the Santa Lucia Station at 3:00 p.m. and board a water taxi. I'm captivated by the view as I am shuttled down the Grand Canal to the city. The driver directs me to a *pensione* down a small alleyway close to the Rialto Bridge.

My room on the third floor has a single bed and a very small bath. But I don't mind because its centerpiece is a large and opulent mirror bordered with Murano glass flowers and stems in a pale fluorescent pink. Some would think it gaudy but I love it because it reminds me of Natale's bathroom and I know it was hand-blown on a little island nearby. I think of him each time I see something new and want to tell him. But I know that to call him too soon would open old wounds.

Immediately, I freshen up and leave the hotel. Trying to acclimate to the layout of the city is a bit difficult since I have a penchant for getting turned around and losing my way. My hotel is two passageways from the famous Rialto Bridge, reminding me of a favorite movie, *Dangerous Beauty*—the story of a 15th century Venetian courtesan. I have dreamt of visiting Venice since seeing the movie years ago.

Musicians, writers, poets and lovers come to Venice, the Queen of the Adriatic. They never want to leave because they are so inspired here. Brightly colored buildings and stone palaces flank the canal, each from a different time-period; the architectural styles are a mix of Byzantine, Romanesque, Gothic and Renaissance which makes each building unique. I can't wait to explore, my passion for architecture almost as great as my passion for painting and sculpture.

Venice is a city for lovers and I wish Natale were here with me. With my head lowered, I roam aimlessly lost in thoughts, my eyes tearing over. I only see the stones beneath my feet as I move them one in front of the other mindlessly, not wanting to lose this feeling of him with his arms wrapped around me consoling me. I don't want anything to interfere with this vision. Not even Venice.

I'm the fool again. Why did I leave? I grow angrier by the moment. This spirit that keeps coming to me ... what does he know of love? Why should I listen to him? Maybe if I call Natale, he will come to me ...

Thoughts of making love and exploring this romantic city together fill my head. I'm lost in my misery and have not even looked up to see where I am. Then, I hear singing and the voice pulls me from my reverie.

I find myself in San Marco's Piazza and before me is a beautiful woman, possibly seventy, in a long black gown holding a champagne glass in her hand. She has dark hair—big hair—and her dress is strapless, only her large breasts holding it up. She dances in circles, twirling and singing in Italian with her glass held upward as if she were toasting the heavens.

Hundreds of pigeons, scurry about her bare feet. She seems out of place. I look around to see if they are filming a movie, she the star. But she is alone, her mellifluous voice and the song she sings mesmerizing anyone who listens.

She stops to sip her champagne and then starts up again. I am now fully present trying to figure out why she's here. Is she drunk on champagne or life? People are standing around her, half of them singing with her. When she finishes the song, she takes another sip from her glass and realizes it's empty. So, she stops and moves out of the circle while the crowd claps.

"*Brava, brava,*" everyone shouts and a few men whistle.

I move to a table at a small cafe and sit.

"*Signora?*" A portly waiter in a white shirt and jacket with a black bow tie asks me for my order. I decide on *acqua minerale* with lemon.

"*Si, grazie Signora.*" I search for the woman in the evening gown but cannot find her in the crowd that has filled the square. The waiter returns and sets a glass of champagne in front of me.

"No, please. I ordered mineral water." I lift the glass to him so he can remove it, but instead, he bows.

"No *Signora*. She is happy. You are sad. *Non buona*. Please, it is my gift to you."

I smile at him for his thoughtfulness and concern.

"*Molto grazie.*" I lift my glass and toast to him as he smiles and walks away. I must look pathetic.

I gaze out over the *piazza*. People are laughing while pigeons land everywhere—even on the heads, shoulders and arms of those holding the food. Little ones are squealing with delight and I find myself caught up in the magic of it all.

I've only taken three sips of the golden prosecco, the champagne of the Italians, but feel its effect ... or is it just Venice? San Marco's Basilica, the Cathedral of Venice stands before me in all its glory. It's the most opulent, grandiose building I have seen thus far. Even from this distance, one would not capture the entire building in one photo.

So much detail ... I know it was built a thousand years ago, and every architectural style is represented in its façade—Byzantine, Gothic, Islamic, and Renaissance, with Moorish and Oriental flares. Greek crosses rest upon its roof ... glorious.

"*Scusi, Signora*, may I sit with you?" My thoughts are interrupted by the woman in the dress. She is as beautiful close up as she is from afar. Her eyes are the color of the Grand Canal.

"Yes, please do." I'm surprised, not sure why she has chosen me to sit with. She reads my thoughts.

"I see you alone drinking champagne and know you are like me. You know how to enjoy life. A toast, *Salute!*"

"*Salute,* to life." We take a sip. Her English is as good as her Italian.

"Your singing is lovely."

"*Grazie*. I used to sing for a living here in Venezia ..." She looks off in the distance, a dream in her eyes. "Yes, those were the days ..." She collects herself. My name is Elana."

Her dress fits her like a glove. Men must adore her.

"I'm Roxanna. Nice to meet you, Elana."

"Roxanna, what brings you here and are you alone?"

"Yes. I was in Rome and decided to stop and see the Venice that everyone talks about."

"Then you must be a painter, a poet or a lover for those are who Venezia calls to." She laughs and takes another drink.

"I paint, or I used to. I'm just getting started again."

"Ah, Venezia. Then you shall be a master by the time you leave here." She's effervescent. "Are you in love, Roxanna?"

I'm startled by the question.

"Yes, I am." Natale's face flashes before me and I feel guilty for I had forgotten him for a moment ...

"Then why is he not here with you?" She asks innocently.

"It's a long painful story, Elana ... one not to speak of on such a lovely day." I try to change the subject.

"Ah, *amore* ... such ecstasy ... such pain. Someone once said that 'the greatest journey is the distance between two lovers.'"

I wait for more but she says nothing else. So, I think about this in the silence that she soon breaks.

"I'm in love as well. He's a gorgeous man who loves me like I have never been loved before ..." She springs up from the table and starts dancing with her eyes closed, all the while humming to her own memories. "La-la-la-la, da-de-da ... hmm-hmm-hmm ..."

Everyone turns to watch her. Her long dark hair is beautifully styled and her voluptuousness sways as she moves. Her lips are painted bright red and her eyes are like two sparkling emeralds. I'm mesmerized.

The waiter comes to the table with two more glasses of prosecco.

"On the house, *le signore*." He smiles as if he's enjoying this.

They must know her. She grabs her glass and toasts to him.

"Per amore."

"To love." I'm suddenly caught up in her passion. She starts to sing a romantic love song. With champagne glass in hand, she makes her way out into the middle of the *piazza* and a crowd begins to gather around her. I smile, supporting her efforts. They love her, and at the end of her song, I find myself clapping.

"*Brava, brava, bellissima.*"

She returns to the table.

"*Mille grazie.*" Thank you, my dear." She sips her champagne and is reflective for a moment. "Roxanna, follow your heart because everything could be gone in an instant." She snaps her fingers together creating a clicking sound and I catch a glimpse of sadness in her eyes. A mandolin plays somewhere in the *piazza.*

The waiter brings bread, olives, meats and cheeses to the table and breaks the moment. I notice his desire for Elana. He looks into her eyes and smiles and suddenly, she is transformed, back to herself.

We enjoy the food and conversation as we get to know each other. I find the romantic tales of her life interesting. However, she is careful not to reveal too much, making the stories somewhat mysterious. No matter who the subject is, even describing a tourist in the *piazza*, Elana's description of them is effusive.

"Look at the way he is gazing at his lover, oh, he is so loving ... *bello.*" Or "Look at this one. She is *molto bella*, so beautiful. Look at the men. They are tripping all over themselves," she laughs.

The woman she's describing is quite plain but Elana sees her differently. Elana's filter can only be described as a thin veil of soft, sweet sensuality, undulating and luscious ... intoxicating. If you are lucky enough to experience it yourself, it stops your breath and blurs your vision so you are suddenly seeing with your heart and not your mind's eyes. Then, ah! It's gone and you feel as if you've been hit by a MACK truck.

We finish our prosecco and she stands.

"Roxanna, it was a pleasure spending time with you. Remember, life is like a tiny soap bubble floating in the air before you. You have to reach for it to feel its magic and only then will you have found happiness." She laughs out loud, big and voluptuous, and says, "I have no idea what I just said, ha, ha, ha."

We both walk precariously as we leave the table arm in arm and make our way to the Grand Canal.

"Elana, please point me in the direction of the Rialto Bridge. I've had too much to drink." We giggle loudly as we bump into each other. I step on her toes.

"Oops, sorry."

"No worries. Come, I will take you to your bridge."

We arrive and I'm still tipsy but find my bearings.

"Grazie e arriverderci, Elana."

The pleasure is all mine, Roxanna. This town whispers that I'm a loon but what they don't know is that I'm simply enjoying life more than they are. It could be gone so quickly."

"Will I see you again before I leave Venice?" I want to spend more time with her, see life through her rose-colored glasses again.

"You will find me. Just look for the staring crowds. *Ciao, bella*." She boldly laughs, and in her black dress and bare feet, she sings and twirls all along the Grand Canal. The street light shines down on her as she pirouettes across a *piazza*.

And me, I find my hotel and fall into bed, light-hearted.

The next morning, I roam the streets with my guidebook which tells me there are 70,000 people living in Venice and 120 churches. I had read how the wealthy commissioned talented artists and sculptors to do work for them in their own personal chapels which would later become the churches of Venice, all 120 of them, on this small landmass.

I roam the streets in search of them and enter the first one I come upon. Here, I say a prayer thanking all that is for uplifting my spirits and for leading me to Assisi and then Venice.

Eventually I find myself in the *Piazza di San Marco* for the second time, but this time, there is no Elana amidst thousands of pigeons ... only thousands of tourists.

Now, my complete focus is on the architecture of the *basilica* and its majesty. Every inch of its façade is covered with detailed design work, gigantic arches, statues and colorful mosaics or Romanesque bas-reliefs. The upper portion of the structure is an elaborate Italian Gothic sculptural composition that is indescribable and above the portal is a 12th century angel, the one who had appeared to Saint Mark. As I walk into the glowing atrium, I notice the marble walls and the gold mosaic mantle. There are domes and portals throughout the *basilica,* too many to describe.

The marble mosaics on the floors and walls and the frescoes throughout the building are numerous. The five chapels are all designed beautifully and filled with extraordinary works of art. The main altar is mounted by a tribune resting on four columns of oriental alabaster and covered with reliefs depicting scenes from the lives of Christ and Mary.

Bronze sculptures of the evangelists and of the fathers of the church, including the famous *Pala d'Oro* by the Venetian master, Giampaolo Boninsegna, are on display. Pala d'Oro, a decorated panel above the altar, is embellished with gold, enamel and gemstones. It contains eighty enamel plaques illustrating scenes from the lives of Christ, the Virgin, Saint Mark and other figures such as angels, prophets, Oriental emperors and evangelists. I had seen it in books but wasn't prepared for it in person. Impressive.

I don't know where to sit because the church is quite large but I decide on the Chapel of the Madonna Nicopeia since the Venetians consider Mary their city's protectress. I close my eyes and say a prayer of gratitude, then all my thoughts leave. Suddenly, I'm brought out of my meditation by someone's anguished cries. At first, I don't open my eyes. I sit and listen. The woman is distraught, now sobbing loudly. I turn and find Elana sitting a few pews behind me, her head in her hands, a black laced veil pulled over her dark hair. She is a far different woman than the day before.

Why does she weep? What could have happened?

I wait for her to stop, hoping her anguish will subside, but it doesn't. I leave my pew and move to hers. I sit. She wipes her tears with a handkerchief. I take her other hand in mine and squeeze it to let her know I'm beside her. She cries louder. The incense is thick, the chanting mystical. I am sure she feels the angels consoling her. Sitting here opens my heart and I think of Natale for a moment and realize how much I miss him.

Elana releases her hand from mine and moves out of the pew. She waits for me to catch up and we walk through the *basilica*

136

where the ceilings seem to be one hundred feet high. Priests are now chanting and the pews are filled with people. The lighting is surreal, a softened gold. Once outside, Elana removes her veil, wipes her eyes and puts on her sunglasses which are large and in vogue. Instantly, she looks like a movie star and not a woman who has been grieving.

"Come, Roxanna. I have a place I want to take you to."

We move through the city, down streets and into alleyways past hundreds of shops selling gold jewelry, Venetian baubles and masks. We pass kiosks selling food, scarves, sandals and wares. It's a shopping mecca but we don't stop. We walk down the *Riva Degli Schiavoni* from the *Ponte della Paglia* along the *Canale di San Marco*, to the *Giardini di Castello,* the Castle Gardens. There along the promenade, Elana takes me to a little cafe.

"Giovanni, *ciao; come va?*" She smiles, her old self again. Giovanni is a foot shorter than Elana. He kisses her cheeks and embraces her.

"*La mia bella,* Elana." He's happy to see her. He takes us to an outside table and snaps his fingers. Two young waiters come to attention and quickly bring bread, olives, cheeses and prosecco.

"This is my home, where I come when I want to be reminded that I am loved." She raises her glass to me. "*Per amore.*" She sips the golden liquid. After a few minutes, the Elana I met yesterday has appeared, no longer any signs of her sadness and grief.

"Roxanna, tell me about your beloved. Now we have nothing but time to talk."

She smiles and clinks her glass against mine. I hesitate, not sure I want to open this door but then I realize I would like to talk with someone about matters of the heart.

"His name is Natale and I met him in Rome. We fell in love and spent six weeks together. He asked me to marry him and I got scared. It was too soon. One night, he went to work and I left him. I didn't even say goodbye because I knew he'd talk me into staying." I take a breath and then swig my prosecco.

"Elana, I'm so confused, not sure if it was the right thing to do. I think I'm insane and my whole life is a lie. What the hell am I doing here? Three months ago, I was living and working in America and my two boys were with me. I worked all day and watched television at night. Now, I think I'm this worldly person who is romancing life and I don't know a damned thing!" My heart beats wildly as I confess my truth to her.

"Oh, sweetheart, it's okay. You're confused. That's all. Let me tell you a story."

The waiter refills our glasses.

"There once was a young woman ... quite beautiful, actually ... tall, voluptuous, long, dark hair. She had to chase men away with a stick. They trailed her like they were the hunters and she the prize!" She throws her head back and laughs big.

"She had big dreams, wanted to sing her way to stardom. She was quite talented, you know. So, she left London in hopes of finding fame. She sang in clubs and made a good living but she was never happy enough with what she had. She wanted more." She takes another sip.

"There was a gorgeous man, a bartender from France named Jean Pierre. He had come to London for work and he was in love with her. They dated and then she moved in with him, lived with him for years. No one ever loved her like he did." She is lost in her dream.

"He had brown eyes you could get lost in and forget your name, a square jaw, thick, curly hair, and his chest ... mmmmmm ... God he was gorgeous. He loved to make love. Those Frenchmen ..."

She picks an olive off the plate, puts it in her mouth and plays with it with her teeth and tongue before chewing and swallowing it.

"He was a beautiful man. But she left him for someone who promised her a record deal ... William." She gulps her prosecco.

"William, a lover of women with his flashy car and expensive suits. He bedded more beauties that long year ... every woman he crossed paths with ... while she was left alone, night after night ... to contemplate her mistake and her broken heart ... and the lie of a record deal. Once she realized she had left the only man she had ever loved, it was too late."

"More champagne, please," she instructs the waiter. She turns to me. "Stupid girl. Before she realized her foolishness, Jean Pierre was back in France married to a pretty French woman. That was over thirty years ago, Roxanna." She grabs my arm and squeezes it hard to get my full attention.

"If you love this man, go to him before it's too late or you will end up a lonely old woman with nothing but romantic notions."

I witness the real Elana—her sunglasses off, her bloodshot eyes filled with old memories and lost dreams.

"I'm so sorry, Elana."

"It's all right. I'm doing well. If I had it to do again, I hope that I would have the sense to make the right choice this time. After all these years, I'm settled in my life and I live each day as if we are together. I sing and dance and dream that we are still a couple." With closed eyes, her face turned upward toward the sun, Elana breathes in as if she can smell him and sighs.

"'I am old yes, but I do not fear death for I have known love.' He read those words to me once, you know. He always read to me … said he didn't trust his own words to describe his feelings for me. Damned French, so damned romantic. They do that on purpose, you know, so you'll fall in love with them. Their words are like foreplay for Christ's sake." She turns to the waiter who hands her another glass.

"*Una sigaretta, per favore.*" He pulls a cigarette from his vest and lights it for her. "*Grazie.*" She turns back to me. "Enough about my history, Roxanna … what are you thinking?"

"I should go back to Rome but I'm afraid. I came to Capri because it was calling to me. It's so crazy." I think of telling her about the spirit but decide against it.

"It's only crazy if you don't follow love. If you must take some time away from him, then do. But return to him before too much time passes. *Capisci?*"

"I understand."

Now, I'm the one lost in thought. We sit quietly, Elana puffing her cigarette, me lost in my memories while a distant mandolin caresses the day. We sit for hours talking and laughing, a little closer like women-friends become after they have undressed their souls for each other.

We walk back along the Grand Canal laughing and flirting with the waiters who stand in front of their restaurants trying to entice us to come in and eat. Elana is at her usual best, bewitching them as she passes. The prosecco has cast a soft glow over both of us.

"It's time to retire, Roxanna. I bid you good night." We are at the Rialto Bridge, not far from my hotel.

"Will I see you tomorrow?"

"No, I have business in Milano, a possible singing job so I will leave early on the train." She pulls a pen and paper from her purse and writes something on it. "Here is my phone number and address in case you ever find yourself in Venice again. It was a pleasure, Roxanna. I enjoyed your company and *grazie mille* for being there today." She smiles sweetly, embraces me and kisses both my cheeks.

"Elana, I'm so happy to have met you. I'm going to miss you. Here's my email address and cell phone number. If you are in Capri or even in the south, please call me and I will meet you." I don't want to say goodbye to my new friend. "The next time I travel, I'll call and let you know where I am."

"Enjoy your life, Roxanna, and remember to follow your heart." She blows me a kiss then leaves me on the promenade.

CHAPTER 22

Natale and I are walking through the streets of Rome laughing. I feel the love we have for each other. Then, he releases me back to myself and disappears. I awaken.

"Please don't go. Not yet."

I ache for him. I fumble for my phone; still sleepy, I call him.

"*Pronto.*" I have awakened him.

"Natale, it's me, Roxanna."

He takes a moment before responding.

"Rosanna, where are you?" he asks solemnly.

"After leaving Rome, I went to Assisi and I'm in Venice now." I ramble on. "I'm sorry for leaving the way I did but I knew that if I waited to say goodbye, I would never have left at all."

Silence.

"Natale, please say something. I'm sorry. I love you."

I hear his heart flutter or maybe I just imagine it.

"Please, forgive me."

"Rosanna, you broke my heart. What do you want me to say? I come home and you are gone … only a note. I cannot sleep, I cannot eat without you."

"It's been hard for me, too." I start to cry. "I'm confused about a lot of things in my life, Natale but I'm not confused about my love for you. It's just the timing of it."

"Then go and do what you need to do, Rosanna. I cannot promise I will be here when you finish. I don't know … don't know. I need to think."

It's quiet on the other end and I picture him with his head in his hands, his fingers wrestling with his hair.

"I understand. I just wanted to call and tell you I love you and that I'm thinking of you." More silence. "Can I call you again?"

Silence.

"Are you there?"

"*Si.* Good luck, Rosanna. I hope you find what you are looking for. I wish you happiness. *Ciao.*"

I put the phone down and weep into my pillow wishing it was him I was hugging. Did I expect him to be happy?

Natale sits on the edge of the bed, his head in his hands. His heart is beating fast and he's angry. He wants to go to her, to get on the next train to Venice. But he knows if he does, he could scare her and push her further away. She said she had to fly free like a bird. She made that clear to him.

"*Non capisc!.*"

His thoughts are confused and running wild. "Why does she need freedom from me?"

"*Merda!*" With his hand, he wipes the night table clean, sweeping everything to the floor.

"Goodbye, Rosanna."

He moves to the bathroom with his heavy heart.

Romantic Venice has not brightened my dark mood. I roam the streets aimlessly, still filled with sadness.

Time ... I just need more time to figure this out ....

I walk through alleyways, over the Bridge of Sighs and through a maze of shops in search of things that will take my mind off Natale. I am back in the *Piazza di San Marco* so I decide to visit the Doges Palace and its museum which are filled with art. This will help distract me.

The palace is the home of the Doges, the supreme heads of state as they reigned over Venice at one time. It's an unusual building, appearing to be a delicate pink and white in color, its façade decorated in the flamboyant Gothic style. Statues and depictions of scenes are everywhere—Adam and Eve in the Garden; the *Judgment of Solomon;* the statue of Venus and the *Robes of Justice.*

The *Staircase of the* Giants is before me, once used for the official crowning ceremonies of the new Doges. Two colossal statues of Neptune and Mars stand guard as I ascend. The Procuratie, once the residence of the prosecutors of San Marco, now houses the cultural institute and the Archeological Museums. The top portion of this neo-classically designed building is covered with statues of Roman emperors and symbolic scenes from long ago.

Inside, its twenty rooms are filled with marble and bronze archeological finds and other antiquities from Rome and Greece— Roman portraits; Greek and Roman reliefs and statues such as Venus and Apollo; a Roman sarcophagus and a 4th century sculpture of Athena, all of which take my mind off my heart.

I'm starting to feel better.

I exit the building and leave the *piazza* to find the most beautiful sight— the church of Santa Maria della Salute in the distance on the far side of the canal. It is domed, has a grand façade and statues and bas reliefs adorn it. The waterway shimmers in the afternoon sun while gondolas covered with brightly colored blue and yellow tarps rock gently upon the water. The scene before me is like a postcard.

I walk through a small neighborhood *piazzetta* where neighbors are enjoying their *espresso* at tables dressed in embroidered tablecloths. Their children are running about playing tag, laughing and giggling.

I turn the corner and find myself on the bank of the Grand Canal. My stomach reminds me that I have not had a meal today so I stop at the nearest *trattoria*. The waiter recommends the

Venetian fish soup. I order it and am happy I did. Lemon, basil and tomato fill my senses as I take my first mouthful. The bowl is filled with shrimp, mussels, squid and whitefish with saffron, fennel, curry and garlic. He also recommends a dry white wine, Soave from Veneto. Both are wonderful. I'll have to remember this meal so I can recreate it and find a wine in the States as good as this one.

As I wait for my bill, I watch the gondolas carrying lovers, some kissing as they pass. Again, I feel Natale's presence but am now in control of my emotions.

Music and laughter fill the street and a man with a black-and-white striped shirt and a red neckerchief has come to play his accordion. The smiles of the tourists brighten my mood and I relax.

It's early evening and I decide to hire a gondolier for a tour of the canals. As I approach three men waiting for patrons, they all smile and say in unison, "*Bella.* You want ride, *Signora?*"

"*Quanto costa?*" I've heard they are expensive.

"*Cento euro per un ora.*" One hundred per hour.

"*Molto caro.*" Too expensive. I turn to leave. The tallest, wearing a barrel-mustache steps forward.

"*Signora*, we work hard. It is one hour. For you, *ottanta*, eighty."

"*Si*, okay."

"Please get in. Take my hand." He helps me into the boat and I take my seat on a red velvet cushion. For a moment, I dream I am Catherine McCormack in the movie, *Dangerous Beauty,* and smile. The gondola is black, lacquered, adorned and embellished with gold statues and scroll work.

"*Molto bella,*" I say in my broken Italian. "Nice gondola." The boatman is pleased. He smiles and proudly nods. He's a good-looking man of about thirty-five with gigantic forearms which I assume are from moving the oar through the water all day. His shirt is black and white striped and his pants are black and he has a red scarf tied tightly around his neck. His skin has darkened from the beating sun.

"*Grazie. Io solo?*" He asks if I am alone.

"*Si.*"

"*Molto bella.*" He winks at me. The sun is low in the sky this time of day creating a sparkling diamond pattern on the water. But here in Venice, the canal is not the color of the sea. Here, the sunlight glitters on the murky water creating an emerald green hue. Its reflection dances upon the facades of the villas along the canal.

"I take you special place … where we live … *non si sono turisti, la mia Venezia.*" He moves his oar in the water and we glide down the canal and turn into a smaller waterway. After a few minutes, he pulls up to a building and jumps from the gondola.

"*Aspetta.*" He disappears inside the building. I lie back on the velvet cushion and enjoy the tranquility, the only sound, the gentle lapping of the water against the boat. Soon, he emerges with two glasses and an open bottle of *vino*. He pours and hands me a glass, then fills his own, all the while managing the oar with his free hand.

"*Salute.*"

"*Alla Vita.* What is your name? *Come ti chiami?*"

"Marco. You?"

"Roxanna. Nice to meet you."

He raises his glass to me and bows slightly. Another gondola passes us, the boatman singing *O Sole Mio*. We all smile. I feel as if I am in a painting.

"Ah, Venezia." He breathes in and puffs up his chest like a peacock.

We float through tiny canals lined with charming houses, *piazzetti* and gardens. The thousand-year-old villas are adorned with terracotta planters holding geraniums. *Ponti*, bridges are everywhere allowing everyone to cross the waterways that run throughout the city. The cafes have brightly colored awnings and planter boxes attached to the wrought iron fences at their edges. Freshly washed clothes hang on clotheslines dry from the day's heat. A grandfather and his young grandson are stooped down at the water's edge, probably looking for fish.

In his broken English, Marco tells me that the canal we are on is where the movie *The Italian Job* was filmed and proceeds to tell me about the shoot. I understand most of what he is saying. He then tells me about each villa, its name and who used to live there.

We travel beneath an arched cement bridge and I look upward in time to see a waterfall pattern of twinkling light on its underside. It glistens with liquid light, a reflection of the waters.

"Marco, look!"

"*Si, la luce del sole,* the light of the sun. *Bella,* quick, *foto.*" I'm awestruck, staring at the shimmering brilliance but quickly pull my camera out just in time to snap a photo. Then, as if minutes have passed instead of an hour, we are back in the Grand Canal moving closer to the dock. I am so grateful that I give him one hundred and twenty euro.

"Grazie, Roxanna. *Sera.*"

I leave him and dance down the promenade toward the Rialto Bridge. Beyond it, the sunlight is reflecting off the buildings along the canal and I want to catch their beauty. So, I chase the sun, snapping photos along the way until I realize I'm in the middle of Marco's neighborhood where the locals live and the tourists never roam. I move through the streets and alleyways looking for more photo opportunities and find many.

Every inch of every building and every bridge is an architectural delight. I come upon the *Piazza di San Paolo.* Four cafes frame the square, each filled with families sitting at tables eating dinner. I choose one, sit and order a limoncello. Families are laughing, talking and singing ... yes, the men oftentimes sing at the end of their meal. These are the sounds of a well-lived life. The little ones are giggling as if they share secrets, and the adults are talking in that Italian way—you know, when they are so passionate with every word, every phrase, speaking in raised tones, talking with their hands and their bodies as if they are musical instruments.

I smell the fresh fish that has been caught today as it waits to be grilled with lemon, Italian herbs, spices and olive oil. This reminds me of the fish Antonio prepared for me. It's the sweet smell of the sea mixed with garlic, basil, and tomatoes, intoxicating my senses.

Once again, my breath leaves my body.

Take it away forever. I could happily die here.

I think about all the moments these past few months that have caused this reaction in me. Then, I whiff the scent of lemons, reminding me of Capri. They're so sweet that you can eat them like oranges. I had watched Enrico in his garden, tending to the lemon trees under the black netting that protects them from the sun. He took care in pruning the trees watering each night, nurturing them and talking to them as if they were his children. Only great things grow with such love.

When I return to my room, I'm inspired to sketch the Santa Maria della Salute Cathedral and the gondolas. I download my photos onto my laptop and start sketching. I also throw open the shutters and am mesmerized by the sounds of people as they pass through the alleyway below.

After an hour or so, my eyes grow heavy so I turn down my bed and crawl between my sheets. The language of love wafts upward from the alleyway below and lulls me to sleep ... *piano, piano* ... *peró ... aspetta ... allora ... poesia.* Poetry.

CHAPTER 23
CAPRI, ITALY

◯

Natale returns to his apartment with a bottle of *vino* and a pack of cigarettes. He hasn't smoked in two years and has been proud he quit. But Rosanna leaving and her phone call has distressed him. His heart aches, his stomach hurts and his hands shake continually.

Ansia. Anxiety, he says to himself, justifying his desire to smoke.

I will stop again soon.

He sits on the balcony drinking the wine and smoking one cigarette after another. Every room in his apartment and this balcony reminds him of her. Her smell is here. He can still hear her laughter. And then he remembers her tears and her fear of commitment. It was too soon. He shouldn't have asked her to marry him so quickly. But it had felt right.

The sun has slid behind a building and the colors of the night appear. She loved the evening light. He smiles as he remembers her passion to paint. He wonders if she has taken the sketches of him and moves into the apartment to look for them. After searching, he realizes they have gone with her. The emptiness he feels is something he has never experienced before. How will he live without her?

"Rosanna *tornerà ... siamo innamorati.* She will come back to me. We are in love." His mind races.

But what if she doesn't?

He starts to pace and realizes he's had too much wine and needs food.

"I must go to her." He dreams, for a moment, that if he goes to Venice, she will fall into his arms and they will be together again.

After drinking the entire bottle of wine, Natale races into the apartment, grabs his jacket and keys and leaves.

The train pulls into the Venezia Santa Lucia station at midnight. He has eaten something but only slept for an hour.

"I will find her. I will go to every hotel if I have to."

I miss Capri so much that I leave the Queen of the Adriatic, this emerald colony of Venice, at noon. On the train, I try and reach Enrico by cell phone but cannot get through. Italia and telephones! *Mamma mia!* It's not an easy feat. I have no place to stay when I return to Anacapri, but Enrico said to call when I return because he might have a nice place for me by then.

As I stand on the deck of the hydrofoil, I am reminded of my love affair with this island. As we move closer, I glance up to the rocky cliffs and make out the faint outline of the bright white San Michele Chapel and Villa, and the ochre colored Caesar Augustus Hotel. Once again, I hear the island whisper my name.

I splurge on a taxi to take me to the top of the island instead of the *autobus* since I have my bags in tow and don't know where Enrico will send me to sleep next. *Mamma mia,* the life of a gypsy is not easy for a woman my age.

As soon as I walk into the cool, marble lobby of the Caesar Augustus Hotel, he greets me in a crisp, blue suit with a wide smile as if he has been expecting me. He's always dressed superbly, looking fresh and well-groomed.

"Roxanna, you are back. Welcome. Did you have a nice trip?" I kiss his cheeks.

"Yes, Enrico, it was wonderful. Do you have a place for me?"

"Yes, yes. I am glad you are here now because the people, they leave today. I will tell you how to get there. Take your luggage and walk into town. You know where the *tabacchi* shop is on the corner?"

"Yes."

"You will find a little alleyway there. Go there and walk down the steps. Keep walking all the way down until you come to the trash bins … you know the ones … and then go to the left. You pass Maruzzella and all the villas. Keep going until you get to the end. You will find a gate that says *Mio Paradiso,* My Paradise. That's where you will stay. The key is in the door, and it is open. I will be down later to check on you. Good to have you back, Roxanna."

"*Grazie, grazie.* Thank you, Enrico. *Ciao.*"

I wave goodbye to him, leave the coolness of the hotel and step out into the hot, humid air. It's as if a wet blanket has suddenly wrapped itself around me. Dampness starts collecting at my hairline and between my breasts. Anacapri is not an easy place to get to. It's not for the faint of heart, mind, or body, especially this time of year. I want to unpack my suitcase and yearn for a more permanent place, somewhere to call home for a bit … and a breeze.

Okay. I'm tired and hungry and have no idea where I'm going. This heat is endless! Drips of sweat slither down my blouse and soak my clothes.

"I wish in this moment, that I am naked with cool water running down my body like an icy cold shower!" I say out loud to no one.

I hear laughter in the ethers and suddenly, my bags are light as a feather. I stop, look upward and smile at the sky. A soft breeze picks up and cools me and I mouth the words, "thank you." No one would ever believe the magic here!

When I arrive at *Mio Paradiso,* the sun is setting behind the Isola di Ischia. A path edged with flowers runs 100 yards along the property and overlooks the sea. The view is the same as the one from the Caesar Augustus Hotel—Ischia to the left, the tiny island of Procida next on the horizon, then the mainland, and

Monte Vesuvio and Sorrento to the far right. It's stunning.

Statues line the walkway. Before me is a stone villa with an attached *terrazzo*, its flooring made of lovely hand-painted tiles. The main house, I would learn later, was the home of Enrico's ancestors and is three hundred years old. The attached building, a kitchen with an outer patio was built one hundred years before by his family.

Herbs, night jasmine, geraniums and roses line the terrace. Fruit trees are everywhere—plums, olives, lemons, peaches and oranges. The gardens are filled with strawberry plants, basil, arugula, rosemary bushes, broccoli, fava beans, lettuce, tomatoes and artichokes. The air is perfumed with their scents.

I set my bags down and sit to watch the setting sun and sky, its colors different shades of salmon and pink.

Then I remember the dream. "... Come, I want to show you where you will live ... you will be inspired to paint here ..."

The spirit ... this is it! The terrace ... the flowers ... the view.

The dream has become my reality.

Mio paradiso ...

Natale has been to most of the hotels in Venezia. He showed each desk clerk and manager a photo of Rossana from his phone. But no one seems to remember her. Dejected, he leaves for the train station. He must return to Rome to work tonight.

"I cannot do this anymore, Rosanna!" he says dejected.

Over the next few days, I hardly leave the villa since I have been blessed with the gardens and the fruit trees. When I do venture out for water, the two-mile roundtrip is a challenge in the heat and the large water bottles are heavy. But soon, I build muscles in my arms and am strong enough. I now have the utmost respect for the islanders and what they do to support their households and families.

I settle into my little villa nicely. Each morning, I sit with the lizards and the birds to welcome the day. I watch the colors of the sea and the sky change with each new wind and each new weather pattern. Enrico comes by to visit daily and to water and nurture his gardens. He describes all the flowers and plants to me, telling me their names. He tells me the winds come from nine different directions on the island, sometimes creating wild storms that blow like a hurricane. I wonder if I should worry.

Enrico's wife Bettina, who speaks only a few words of English, has come by to introduce herself. She's an attractive woman, always smiling and singing as she works on the property. I'm amazed at her energy and her hard body which is lean and muscular. She pushes wheelbarrows filled with tile, rock, branches and dirt from one end of the property to the other. Enrico and Bettina have a daughter, Maria who lives on the other side of the property with her husband and two daughters. I often hear the children's laughter and it makes me smile reminding me of my sons.

Maria who is as beautiful as her mother, speaks excellent English. She brings me homemade tomato sauce and wine from the cellars and I thank her for her kindness. It's nice to know her family is just on the other side of the gate if I should need anything, especially if a storm should blow through.

I have been at the villa for two weeks and my madness has returned. My anxiety is high and I am doubting my every thought. Natale is constantly in my thoughts. It's as if he's thinking about me as I am him. I want to run to the phone in the *piazza* to call him but I feel that if I do, he will be angry, or worse, not pick up the phone. And I'm not sure what I will say to him since I have not made a decision.

This night, the spirit visits me.
"Roxanna, ninety percent of what you are feeling is not yours. You humans feel what everyone around you is feeling and take it on as your own because you are all connected. And when you are connected to a beloved as you are, you feel what he is feeling as well. When your body and heart feel heavy, say, '*Who does this*

belong to? Is it mine or someone else's?' If it is not yours, say, *'Return to sender.'* This will clear you and make you whole again. Let all the swirling emotions and feelings move around you as if you are a boulder, massive and strong. Then you will know the difference between what is yours and what belongs to him or anyone else. You will breathe easier and life will not seem so insurmountable."

So, I practice this each time I feel him. I am thankful it is working.

I'm soon overcome with sadness, not only missing Natale but also my boys. And what of my future? I don't know who I am anymore. The longer I sit here alone, the faster my mind races backward toward insanity and self-doubt. I finally slap myself out of it and decide it's time to go into town and be with people.

I dine at a *ristorante* where a petite woman named Patricia waits on me. I like her immediately. She's warm and friendly with soft eyes and a bright smile. I am fortunate that she speaks English well enough for us to communicate. I take her recommendation and order Italian herbed, roasted chicken, which no one does better than the Italians.

As she serves me, she asks me where I have come from and where I'm staying. I tell her. We talk about our children and soon we bond because we understand what it means to be a mother. She tells me the story of how difficult it was for her to release her 25-year-old son to his new wife and how she wept and wailed for a week, her heart broken. She said she loved her new daughter-in-law, but it was the act of giving her son away that was difficult. She said no one understood her grieving. She asks me if she is the only mother who has experienced this.

I share my story of how my sons are now sixteen and seventeen but I still treat them as little boys, never wanting them to grow up.

She explained that we as women birth them and love them, protect them and teach them to be good men. Then, it is our job to give them away to another woman. She laughs and apologizes as tears escape her.

"*Mama mia*, Santa Maria, bless us mothers," she says with cupped hands. We both laugh. When I'm finished with my meal and our mother-to-mother talk, I hug her and I promise to come again.

I dream of Natale ... you know, one of those dreams that continues all night, even after you have awoken and try to shake it off. In it, I walk from room to room chasing him but he cannot see or hear me. I run after him, fear and loneliness creeping into me like a demon. I want to feel his warmth and embrace him. It's horrible.

My sanity is finally restored once daylight comes and I walk out into the gardens overlooking the sea. I know I must be strong enough to take care of myself before I give myself away again.

What a strange idea that we women can only have love if we give ourselves away ...

I ponder this for quite some time.

No. I will not give myself away. I want a partnership. I want to be equal. I am valuable. When I finish this journey, I will have the relationship of my dreams. I nervously pick at my nails. *I do hope Natale waits for me, if I haven't lost him already.*

I shiver at the thought of my past and what I've come through. Maybe I'm just afraid Natale will tire of me and eventually leave me for another woman. My head starts to sabotage my thoughts. Sometimes, I think I need my antidepressant again.

Stop! That's not who you are anymore. You are strong and you can accomplish anything!

After days of dissecting myself and noting all my fears and flaws, I realize I need a break from this self-deprecation. Travel ... an adventure ... that seems to be the thing that shifts me. If I am ever to be ready to go back to Natale, I must be strong and confident.

If I had been a different person when I met Ed ... stronger, more confident, I wonder if my marriage would have survived ...

CHAPTER 24
FLORENCE, ITALY

Painters and sculptors flock to Florence. She lies before them spread out like a lover waiting to be taken—to be painted or sculpted, of course. Her skyline with its ancient tiled roofs atop multi-colored medieval buildings paints the horizon like no other place in the world. The turrets, the towers, the *basilicas* and their facades, the famous *Duomo di Santa Maria Del Fiore,* all a mixture of Florentine Gothic, Baroque and Romanesque styles. Every artist, sculptor and architect who has come here before me has left their mark, not only in the museums and palaces, but also in the outer structures of the buildings, their exteriors and the squares.

I fall in love with the city the moment I arrive. I sit in my hotel room and look out at the *Arno Fiume*, the sounds of the night music to my ears. Aromas from the cafes waft up to me carried by the breeze that has come to cool the day. Firenze is what it has promised to be, a great lover, for I feel my heart beating wildly with anticipation. I hardly sleep for I cannot wait to explore as soon as dawn breaks.

At 6:00 a.m. I ready myself and walk the streets and alleyways in search of *espresso*. The tourists have not risen yet so I have the city to myself.

I stroll over the *Ponte Vecchio*—the old bridge, and through the *Piazza della Signoria* containing the *Palazzo Vecchio* and Arnolfo's

Tower. I enter the *Loggia dei Lanzi* and am awestruck. The building is divine ... gothic with its soaring clustered columns and trefoil arches. There are colossal works here such as Giambologna's *The Rape of the Sabines* and the *Perseus* by Cellini. I come upon (a copy) of two sculptures by Bandinelli—*The David, and Hercules and Cacus.* On my far left sits the *Fountain of Neptune* by Ammannati, a large figure of the sea-god Neptune with three tritons (mermen) on a light chariot drawn by four horses.

Florence is the seat of the art world and I feel as if I've traveled back in time. Between the 8th century B.C. and the 20th century A.D., passionate painters, sculptors and architects left their mark here. Wherever I roam, there is a building with an exquisitely decorative façade, a *piazza*, a sculpture, a monument or a church. Each time I walk the streets or enter a building, I find works by the great masters.

Florence has a long history of dissension and conflict but these days, the streets are filled with lovers and artists. It has survived barbarian invasions, the time of revolutions from the 13th through the 16th centuries, a revolt due to Spain's presence, and French domination. Despite its history, art has flourished here.

During the 13th century, Gothic style structures started to appear such as the *Duomo* and the *Palazzo Vecchio.* In the 14th century, this work continued as the *Ponte Vecchio, Giotto's Campanile, Orsanmichele* and the *Loggia del Bigallo* were constructed. The Pitti and Medici families came into wealth and power in the 15th century and numerous *palazzos,* palaces were built as well as other monuments. From the 16th to the 18th century, many libraries, museums and other important buildings were built including the Uffizi Museum, the Boboli Gardens and the *Mercato Nuovo.*

For days, I walk through gardens, galleries, museums and buildings, all containing great masterpieces. My mind has been swimming, my breath caught in my throat. With my digital camera in hand, I try to capture all of it knowing one photo will not do it justice.

I feel the masters in every fiber of my being and their fingertips upon my soul—Lippi, Botticelli, Donatello, Leonardo, Michelangelo,

Bandini, Giotto, Caravaggio, Reni, Sanzio, Rossi, Lorenzetti, Buoninsegna, Fabriano, Raffaello, Bonaiuto, Cellini, Cimabue, Verrocchio, Ghiberti, Brunelleschi ... and yes, Gentileschi and Cecchi—the only two female artists I could find from the Renaissance period; it was illegal for women to paint during that time.

The *Piazza dell Duomo* is considered the religious center of the city. It's known for its famous *Duomo,* the dome of *Santa Maria Del Fiore,* the great cathedral, *Giotto's Campanile,* and the *San Lorenzo's Basilica*. Its façade is so busy that they say it took a thousand years to plan it, build it and then rebuild it again. Every inch of it is opulent—decorated, carved, frescoed and containing mosaics bas-reliefs, pilasters and niches holding statues.

The *Campanile*—the bell tower stands alongside the *Duomo*. It, too is made of colored marble. It stands at 277 feet tall with columns, arched windows and bas reliefs decorating its façade. I could study it for hours and still not see it all.

I know Florence is called the "Cradle of the Renaissance," but after roaming the streets and seeing all I have seen, I now call it the "City of the Masters."

I sit in a café, Italian music playing in the background as I watch the tourists and locals. I notice many of the women have dark hair but light-colored eyes. They are dressed beautifully, their clothing and shoes from fashion magazines.

After leaving the cafe, I roam the alleyways and small streets to study the architecture of the old medieval buildings. I come across an open-air market and stop to purchase a few things to remember Florence by before returning to my room to sketch.

The sun sits high in the sky this day. I walk across the *arno* toward the *Palazzo Pitti*, the Pitti Palace. I thought the heat and humidity were only relentless in the south, but now I realize that's not the case. I walk slowly and fan myself with the decorative fan I purchased from a street vendor.

I arrive at the palace on the slopes of Boboli Hill, which was built for the Medici family and was their residence for six generations. The gardens are magnificent, framed by flights of steps that lead to the upper hill, a fountain and a small museum.

The terraces below contain a large granite basin in the center, originally from the *Baths of Caracalla* in Rome, and an Egyptian obelisk from the *Temple of Amon* in Thebes. Statues from famous 16th and 17th century artists line the perimeter.

The "great masters" await me as I enter the royal quarters known as the *Galleria Palatina*. Each room has its own name— Allegories Room, Room of Fine Arts, Hercules Room, Psyche Room, Music Room, Flora Room, Iliad Room, Apollo Room, Venus Room, etc. Next are the Royal Apartments which are broken up into the Green Room, Throne Room, Blue Room, Chapel, Queen's Apartment and the King's Apartment. All are quite large.

The ceilings are decorated with frescoes, bas-reliefs, trompe l'oeil and sculptures. Marble or alabaster columns decorate the halls. And if this is not enough for the senses, painting, sculptures and ornate tables of bronze gilded malachite or decorated marble grace each room.

The first room contains a collection of pen and ink drawings. Black or red sanguine pencil was used by each artist, then a brown wash creating a highlighted or colored effect, giving the drawing the feel of a completed work. I study each one ... like these ... *the Council of Ephesus* by Giuseppe Nicola Nasini and *The Last Supper* by Giuseppe Cades ... amazing definition and shadow created with pen and black ink with a brown wash. Such exquisite detail in Baldassarre Peruzzi's *Adoration of the Holy Child* as he has used a brush, brown ink and then highlighted with black pencil which brings light to the drawing.

Ah, I shall try this technique.

In the apartment of the Grand Duchess the entire room is filled with incredible trompe l'oeil by Castagnoli. The Music Room, *Sala della Musica* is filled with marble columns, detailed bas-reliefs, tromp l'oeil and frescoes.

Then, I come upon the masters I have been waiting to see, the ones that make my heart thump inside my chest. Raphael—*The Veiled Woman, Madonna of the Grand Duke, The Vision of Ezekiel,* and finally, his *Madonna of the Chair, Madonna della Seggiola* ... my breath becomes heavy. Her face is so young, so serene. Her eyes, her lips, her ears, her nose ... all so perfect ... She holds her child close showing such intimacy, and the Christ child's face is the most precious I have ever seen.

Others also make me purr—Caravaggio's *Sleeping Cupid,* Andrea del Sarto's *St. John the Baptist*, Titian's *The Magdalen* and his *Portrait of a Man*. There is Artemisia Gentileschi's *Judith.* She was the young female painter during the Renaissance who had a profound influence on Florentine painting and one of the first artists to show true, deep emotion in the faces of women on canvas ... the details of their hair ... their clothing ... the scarf around the head ... the flesh on the bodies ... profound.

There are many works by Botticelli, but three hold my attention—*Adorate il Bambino,* Adoration of the Child; *Madonna del Mare,* Virgin of the Sea; and *Madonna col Bambino,* Virgin with Child. In the latter two, the Madonna's face is angelic with soft pale skin. In one, her eyes are lowered, gazing downward toward her child, and in the other they are looking outward as if she is dreaming. The colors of the fabric, the detail, the lace about her face, the thin golden halo around her head ... In the *Madonna del Mare*, there is a beautiful star painted upon the shoulder of her robe.

Although I am light-headed with all I've seen, I don't want to stop. I walk back over the *Ponte Vecchio* above the *arno* toward San Marco's *piazza* and into the *Galleria dell' Accademia*, the great museum that holds the original Michelangelo's *The David*. It also holds the famous statue by Giambologna—*Rape of the Sabine Women,* which is exquisite. The museum is small and I take my time studying the four Captives of *The David*.

I move into the great Tribune at the end of the hall of the *Accademia* and come face-to-face with this god that has been birthed from someone's soul ... *The David* ... Michelangelo's masterpiece ... the symbol of the entire Renaissance and of Florence. I can feel the energy of it—his strength, his youth and his beauty. Once again, my soul weeps and my heart pushes against my breast begging for release.

I suddenly notice someone standing so close to me that I feel his moist breath upon the back of my neck. He speaks to me in Italian but it's so soft, I barely hear him.

CHAPTER 25

"**A**h, you are *Americano*; I thought you *Italiano*."

His eyes are dark, his skin translucent, smooth for a man. I look him over, his black tee-shirt outlining his abs. I blush and lower my eyes. The only reason I would look there is because I am standing in front of *The David*.

He speaks.

"I was saying, there is a theory that this was a likeness taken of him after he slew Goliath. You see his face as he looks out into the distance as if he is contemplating or meditating, lost in thought. There is no ... how you say ... cockiness ... no ego about him after he has won the battle. Do you see how his arm hangs at his side and the bow is slung over his shoulder?"

He smiles, his eyes never leaving the *The David*. His accent is thick but his English is near perfect.

"I have never heard that theory," I whisper, "but I see what you mean."

"Yes. Oh, please, allow me to introduce myself. My name is Valentino. Valentino Lorenzo. And your name?" He reaches for my hand and kisses it.

"Roxanna." He's charming.

"Rosanna." He smiles.

We are quiet for a few moments. Then, he breaks the silence.

"I come here often to study his proportions. See how his feet and his hands are so much larger? It gives the piece perspective. Look ... the muscles in his legs," he points to them, "and the way they are slightly bent at the knees. His rib cage and his collarbone.

Do you see how he created the veins in his arms and hands? Such detail. *Perfetto.*" He kisses his fingertips and spreads them as if he is releasing his words into the air.

"You view art as if you are a sculptor."

"*Si.* I come from a long line of sculptors, a descendent of the great Ghiberti Lorenzo. Do you know his name?

"No, I haven't."

"He was a great Florentine sculptor, painter and architect responsible for the Baptistery of San Giovanni in the *Piazza dell Duomo.* Have you been there?"

"Yes. Was he the architect that designed the structure?" I'm excited that here before me is a descendent of a famous sculptor from the past. We both start to walk toward the exit as we continue our conversation.

"He actually designed and built two of the great bronze doors—the one on the north side and then the one on the east side. It took him thirty years to finish this work. Michelangelo called the one on the east side the *Porta del Paradiso,* the Gate of Paradise. It is a group of panels with twenty-four niches and bas-reliefs representing stories from the Old Testament and statues of biblical figures. It is *magnifico.*"

He has a fire in his eyes as he talks about the panels.

"They moved the original panels to the *Museo dell' Opera del Duomo.* They move everything here in Florence, you know ... for safe keeping. It is a masterpiece. You should see the original."

"That's quite a heritage."

"He also produced work for the *Duomo* and the Church of Orsanmichele."

"You must be proud ... and talented."

"Proud, yes; but no, I do not have the talent he had in his little finger." Valentino lowers his head in reverence. "Each time I begin a sculpture, I always say a prayer to San Lorenzo and to Ghiberti." He makes the sign of the cross upon his own skin then kisses the small golden one which hangs from a thick gold chain on his neck.

"Well, Rosanna. It is time for my *espresso.* Would you please join me?"

"*Si, grazie*, Valentino."

We walk through the *piazza* toward a bar, enter and he orders two *espressos*. This is the Italians' pick-me-upper this time of day that holds them until dinner in the later hours. I never understood why they eat so late in this country.

"So, Rosanna, are you *solo?*"

"Yes, I have come to see the art in Florence. Do you live in the city?"

"*Si*, I live in an apartment near the *Duomo*. It has been in my family for the last two hundred years. The buildings are very old here, no?"

I'm enjoying the conversation and his company as we sit at an outside table talking about Valentino's family. He tells me that his work is shown on Via de' Vecchietti, a street filled with art close to the *Duomo*. His pieces are half-life and full-life marble sculptures, very large works. He says he has sculpted copies of the gods but has not yet attempted *The David,* although he comes to study him every week and says he will know when it's time to do so.

"My favorite pieces are those of women but I have to touch them to be able to create their likeness."

"Do you sell many, Valentino?"

"Enough to buy food and clothing. My family supports me so I am okay. What do you do in America, Rosanna?"

While he waits for my response, he sizes me up looking at my face, my cheekbones, my nose, the curve of my lips. It's as if he's touching all my intimate parts. I squirm in my seat.

"I'm not working right now but I'm a painter." Funny how I can call myself one when I haven't picked up a brush in years.

"Painting is like sculpting. You must have the sight. You must become what you are creating, get inside it, feel it. Is that what you do when you paint, Rosanna?"

"Yes, I do. Sometimes, I lose time." I remember when the boys were young. I started my first landscape. They were down for a nap. Two hours went by as if it had only been twenty minutes. I had no idea where the time had gone.

"When I am creating, I stay inside my studio for months. Sometimes I see no one. I don't sleep for days and I forget to eat. You see?"

He pulls up his shirt exposing his abdomen. Although he is tall and of medium build, his stomach indents there and I can see he works out because of the well-defined muscles. I blush and quickly look away.

"Sometimes I am crazy inside my head, you know? No one understands what it is like to be filled with a love for something so deep. I cannot explain it." He is pensive.

"I understand, Valentino. I know how you feel." My memories have come back to me.

"You do understand me." He reaches for my hand and brings it to his lips, kissing the back of it. Now his eyes are smiling. "Ah, companions. We are so blessed in this life, are we not? Rosanna, would you please have dinner with me tonight?"

I close my eyes for a moment and think about Natale. Valentino senses there is someone else, as if he has witnessed my love leave my body and go elsewhere.

"No, no. I can tell you are in love. It is only dinner. I enjoy your company. I will meet you at the restaurant, a place not far from here. It is halfway between *Santa Maria Novella* and the *Duomo* on Via dei Panzani on this street." He points. "*Ristorante Giglio Rosso.* Will you meet me there at 19:00?"

"Yes, I will see you there."

Valentino is outside the restaurant when I arrive and this time, half his long hair is pulled back and up into a ponytail, the rest hanging straight. He looks like a true *artista*.

"Ah, *bella donna,* you are a Roman goddess." He kisses both my cheeks and then my hands.

"*Grazie*, Valentino." The owner, a friend of his, ushers us to the best table in the house. Valentino asks for a bottle of Chianti Classico 2000 which is smooth, bold and full-bodied. "This is excellent, Valentino. Is it from Tuscany?"

"*Si,* it is from the *Castello di Lorenzo* in the Chianti region, not too far from here. It is 95% Sangiovese grape and 5% of another grape that is grown in this region called Canaiolo. Then, it must sit in the barrel for three years before it can be poured. This is the reason it is so good." He takes another sip and continues. "No one can label their wine as Chianti Classico unless the grapes are grown in this region. It is a law of the winemakers and it is a well-respected one."

"How do you know so much about wine?" He hesitates for a moment but confesses.

"Actually, the winery belongs to my family. I grew up working the vineyards and in the tasting room. I love this place. It used to be the summer house of the Pitti family in Florence. Luca Pitti was a knight and a banker who worked for Cosimo de' Medici. Have you heard of him?"

"Yes, I've read a lot about the Medici family."

"It was given to my family in the last century. It's not far from here. I will take you tomorrow and you may taste other wines if you like."

"I'd like that." I wanted to tour a vineyard in Florence; it will be nice to have my own private tour guide.

We dine on special foods chosen by the owner, each one a delicious Tuscan or Florentine dish. The first course or the *primo piatto* is *panzanella,* a cold summer dish made with moistened bread crumbs and onions, tomatoes and basil, and then topped with oil and vinegar. The *secondo piatto* is *ossobuco alla fiorentina,* slices of veal stewed in tomatoes, with garlic, rosemary, sage and lemon. The salad is fresh arugula with gorgonzola cheese, lemon, olive oil and salt. Other dishes are served but I'm lost in conversation and don't remember their names. I do know my palate is enjoying every bite.

For dessert, they bring *panna cotta*, a pudding made of crème, eggs and lemon served with a chocolate sauce, and next, the traditional *tiramisu* which is a truffle with lady fingers dipped in a sweet liquor and dusted with cocoa. Another night of making love with food.

"Valentino, this is one of the best meals I've tasted since I've been here."

"I knew you would love it, Rosanna.

We talk through dinner and get to know each other discussing our lives, my children, his family and the fact that he cannot keep a girlfriend because he hasn't been able to commit to anything other than his art.

We walk back to the hotel arm-in-arm. At the door, he kisses my cheeks.

"I will come by for you on my scooter tomorrow at 13:00. *Arrivederci*, Rosanna."

I open the shutters in my room and gaze out over the Florentine skyline and its rooftops. The city is still alive and once again I hear music somewhere in the distance. What a magical place and a perfect day it has been.

"Ciao, bella." Valentino arrives on time and we travel on his scooter into the Chianti countryside. The scenery is decorated with vineyards and olive groves and the woods are filled with cypress and oak trees. Scattered throughout the land are Romanesque churches, farmhouses, villas and castles. Ancient hamlets, medieval villages and large estates sit atop the hillsides; most are hidden by cypress trees. The landscape rolls out before us like a magical carpet. Once again, I'm on the back of a scooter with my arms wrapped around an Italian.

"Rosanna, do you see all this beauty? I live in *paradiso."*

I enjoy the ride, lost in the ecstasy of the wind upon my face and the sun in my eyes as we maneuver the turns on the winding road. He takes them with ease as if he and the bike are one and he has driven it a thousand times. My body tingles with life, filled up like a glass of champagne, all the bubbles trying to escape.

Valentino has turned onto a long tree-lined driveway which leads to a castle. The entire property, as far as the eye can see is filled with vineyards and olive groves. Gardens and grassy areas surround the building. A lily pond sits in the middle of the yard and two peacocks are roaming about. One has blue and green feathers and the other is an albino. How strange ... peacocks in Italy.

This is a fairy tale.

We dismount and walk through the side door into a large marble foyer with a winding staircase and a drawing room at the far end of the hall. The marble floors are covered with carpets and heavy draperies cover the windows.

"Do you like it? It is *grande,* eh Rosanna?"

An elderly man enters. He's tall and dressed in a linen suit, hand-woven shoes on his feet. His eyes are deep-set, his face aged; Valentino resembles him. He throws his arms around Valentino and proceeds to hug and kiss him.

"*Mio nipote e bello. Si, si.* My beautiful grandson."

He continues to hug him as they both speak their native tongue. Valentino introduces me to his grandfather, Dante Lorenzo.

He says, "*Benvenuta.*" He is happy to see us.

"My grandfather says welcome and that it is good to see you. He says you are very pretty."

"*Grazie.*" I turn to him and smile.

Valentino and Dante exchange a few words and his grandfather leaves us.

"Today, he will leave for Roma, Firenze, Milano and Napoli. The *vino*, you know. But he wants us to stay and enjoy the house."

Valentino leads me from one room to another while he tells me stories of his childhood. He shows me the room he sleeps in and an enormous music room, a grand piano sitting in the center. He sits to play an Italian tune for me and sings. Not only can he sculpt but he's also a musician.

We walk out to the garden and I follow him to the olive groves.

"We make our own olive oil here. One tree gives us one liter of *olio d'oliva*. We must hand-pick the olives when they are young, not at the end of the season because they will not be as fresh and not have as much oil. Then, we process them within twenty-four hours so we can certify it as 'extra virgin.' The olives have a very different and spicy taste in this region, you know. I will show you when I make food for you later; then you will taste the difference."

I am one luck girl, on a private tour of a vineyard in the Chianti countryside. Did I just fall from the sky into an Italian dream? How could it possible get any better than this?

We have entered the vineyards and Valentino checks the grapes. He says he's making sure none are diseased and that they are growing perfectly.

"Rosanna, do you see how perfect and how firm they are even

though they are still young? You see, the picking season is not until late September or early October. My grandfather taught me how to make perfect *vino* at a very young age. He said 'Lorenzo, you treat them as if they are your children. You come and talk sweetly to them every day. You touch them, caress them and love them. You sit and tell them stories before they go to sleep at night, stories about the *vino* they will make someday. You make sure they are not thirsty and that they have the love of the sun on their skin as they grow because they are like babies. Then, when it is time, they will give you all the love back that you have given to them. That is what makes *il migliore*, the best Chianti Classico. This is all you need to know, *mio nipote*.' My grandfather is the best winemaker in the region."

"Valentino, have you ever thought of going into your family business? You have so much knowledge."

"And give up my art? Never. I have no time to give! *Morto!*" His eyes darken. Obviously, I have hit a nerve that has been poked at by his family.

After a few moments of silence, the darkness is gone and we walk through the rows of vines. He talks to the leaves and the babies that bask in the sunlight. He grabs my hand and pulls me back toward the castle.

"Come."

We move into the coolness of the wine cellar, a reprieve from the blistering Tuscan sun.

"Here, we have only the best barrels in the world which we buy from France and America. You see?" He points out insignia carvings on the barrels and shows me the *bianchi,* the white wines, and the *rosso bianchi* which are a mixture of the Sangiovese grape and the Trebbiano white grape from the region. Next, he takes me through the Chianti rooms where hundreds of bottles of red table wines—Chianti and the Chianti Classico are stored. He uncorks a dusty bottle of Chianti Classico and pours a glass for each of us. After swirling it, sniffing it and then sipping it slowly, he closes his eyes.

"Ah, *la dolce vita, la dolce vino*."

"This is heavenly, Valentino." I take another sip and breathe it in deeply as it dusts my palate.

"*Mio famiglia.* They are the best winemakers," he says proudly slapping his chest. "My grandfather, my father and my brothers love the grapes like I do. Come. We take this *vino* to the kitchen and make something to eat and enjoy it together. This way."

CHAPTER 26

I am intoxicated from the wine or maybe it's my imagination since I have only tasted a half glass. Maybe it's because I'm in Italy ... in a castle ... I feel as if I'm with Valentino's ancestors, as if we are somewhere else in time, and the year is not 2006 but maybe 1406 instead.

He leads me out of the wine cellar and up to the next level of the castle where we walk through two halls and two rooms before we reach the kitchen. The stove is *molto vecchio*, very old. A large wooden table sits off to one side where I imagine the servants used to eat.

"*Aspetta,* I go to the garden for *verdure*, vegetables. Would you like *insalata*, bread and cheese?"

"That sounds good. Can I help?"

"No, no. Sit. Rest. Enjoy the Chianti. I be right back."

I notice the stone flooring beneath our feet and the leaded windows that run from ceiling to floor. Pots and pans hang from hooks above the stove, and ceramic tiles of painted scenes of the four seasons—*Inverno, Primavera, Estate* and *Autunno,* hang on the stone wall. To live in a grand castle such as this ...

We dine on the terrace on fresh greens from the garden, fresh cheeses, olives and homemade bread topped off with the olive oil and a bottle of Chianti Classico. A delicious meal.

"Now, can you smell the *olio* d'*oliva*? Does it not smell like fresh olives, *si*?"

The scent ... perfume. I close my eyes and breathe it in. He drizzles oil on a plate and breaks off a piece of bread for me.

"*Adesso prova questo,* now taste this."

As I bite into it, the oil drips down my chin.

"Mmmm ... this is wonderful."

Valentino takes his finger and wipes it from my lower lip and chin. I blush.

"You know, Rosanna, you have a unique look. Your eyes are different from anyone else's in Firenze and your skin, *porcellana.*" I turn away from him, embarrassed.

"No, look at me!" Valentino says with intensity, startling me. He reaches for my chin and pulls me toward him as he studies me again.

"Look, your cheekbones ..." He runs his fingers along my face. "Your nose, it is strong ... and here," he touches that place above my lips, "well defined ... *belissime labbra,* beautiful lips. These are the places I love most to create."

I sit patiently, but am uncomfortable with this intimacy. His fingers move down my throat to my collar bone. He takes my hand in his and studies it, then traces the outline from my fingers all the way up to my wrist. "So delicate, *perfetto.* Give me your foot."

"Valentino."

"Please, I have to see it." He kneels on the floor in front of me and before I can protest, he removes my sandal. His face is so close that I think he will kiss it; but instead, he outlines every inch of it—the top, the bottom, my arch, each toe and my ankle. He pulls my leg out in front of him so it is inches away from his face. He extends it to the side to get a better view. I am speechless. I feel as if all of me is naked and under a looking glass.

"Ah, *bellissima.* Your legs ..."

He moves his hands along my leg until he reaches my skirt and then inches his way up my thigh. I am unsettled. I know he is starting to become aroused.

"Stop." I grab his hands and push him away. "Please."

"But Rosanna, you are a work of art. I want to feel you, touch you, make love to you."

I walk quickly to the end of the terrace.

"I'm not interested in making love to you! Take me back to the hotel now!"

"Please forgive me. I only want to sculpt you. May I, please?" He walks toward me and I back away.

"Valentino, I have someone who is very special to me and I don't want to be with anyone else."

"Oh, *bella*. I am sorry. *Capisco.*" He comes to me and gently embraces me. "Sometimes I cannot think of anything else except the art." He embraces me.

"Thank you, Valentino, for respecting my wishes." He kisses my forehead.

"Rosanna, please may I sculpt you.?"

"What does that mean? Do I have to pose naked?" I ask nervously.

"*Si*. That would be good."

"I can't do that, Valentino."

"Rosanna, the naked body of a woman is a beautiful thing."

"No. I cannot and will not pose for you naked so I guess you'll have to find someone else to sculpt."

"But there is no one like you." After a few moments of pacing, he relents. "Okay; you may wear your clothes. I will do your face, your arms, your wrists, your legs and feet. I will find someone else for your torso but it won't truly be you, Rosanna."

I chatter nervously. It's probably the wine and the fact that I'm negotiating for my clothes. At this, his intensity shifts and he starts laughing too. And I know that the sweet and trusting Valentino is back; the air around us has softened.

"Please, consider it."

We sit at the table and talk easily as we finish the wine and our meal.

"Tell me about him, Rosanna." He fingers the rim of his glass like he does with everything, giving away the fact that he is a sculptor.

"I met Natale in Rome. I left him to travel but I will visit him again ... soon." I do not want to reveal too much, so I move my eyes to the hills and the olive groves as I remember Natale's touch.

"Ah, you are in love. I know that look. Unfortunately, I cannot hold onto a woman. They are all jealous of my work, because I never give them enough time. They always want more of me. When I go into my studio and do not come out to call them or be with them, they become angry. You know, Italian women are very jealous. Do you want to know a secret? I sleep with my marble." He is embarrassed by his confession. "I love its coolness on my skin."

He laughs at himself.

"Come, I will show you where I create." He takes my hand.

We walk down the stone stairway and through the gardens to the back of the property. Once inside his studio, I realize the room is as big as my small villa on Capri. The ceiling is two stories high and golden light enters from a windowed wall. Blocks of marble lie everywhere, many, captives half-finished. Sketches have been tossed about as if he were a madman trying to perfect a vision. A long bench holds a half-built armature and a few clay models of male figures. Marble dust covers the floor.

"My room ..." His eyes glaze over. "This is the place I love most in this world." His eyes light up and I sense the presence of Ghiberti who has sculpted here before him.

"Let me show you how it feels to have marble touch you." He leads me to the large stone table holding a four-foot block of the stone. "Here." He places a chisel in one hand and a heavy mallet in the other. Then he stands behind me, his hands over mine.

"Hold it like this." He guides me as we hammer at the marble and slowly, we start to whittle away at its hard surface. I sense his passion as it takes hold of him. He breathes hard and presses into me, not because of me but because he is merging with the piece. Much time passes before he stops. I step back and admire the arm we are working on as it begins to take shape. I think of young Michelangelo carving his sculptures and the passion he must have felt. I turn to Valentino and realize he seems possessed.

"It is a sacred thing to be able to cut something so incredibly hard and create form." He speaks more forcefully and with a deeper voice.

He quickly moves me to the chaise at the far end of the room and sets me down. He finds his sketch paper and pencil, and turns his eyes toward me. Every few minutes he rearranges my position so he can observe me from a new angle. He scrutinizes my nose and my lips, and then touches them as if he were a blind man. He has an insatiable desire to touch these parts of me, to draw them. I sit for an hour before I can take it no longer.

"Valentino, I have to use the bathroom and I'm stiff from sitting here." The glaze is gone from his eyes and I have his attention.

"I will show you." I follow him to the back of the house where I use the bathroom and stretch my back; when I'm finished, his mood seems lighter.

"It's 19:00; should we head back to Florence?" I ask. I know if he could work through the night.

"Rosanna, I will take you to your hotel if you will promise to accompany me to the *museo* tomorrow and then I want to continue sketching you. Please? I would be honored."

"Yes. I'll go to the museum with you. And yes, you may sketch me."

"I will show you the sketches when they are finished, *si*?" He says excitedly.

When I finally bathe, and climb into bed, I realize how weary from the day I am and fall asleep instantly. The spirit comes to me in my dreams this night, and instead of walking with me along the cliffs of Capri, we are in the Boboli Gardens at the *Palazzo Pitti*.

"Are you enjoying yourself, Roxanna?" I nod yes and he laughs. "Good! This is the reason you are here. This Valentino has the blood of Ghiberti inside him. They are one and the same, you know. He is not of this world, but a gift from the gods for a very short time here. You would honor him by allowing him to sculpt you, all of you. And you will truly honor yourself. You were a great lover of Ghiberti's when he was alive. Human flesh is nothing but an overcoat for the soul where the real beauty lies. He is feeling your soul, not your flesh."

My mind races back over our time together.

"The body is only a covering that protects us from the winds of time. It is only flesh, bone and blood, Roxanna. Be naked and be free and drop the puritan attitude that you have carried with you from your homeland. You are in Italy now and everyone wants to paint and sculpt. Live life. Love. Let your form be created to last through eternity. Go down in history with him this time when he passes from this earth."

In the blink of an eye, he's gone and I'm left alone in my bed at 4:00 a.m. wide awake, worrying about my naked body. Being naked with a man other than someone you are about to make love to is something I've never thought about doing. It just doesn't seem right.

My head swims trying to figure it all out until I drift off to sleep hearing his words, *"Human flesh is nothing but an overcoat for the soul where the real beauty lies. He is feeling your soul, not your flesh. The body is only a covering that protects us from the winds of time ... It is only flesh and blood, Roxanna ..."*

It's another hot, steamy day in Florence, the weather relentless and everyone everywhere is shouting, *"molto caldo,"* too hot! Valentino is waiting for me at the *Museo Nazionale del Bargello,* his special place where he comes to study and think. On the ground floor, we visit the Room of Michelangelo and his 16th century sculptures. Valentino's favorite and the first one we study is *Brutus* and *Apollo,* one of his biggest achievements, a work that was commissioned by Cosimo de' Medici. Next is *Bacchus,* his first large scale free-standing sculpture.

We move to another room where we find the works of Sansovino, the *Bacchus;* Bandinelli's *Bust of Cosimo I*; numerous pieces by Cellini including his famous *Bust of Cosimo I;* and *Hermes* by Giambologna. Valentino walks through each room as if he is seeing them for the first time but I know he has been here a thousand times before because he told me so.

We move through the Room of Medieval Sculptures and next, into the Room of Donatello where we find Luca della Robbia's *Madonna and Child with Two Angels* and *Madonna of the Rose-Garden.* At last, we arrive at the great panels. Valentino stops before them—one by Brunelleschi and the other by Ghiberti.

With great reverence, he whispers, "This, he created for the Baptistry competition in 1401. It's called the *Sacrifice of Isaac.* Look at the detail." He smiles with eyes closed and outlines the relief in the air since he cannot touch it. Maybe the spirit was correct when he said Valentino was the reincarnation of Ghiberti.

"From this, he was awarded the panel work on the Baptistery, the *Gate of Paradise.*" He blesses himself with the sign of the cross and we linger until he is finished paying homage.

We talk about all we've studied as we walk the *Piazza Santa Croce*. Valentino tells me about each sculptor's style and how he believes Michelangelo was the best because his works were anatomically perfect. He speaks about Sansovino's *Bacchus* and how it stands up to the works of Michelangelo because it, too is near perfect.

We turn the corner and step into the *Piazza Signoria* where we stop to admire the Fountain of Neptune.

"I have decided that I will pose nude for you." There, I have gotten the words out. Valentino stops.

"Oh, Rosanna, thank you, thank you. *Grazie.*" He kisses my hands and bows down before me. "You will be pleased." He dances around the fountain singing loudly while the tourists stop to look.

I shyly say, "Well, I'm still a little nervous about taking my clothes off in front of you ... you must know it's not natural for me ... I'm an American after all."

"Rosanna, you are a sacred thing; I will honor you and respect you. I promise you." He collects himself, steps away from the fountain and takes my arm.

"But why me, Valentino? I have seen the women in Florence. They are all so beautiful, far more beautiful and younger than me."

Valentino is deep in thought as if he is deciding what words to choose.

"I want to touch your soul and place you in marble through eternity. In my eyes, you are more beautiful than the rest."

We walk on, quiet with each other.

CHAPTER 27

Again, I travel to *Castello di Lorenzo*. I'm sweating bullets ... not because of the Italian summer heat and humidity ... but because eventually, I will have to face my own unveiling.

"Tonight, I will start with your face but I need you to remove your clothing and lie on the chaise in the same pose I will carve you in. For now, I will give you a robe to drape over yourself until you are more comfortable."

He hands me a crimson robe which smells of him. He piles my hair high upon my head and fastens it with a barrette letting a few curls fall loosely.

He has done this before.

He moves me about until I'm in the correct position with one hand draped lazily over my hip, the other resting on a pillow on top of the chaise, my head resting upon my arm.

"I feel like Canova's *Paolina Borghese.*"

"Yes, this is my intention but you will not cover those beautiful legs with that fabric. Now, look down at your feet. Tilt your head upward. I want to see the curve of your neck. That's right. *Si, si.*" He is the intense sculptor, once again.

"Think of something beautiful, Rosanna ... the sea ... the mountains. Think of the vineyards and how they smell at night ... or a bouquet of beautiful flowers ... or your Natale."

This does it for me. I'm now far away from here, lost in thoughts and feelings that have been evoked just by hearing his name.

"Yes, that's it. You have captured it. Do not move. Hold it ... Ah!"

He's like a madman, obsessed. Every few moments, he completes a drawing and starts another, tossing the finished sheet over his head into a pile on the floor behind him. He comes over to me in between each one to touch my nose, my lips, the curve of my face. After a few hours, he has finished my head, my face, and all the features upon it. Next, he starts working on an outline of my body. He watches me fidget, nervous that I might have to remove the robe. He suddenly becomes impatient.

"Ah, no good! You keep moving. We finish tonight. Tomorrow, we will capture the outline of your form. *Capisci?*" His voice is loud and firm and he coldly turns away from me.

"*Capisco*. I will be ready tomorrow." Two minutes have passed and he places his notepad on the table, then comes to me, now softened.

"Rosanna, will you stay tonight? I will begin in the morning when the light is best. I have a private room for you here. Please?"

I have no toothbrush. Will I be safe here? I must get back to Capri. Random thoughts cross my mind. He notes my hesitation.

"There is a lock on the bedroom door."

"Yes, I'll stay. But I don't have a toothbrush."

"Is okay. I have extra." He smiles tiredly. "Come. I will show you where you will sleep."

We move to the second floor. He opens the door to a large bedroom with high ceilings. It's fully decorated with lace curtains and a canopy bed, obviously, a woman's room.

"Whose room is this?"

"It is my sister's when she is here. You will be very comfortable. Do you need anything before you sleep? Food?"

"No, thanks. Night, Valentino." He pulls me to him and holds me tightly. Then he kisses my cheeks and my hands ... always my hands.

"Rosanna, I don't know what it is about you that I must have ... this sculpture ... this ... I don't know. Please forgive me." He's confused. "Thank you for the wonderful gift you are giving me, Rosanna. I will never forget this and you will be pleased. *Buona notte e sogni d'oro,* good night and sweet dreams."

"You, too. Good night." I move to the bathroom and fill the tub. As I step into it, there is a knock on the door.

"Rosanna, your toothbrush." He opens the door.

I forgot to lock it ...

"I will leave it on the table near the door. If you need anything, I will be in my studio."

By the time I finish the thought, he has politely opened the door and stepped inside without looking toward the bathroom.

He leaves quickly and I sink into the tub, all thoughts dissipating in my tired mind. I think of Valentino and how his mood changes when he is drawing or thinking about sculpting. He is clearly not himself. It's as if someone has taken him over.

This night, I dream I'm lying on the chaise while Valentino sketches me. He comes close and tells me he loves me. Then, he bends down and kisses me. I do not protest. In this dream, I am in love with him.

"My beloved, I will finish it this time. I promise you."

Valentino's knock on my door awakens me.

"Rosanna, it is early I know, but the light! The light! *It is perfetto!* Can you come please?"

"Valentino, give me a few minutes. Do you have *espresso*?" I didn't realize how demanding this would be.

"*Si.* Come." I quickly dress and go to his studio where he's already deep in thought, head hung over his sketchpad.

"There." He points to the stone table without looking up.

I move toward the cup of *espresso* and a *cornetto*. I need to eat something; it will be hours before we stop. I sip my *espresso* and examine his work.

"You have captured me for sure. My nose ... I never realized it was that big before and I've never seen it quite from that angle."

"We never really see ourselves, Rosanna. I still need to make a few changes, but we have accomplished much. Sit."

He's already in the unwavering sculptor persona so I try to pose as I did yesterday. He adjusts me a bit and fixes my hair.

"I like you this way. No make-up." I feel invisible without the aid of powder or lipstick.

I'm bare beneath my robe, its fabric brushing against my skin. I wonder how he sees me. How do I appear, through his eyes, at fifty? I've never really looked at myself that closely in a mirror.

"Be still," he commands. He moves toward me and removes the robe roughly without warning. I'm horrified. I hold my breath and shiver. He doesn't look at me but instead turns back and walks to his chair and sketch pad.

"Valentino, do you have any limoncello?"

He comes back to himself and looks puzzled, probably because it's such a strange request this early in the day. He quickly realizes my nervousness.

"*Si*, I understand." He leaves and returns with two small glasses and an iced bottle. He fills them and hands me one. My hand shakes as I take it. I drink it quickly.

"More, please." I smile at him.

In a matter of minutes, I find myself more relaxed and wonder what all the fuss was ... I feel beautiful. I remove my robe and throw it across the room.

I am Venus.

With eyes closed, I imagine the sensations I felt sunbathing topless at the fort. The wind caresses my nipples as if I've been transported there and I taste freedom once again. For two hours, I stay in this pose, thoughts of the wind and the sea washing over me. I'm in a meditative state, flowing with each of Valentino's graphite lines. I can almost feel the touch of his pencil upon my body, every stroke, as if they were his fingertips.

He comes to me and draws upon my skin—from my neck downward, over the curve of my shoulder, down the length of my arm to the curvature of my wrist. He then moves to the space between my underarm and downward to that area where my torso and hip are connected. I shiver, not knowing what to expect next. As I hold my breath, he runs his fingertips ever so lightly around the underside of my left breast and then up to its nipple.

"*Belissimo* ... You will go down in history with me." I hold my breath and he places his lips gently upon mine. He gathers me up in his arms and holds me tightly to his chest. He buries his face in my neck and weeps. Is this Valentino or the sculptor Ghiberti? We stay this way for quite some time and I'm not afraid. But then, he pulls away from me and I pick up the robe and cover myself.

He collects himself.

"I am sorry, Rosanna. I don't know what happened to me. Please forgive me." He moves away, retreating to his sketchpad.

"Valentino, I need to stretch and take a break, please?"

"*Si, si* ... how thoughtless of me. Go. I am sorry for kissing you, Rosanna. I promised you I would respect you and I have ... I mean I do. I don't know what came over me."

"I understand. You lose yourself in your work and sometimes don't know who you are."

"Thank you. Would you like something to eat?" I nod yes. "Then come."

We move to the kitchen where he makes eggs, juice, and fried bread with jam.

"You're good in the kitchen. Have you always cooked?"

He laughs. "Out of necessity. I have learned to take care of myself."

We eat and return to the studio where we stay until late afternoon. Then we both agree that I should check out of the hotel and move my things here so he can complete his work more quickly. Soon, we drive to Florence, pick up my bags and return to the restaurant we ate at that first night we met. After dinner, we make the journey to *Castello di Lorenzo*.

For the next few days, we work long hours in the studio but we also take long breaks so Valentino can prepare delicious meals for us which we pair with the best Chianti from the wine cellar. We take long, leisurely walks through the vineyards and watch the sun set over the hills in the distance.

I share my heartaches with him and he tells me much about himself, revealing his unease with the changes that overtake him when he sculpts. He admits that it's as if Ghiberti is inside him, guiding him to sculpt which causes him much rumination. He tells me his deepest darkest secret ... that it's not he who has the talent but Ghiberti. He struggles with forgiving himself for keeping this secret from everyone, including his family. He weeps and I console him. I weep for Natale and he consoles me. We have become close.

Valentino has chosen a beautiful white marble which was delivered today. He carefully removes its protective covering and gasps.

"Ah, *incredibile*. I chose this marble because it appears translucent, like human skin. It will give the sculpture visual depth beyond its surface and evoke a certain level of realism. See, Rosanna?"

"*Si*, it's beautiful." I love its translucency and the feel of it.

He takes his tools and starts to chip away.

"It is soft and easy to work with," he says.

He continues to chisel. I turn and gather up the drawings that are strewn across the floor.

"These sketches are good, Valentino." I hardly recognize myself. My body … I have aged but I appear beautiful. How odd, I never thought I was. What a great gift Valentino has given me.

My thoughts are interrupted by a familiar voice only I can hear.

"*Brava*, Roxanna. Welcome to who you are," says the spirit.

"So, this is Roxanna …" I say it out loud and smile.

"*Bellissima*, Rosanna; you are far more beautiful than Paolina. You will see when I finish," says Valentino.

"Thank you." I reach up and kiss his cheek and he embraces me.

"Please allow me to take you to dinner tonight before you leave. I have been so busy with my work that I have not treated you well. I want to make it up to you."

"That would be nice." I yawn, a little tired from the day.

"Please, I will stay and work. You go rest. I will come for you later."

As soon as my head touches the pillow, I fall into a deep sleep. Ghiberti is before me, bent over a large bas-relief in the studio at *Castello di Lorenzo.* He's so focused that he doesn't notice I'm in the room even though I have called out to him. He has the same intensity and focus that Valentino has when he's working. I feel his immense love for me even though he has not acknowledged me. My heart swells with love for him, but it is soon replaced with loneliness and longing.

When I awaken, I lie in bed and contemplate what I have just dreamt and felt when the spirit speaks to me.

"Now you know, Roxanna. He never completed the sculpture of you he had promised you. You were the only woman he loved in that lifetime but his passion for his work took him over. Once the *Porta del Paradiso* came along, it took him thirty long years to complete. You died at sixty-seven, ten years before he passed and he was tormented for the rest of his life. He never forgave himself for his broken promise. Now, he has come through Valentino to finish his gift to you. Don't think too much about it. Just breathe. It is done."

I try and digest all I have learned. I'm sure Valentino has no idea the part he has played in all this. Or does he? Nothing is as it seems. I'm happy to have posed for him and in doing so, given my heart and myself back to Ghiberti.

Over dinner, Valentino and I discuss his uncle.

"Valentino, do you know anything about his life? Was he ever married?"

"No, he is like me. He was married to his work. He could not keep a woman. They say he was in love once and she was the only one who had his heart. I understand she died before him and he mourned her death for the rest of his days. He never recovered from his guilt." His eyes grow dark as if he himself feels the pain of it.

I change the subject.

"Valentino, you are very talented."

"Thank you, Rosanna." His eyes brighten. "I am pleased with how far we have come. I wish you could stay longer."

"I would love to but I also have work to do. I haven't done anything since I arrived. I'm happy we have met and had the chance to spend time together. You are truly a gentleman and I will never forget you."

Lost in gratitude, he reaches for my hand. He runs his fingers along the top of it and traces the veins and the tiny scar on my wrist. He turns both over and touches each line.

"These are hands of beauty, *bella*. These are hands filled with

182

life lived and with much love." He reaches for my face and rubs it with the palm of his hand.

"You have the eyes of the sea, the *Mediterraneo*. It's as if you belong to it." He sweetly kisses my hands then moves them to his cheek.

After we finisher our dinner and the wine, he makes *espresso* and lays sweet desserts on the table. The night is memorable.

He walks me to my bedroom door and pulls me close kissing me hard on the lips. His hands are everywhere rubbing my hair, my face and my back all the while breathing me in. He intertwines his fingers with mine and pulls me closer. I can feel all of him but mostly, I feel his soul reaching out to mine.

I relent for only a moment for it seems the right thing to do. I allow him to move into me, not physically but as if skin and bone does not separate us. We become one in this moment.

"*Mio bella* Rosanna, I want to make love to you; I love you, *amore mio*." I hold him as tightly as he holds me.

"I'm sorry. I'm in love with ..."

"Yes, Natale ..." He releases me. "I understand your heart when it speaks. I will never forget you, Rosanna. I will write to let you know when I'm finished. Maybe you will come to see it. *Ti amo. Sogno d'oro,* sweet dreams."

The next day as we ride to the train station, I hold on to him tightly ... not because I'm afraid of the turns in the road but because I have a love for him and know it might be the last time I ever see him again.

After we say goodbye and he departs, I wonder if all this really happened or if he was just a ghost.

"Thank you, Florence. And thank you, Valentino ... for showing me myself. I now accept who I am. I have truly been birthed in *Italia*!

CHAPTER 28
BASILICATA & CAMPANIA REGIONS, ITALY

I'm elated to be back at *Mio Paradiso*. God, I've missed it.

"Roxanna, *journo*."

"*Journo*, Mario." He has stopped by to ask me something. Since he's speaking in Italian, he talks slowly, hoping I will understand him better. After all my travels, I feel more confident with the language. I understand *domani ... basilica .... Sorrento ... amico*, Giuseppe ... and he points to himself. He's asking me to accompany him and his friend Giuseppe to a *basilica* in the south of Sorrento tomorrow. See? I'm good. I even understand the time he will pick me up—*alle sei di mattina*, 6:00 a.m. to go to the port.

"*Grazie*, Mario, *ciao, ciao, a domani.*"

The next morning, we walk the mile to the outskirts of town where we meet Giuseppe who is waiting for us in his automobile. He's a very tall man with thick curly hair and sparkling eyes and he looks as though he knows a secret but can't tell, even though he wants to. He talks like Vito Corleone in *The Godfather* so I imagine he's Sicilian, although he tells me he is *Napoletano*.

We stop in the town of Capri for a quick shot of *espresso* and I belly up to the bar with them and drink like a local. Back in the little car, we drive to the port, Marina Grande, to catch the hydrofoil which will take us and the car to Sorrento.

Once on the mainland, we drive for hours. I sit back and listen to them talk to each other like two high school boys. Even though they are both speaking Italian, I hear lots of *"capisci" and "no, no capisco"* which means they don't understand each other. This language is such a strange one. From one region to the next, the dialects are different, the pronunciations are different, and sometimes even they don't understand each other, although they're all Italian. With their thick accents, their passion and the way they talk with their hands, I can't help but laugh and get caught up in this scene taking place in the front seat.

It's about 105° in the south of Italy and everyone is sweating profusely. Mario turns around every fifteen minutes and says, "Roxanna ... *molto caldo,"* as he smiles and wipes the beads of sweat from his brow with a damp, white handkerchief. The traffic is heavy and it seems to be taking forever but I enjoy watching families and couples in the other cars as they, too are driving with their windows open. No one seems to have air conditioning here.

The countryside is filled with flowered fields and rolling hills. Every now and then I see a hamlet, a castle ruin or lush vineyards. Mario says they make *bene vino bianco*, good white wines in the Campania region. This region is so beautiful and so close to the sea which is why I love it so much.

After four hours, we arrive in Padula and drive to the *Certosa* di *Padula,* the Monastery of San Lorenzo which stands beneath the Apennine Mountains and the little city of Montesano. After visiting Florence, Pisa, Rome and Venice, I'm not sure any church or monastery in the south will be as grand as those I've seen thus far.

Have you ever been a lover of books, walked into a bookstore, and had so many to choose from that you were dumbfounded, not knowing which one to choose because you loved them all? Then, one falls off the shelf and hits you. You pick it up and try to read it but never really see the words that are written there. It's all a blur—except for the fact that you need this book ... must have it. You can't release it back to where it came from; you must own it, take it home and sleep with it.

Not until you get it home do you realize that you have a secret gift that was only meant for you. It isn't so much the book itself, but it's the way it makes you feel when you hold it in your hands. Your eyes are glazed over and you cannot seem to comprehend what you are looking at. But you receive the message as the fingers of your heart move across the pages as if it were Braille. Each word is a chord that makes your heart sing.

This is how I feel as I enter the monastery.

Everything is in Italian so I have no idea where I am or what I'm looking at except that it's a very old monastery. I don't even know the name of it at first. I only know its effect on me since I have walked through the gates. I wander through the outer courtyard, into the church, from one room to another, through the great cloister, through the park and into the cemetery.

I feel San Michele walking beside me with each step. I want to stay here for the night ... ask for a room ... I want to sit and meditate ... to pray to all those who have been here before me and who are still here. But I know I cannot. I know I must go back with Mario and Giuseppe. Instead, I hide my face and my tears of deep love and gratitude and trail quietly behind them.

It's only later when I am settled that I learn the history of the place. The monastery was founded in 1306 by Tommaso Sandeverino, Count of Marsico, and eventually given to the Carthusian monks. The church of San Lorenzo would soon follow. Another gift. Then, the inner cloister was rebuilt and enlarged and was called the *Great Cloister*.

The *Divino Michelangelo,* as they call him in this part of Italy (this is the reason why I love the Italians so much) created the *Fountain of the Dolphins* before me, the precious ivory crucifix and the *Great Cloister*—although it has never been proven except for the sketches of these things that were amongst his possessions when he died.

It is said that of all the monasteries of the Carthusian order, this is the most beautiful one and I believe it to be so. The outer courtyard is filled with magnificent Italian stonework. I'm enraptured by its beauty and try to snap as many photos as I possibly can before Mario drags me away.

We visit the Prior's Apartment and all its rooms. Next, I come upon the Chapel of Archangel Michael, the patron saint of Padula.

He is everywhere for I feel him. How can he be in so many places at once?

I'm quiet as a monk for a long time, but soon it's time to leave and Mario and Giuseppe must tear me away. We drive half way up the mountain to Montesano and visit yet another splendid cathedral, the Cathedral of Saint Anne. It's not a large church but it has spires that climb upward toward the sky. It's Byzantine in structure with three great arches on the front façade and sculpted walls. I apologize to every Italian from the south of Italy for assuming the churches and cathedrals in the north were far more elegant and majestic. I was wrong.

I am experiencing a first communion of sorts, a ceremony ... a rite of passage. I've been guided on this sacred pilgrimage by San Michele, and Mario and Giuseppe are his angels holding my hands, leading me each step of the way. What a great gift that they have brought me here—one my private driver and the other my tour guide—to show me southern Italy, the "Seat of the Sacred." This is my new name for this area.

We stop at an *albergo*, a hotel. Mario knows the owner who is an old friend he hasn't seen in many years. After hugs and Italian kisses, he asks to "see a room." Giuseppe waits in the car as we talk with the owner. I'm confused and cannot comprehend why we need a hotel room. What's he thinking and what does he have in store for me? Aren't we going back to Capri now? My female antennae shoot straight up out of my head as I remember that I'm in romantic *Italia* where the men love all women.

The owner doesn't speak a word of English, nor does Mario, so no one can explain to me why we are looking for hotel rooms in the middle of the afternoon. With my dictionary, I try to communicate with them but Mario speaks rapidly and I can't understand a word. He speaks more slowly when I ask questions, but my mind has blocked out all language and reasoning. I realize I am a woman alone in a foreign country with two Italian men I really don't know well at all ... why didn't I think of this before? Alarms go off in my head, stopping all neurons from sending messages to my brain for understanding or translation.

As I would do in America, I say to the manager, "*No grazie*." I ask for a business card, shake his hand and quickly walk to the car. Mario trails behind me trying to keep up, all the while mumbling to himself, "*Mamma mia!*" as he slaps his forehead.

There's nothing to do at this point but go to lunch. So, Giuseppe drives on. We stop at *Agriturismo Macchiapiede di Vespoli Michele,* a bed and breakfast on an organic farm with a small restaurant attached. Here, they grow their own organic produce and serve healthy meals. They also have a vineyard and make their own wine.

Mario proudly orders for us. Meanwhile, I have my dictionary out and am writing down sentences so I can ask him why we need a hotel room. We try to communicate for thirty minutes without much headway. Meanwhile, the wine has come, the bread has come and then the food. I nervously sip in between my sentences, trying to figure out how to get out of this predicament.

Mario and Giuseppe are in a spirited discussion as they try to find the words I might understand. No one here speaks English so no one can help me. The whole time, Mario slaps his forehead and says, "*Mamma mia,*" and "*capisci*" a thousand times, as if this will help.

Then suddenly, I start to understand. The traffic getting here has taken twice as long. It will be a three-to-four-hour drive back to the port in Sorrento to catch the boat to Capri and the last one leaves at 5:30 p.m. We cannot possibly make it, so we will have to stay the night. Did we know this when we started out so I could have been more prepared? Now I start to say "*Mamma mia,*" and slap my head!

After I resign myself to the fact that I have only the dress I'm wearing, which I have been sweating in all day, and no toothbrush, we all start to relax and enjoy the food. Before I know it, I understand every word they are saying to me.

Giuseppe tells me he is my age, fifty, and Mario says he is almost fifty, although they both appear to be much older. I'm slightly bleary-eyed so I'm not sure if they are telling me the truth. We talk about where we will go after we eat and then discuss the plan for the next day. Maybe when you purchase an Italian-English dictionary, a bottle of *vino* should accompany it? I think I'm having a wonderful time.

After lunch, our next stop is the *Grotta di Pertosa,* an underground grotto with natural caverns that were discovered five hundred years ago by a monk from Bologna. The monks lived everywhere in Italy; I wonder where they all are now.

Inside the caves, we see stalactites and stalagmites, beautiful waterways and rock formations. An altar sits in one of the caverns but I don't know why until Mario explains to Gino our guide that I speak only English. He asks him if he can give me the English version and I am quickly moved to the front of the line. Each time we move from one area to another, Gino speaks to me in English then turns to the others and speaks in Italian. I feel like someone special, sent to the head of the line to walk beside this young, handsome docent.

He explains that from the archeological findings in the cave, and from the sizes of the stalactites and stalagmites, they are estimated to be 35 million years old. He also mentions that the water is sacred. He tells me he has been a tour guide at the grotto for the last ten years and that this place pulls at him so much, he can't seem to leave it. I tell him I feel the pull as well. There is such a sense of peace and sacredness here. I'm not a fan of dark caves and never thought I'd like to live in one, but here I do. He tells me the monks used to live here and built little altars for themselves. We pass by two and he points them out to me.

Half way through the tour I ask, "Gino, what does the name mean, *Grotta Dell'Angelo*?"

"These are the Caves of the Angels of Archangel Michael. He is everywhere. Excuse me. I have to explain in Italian now."

He moves back toward the crowd and leaves me alone. Suddenly, I am surrounded by the most heavenly music. I look out into the darkness and let the tears of my soul flow like waterfalls, down my cheeks and onto my breast. They don't want to stop and I have no control over them. I feel the electricity of Him beside me, his hand on my shoulder, and I'm suddenly overwhelmed with love as if I've been infused with light. In this moment, I know Saint Michael and the spirit are one and the same as he reveals this to me now. I turn and catch sight of his face, his golden hair and his piercing blue eyes.

"You will never be alone, Roxanna, for I am always with you. Ask for anything you want and you shall have it. And remember, always follow the calling of your soul for this is the road to happiness."

I feel a puff of warm air so I close my eyes. When I open them, he is no longer with me. I collect myself. My tears dry and I realize giddiness and laughter are spilling out of me.

I'm three feet off the ground for the rest of the tour and each time Gino guides me in English, I nod as if I hear and understand him but I do not. My mind is lost in lightness, my heart lost in memories as if I have been kissed and still caught up in the rapture of it.

My life flashes before me and I remember how as a child, I knew the angels were my family. I belonged to them and my relationship with them had no boundaries. I knew their house of prayers intimately. This Cave of the Angels... San Michele ... the entire trip was for me and this moment. He is everywhere and he has nudged me to come and be with him to see his place of respite on Capri and all the other places he loves in Italy. No wonder the Italians have the word *paradiso* in their language to define both heaven and paradise.

I'm quiet for the rest of the tour and in the car as we drive on to the next place.

"Roxanna, *L'acqua di Santo Stefano, acquedotto naturale* ... *bene. Tu vieni?*" Lost in thought, I realize Giuseppe has driven down a long dirt road somewhere near Pertosa. I'm instructed to take my water bottle with me and we move down a trail to a flowing spring.

Giuseppe smiles as we move toward the spring, and when we arrive, he and Mario bless themselves by making the sign of the cross on their bodies. We wash our faces with the cool water as if we are being baptized and then fill our bottles, drinking as much as we can. My head is spinning with all this and I'm not sure what's real and what's not. Are these truly sacred waters? Will they heal anything? I decide I'm officially having a religious experience and I will call this day the *Festiva de San Michele,* my own personal holy day. Walking back to the car, I realize we are all having our own religious experience. We seem to be drunk, intoxicated by the holy water. Is this at all possible?

My senses cannot take anymore and I realize this is probably why Italians drink wine with their meals. All these saints hang out in Italy and if you pay attention, you could run into one at any given moment. This is a staggering event that makes you want to sip limoncello or *vino.* So, what do you do when they leave? You drink something to shake off the ecstatic stupor you are in and come back to earth.

We are all quiet as we head back to town and a *farmacia* in search of toothbrushes. Naturally, no one speaks English, so I use the little words I know like *capella,* hair and *lavare,* to wash, for shampoo. I don't know the word for toothbrush so I make the motion with my hands as if I'm brushing my teeth. They are more than happy to help me and probably happier with themselves that they understand. They smile wide and give me all sorts of toiletries gratis, free—a hairbrush, toothbrush and natural conditioner. I realize I'm surrounded by angels. People in the south of Italy are wonderful, living life with open hearts.

I have twenty minutes before I am to meet Mario and Giuseppe in the lobby for dinner. We are returning to the *Agriturismo* since lunch was so delicious.

When we arrive, they greet us as if we are members of their family who have just returned from a long holiday. Vincenzo, his wife Simona and their new baby take us to our outdoor table and graciously serve us the specialties of the evening.

We dine on homemade pasta followed by grappa and limoncello. All throughout dinner, Mario, Giuseppe and I talk in Italian and I communicate well and understand everything, until the limoncello, when my *cervello* becomes *stanco,* my brain becomes tired. I open my dictionary which is like my bible and tell them why I no longer *capisco*, understand and they laugh saying, "*Si, si.*"

With the heat and humidity of the day, I wash my things in the sink—my bra, panties and my linen dress. How will I iron the wrinkles out? Do they have irons here? Will it dry? How will I dry my hair without a hairdryer and brush? All these civilized American female thoughts race through my mind as I brush my teeth.

Am I in for a surprise, because the windows have thick metal grates over them to keep the cold and heat out and they have little tiny holes in them to let the air in along with those little nasty creatures called "no-see-ums." It's too hot to sleep the entire night and I'm busily swatting tiny invisible things who continually land on my body, relentlessly tormenting me. I constantly move from the bed to the sink and back again, to soak the linen towels with cold water and then drape them across my torso. But the heat in the room is so intense that the towels dry quickly. Undoubtedly, my dress and underthings are dry and wrinkle-free by morning, more so than me.

CHAPTER 29

It's early morning as we leave the hotel in search of *espresso*. I find it amusing that Americans live in such a fast-paced society and yet they linger over their coffee like a morning meditation. Italians enjoy a slower pace of life but drink their *espresso* quickly while standing. Who can figure this out?

After my hurried *espresso* and *cornetto*, we leave in search of the *Monte de San Michele* which is somewhere close to Sala Consilina where our hotel is. Within fifteen minutes, we find it. Six hundred meters above the town is the mount and the church. Mario tells me it's a thousand years old.

I have the same experience walking through this church as I did yesterday. A sacred peace envelops me. I could live in this bliss forever. Eventually, I collect myself and move outside where I take in the view of the valley below—Polla, Pertosa, Padula, Montesano and Buonabitacolo. The peacefulness here reminds me that there is nothing I want or need in this moment.

The next leg of the trip is three hours. We drive in a northeast direction toward Matera which Mario pronounces **Mee**-tra ... although other Italians pronounce it Ma-**ter**-ra. I don't realize until we arrive that this is the town where Mel Gibson filmed the movie, *The Passion of the Christ.* I never tire of the scenery—the lush countryside filled with olive trees and vineyards. We travel through Potenza and further into the Basilicata region where there are forests thick with trees and running rivers. I ask my companions the types of trees that dot the landscape and think they say *pioppi* and *faggio*, poplar and beech trees. Wheat fields lie everywhere, their grains a soft golden color.

Occasionally, villages and hamlets dot the landscape and a castle stands in the distance. Sheep and goats lazily graze as the sun heats up the day. I enjoy the scenery and the sounds of Mario and Giuseppe speaking in their native tongues. Oftentimes, they speed up and start to talk faster. This is when Giuseppe sounds most like "the Godfather," his deep, throaty voice and words rolling into one another like marbles racing across a floor.

As we move closer to Matera, the landscape changes into a more arid and rocky terrain. Cacti fill the dry landscape reminding me of Arizona.

We stop at another monastery, *Santa Maria di Orsoleo in the town of Sant'Arcangelo*. The building is dated 1192 and still standing with its elegant marble work and frescoes. Another sacred site, another religious stupor ... My favorite Rumi poem comes to mind:

> *"If your every single breath became a prayer*
> *You'd see atoms as angels and hear in each wind*
> *The Whirr of Love's wings, and feel in each moment*
> *The Beloved pulling you into His heart."*

This is how I feel with each breath I take in Italy, especially when I am inside the churches and cathedrals.

Back in the car, it's another hour to Matera but I'm enjoying this continuation of my *Festiva de San Michele*. We stop along the roadsides and fill our water bottles with water from old fountains which are scattered throughout the countryside, same as they are throughout Tuscany and Umbria. Mario tells me this is the best water ... *l'acqua piú buona*. He's right, for it's cool and refreshing and tastes like the springs of San Stefano.

Next to the fountain, I notice a crate of nectarines. They don't have a sign on them so I am not sure who they belong to.

"*Perché sono qui? Sono endate a male?*" I ask why these have been left here. Are they bad?

Mario understands and says, "*No, no, bene,*" and hands me three nectarines. As we drive away, I bite into one and it melts in my mouth. My senses are suddenly overtaken by its perfume and for a moment I feel intoxicated ... captivated ... my body flutters. This is the most delicious fruit I have ever tasted and I savor every bite. I wish we had taken the entire crate.

We stop at a place with the word *Panificio* painted on the door. Here, we purchase homemade bread made with grains fresh from the fields—so fresh that I smell the sweetness of the earth in it, if this is possible. It's sweeter than any I have ever tasted ... or am I just intoxicated, a state I have been continually in since landing on Italian soil.

We arrive in Matera, the town of the *Sassi*. *Sasso* means stone or rock and there are stones and boulders everywhere. It's as if the whole place has risen out of them. As we walk the lower town, we realize that the churches and homes have been carved out of tufa rocks, creating cave-like dwellings.

The town reminds me of Bethlehem, all the buildings white in color. Although Matera is believed to go back as far as the Paleolithic Period, the rock churches were dug out by monks between the 8th and 12th centuries.

We walk through the two lower districts and visit all twelve churches. They're small and simple, a few religious artifacts and frescoes still intact. I cannot believe people lived in them. And I'm amazed at how they have survived through the centuries.

After exploring each one, we climb to the top of the hill that leads to the piano district where more churches and castles stand, all built in the 16th and 17th centuries. I realize how unusual it is to see this contrast—a town that could be Bethlehem beneath and the more modern district above with its Gothic, Baroque and Renaissance structures. There are numerous churches and the *Aragonese Castle* of Count Tramontano—a count who in 1497, was given the city of Matera (as his country) by King Ferdinand II of Naples. What a stark contrast between these grand architectural buildings and churches high on the hill and the *sasso* caves below.

In the piano district, we try to make our way to the churches but the heat is stifling, 115°. It's an effort to hike around in the blazing sun. The water we are drinking is not helping as it heats up in our hands before we can get it into our bodies. We do manage to visit the cathedral built in 1270 which is at the highest point in the city, a statue of Archangel Michael guarding its portal.

We also walk through the churches of San Francesco and Saint Claire but the heat holds us back from pressing onward. Instead, we stand in the shadow of a building comparing our map to the landscape where we point out San Domenico's Church, La Palomba the Church of the Holy Spirit and Santa Lucia alla Malve. San Michele is omnipresent as he stands guard from their rooftops.

Soon, we are in the car driving the long distance back to Sorrento and to the port where we barely make the last hydrofoil. Although it has only been thirty-six hours since I left my villa, it feels like seven days ... yes, seven days with San Michele, the Guardian of Truth and the Keeper of the Veil. A lot has been revealed to me on this sojourn and I'm yearning for quietude.

Il tramonto, the sunset waits for me until I arrive home and take my place on the *terrazzo*. My heart is full and my soul is singing. I realize I'm now wise enough to know that if I listen to the signs and my inner voice, they will guide me through much happiness and the world will open wide for me.

CHAPTER 30

Life is sweet on the island of lemons, limoncello and Caprese salads. I wander about watching the tourists, sketchbook in hand. My feelings are spilling out of my heart onto the pages at every turn. I've decided I want to sketch as many people as I can. So, I sit on the bench that Bruno and I used to share. I've not seen him since that day we were so intimate at the fort and I realize I miss my friend.

At midday, I return to my villa for a *siesta* since the temperatures have soared. After a short nap, I sit on the *terrazzo* and sketch the lizards as they play and the grapes as they grow plump. I'm bathed in the soft, late-afternoon light, the sounds, the wind, and the sea. Where does the time go? How delicious and decadent it feels to be able to play hooky from life, shun all responsibilities and only pay attention to my own needs and desires.

Donata calls to remind me of our dinner plans; I move inside to change into the cool cotton shift Louisa had given me as a gift. The walk will take me about one hour but it's a glorious walk. The flowers are in bloom and all along the way, the cats come out to greet me.

I look up just as Antonio steps onto the path before me. He is startled, not sure how I will react. I quickly put him at ease.

"Antonio, it's good to see you. How have you been?" I kiss both his cheeks. After all, I have already forgiven his innocence and my own.

"Ciao, Roxanna. How are you? I have not seen you in a long time. Is everything good?" He begins to relax.

"I'm good. I've been traveling throughout Umbria and Tuscany so I haven't been on the island much. How about you?"

"Oh, you know, sometimes I am busy as a tour guide for the tourists."

You mean the women, I think to myself but do not say it aloud.

"I met a girl, you know. She is from Florida and was here on vacation for two weeks. She asked me to come live with her there. I will work in a restaurant and then I will take care of her." He smiles wide, his perfect teeth glistening in the sunlight.

"Good for you, Antonio. I know it was your dream to go to America."

"Yes. I must go now. But when I move there, maybe I will come visit you," he says.

"Yes, maybe then, Antonio. Congratulations and enjoy your new life."

"I will, *bella. Ciao.*"

"*Ciao, bello.*" As I walk the path, I remember our last night together and laugh out loud. I must have been quite a fright!

When I arrive, Louisa and Mario greet me in the garden.

"*Ciao, ciao, Rosanna,*" they say.

Mario's daughter and her husband Marcello come to embrace me.

"We are so happy you come," says Donata.

"*Sera*, Roxanna, *benvenuta,* come in please," says Marcello.

"*Grazie*, Marcello. *Come va?*"

"*Bene, bene.* Life is good, no?"

"Yes, it is. Especially if you live here in paradise." I smile wide, thankful I am here. I kneel before Luca and extend my hand with the candies I bought for him in the village. "Luca, I have something for you."

He hides behind his papa's pant legs. His cheeks are rosy and his eyes are dark shining pools. Although he's shy, he's happy to see me. He's a beautiful little Italian boy who will grow up into a beautiful Italian man.

"*Regalo, per* Luca." He comes immediately and takes the candy. He quickly kisses my cheek.

"Roxanna, *bella. Bene, bene,*" Louisa says with pride. After hugging and kissing me, she points to my dress, admiring the beautiful gift she had given me.

"*Grazie, fresco.*" I tell her it's cool and fresh.

The women move to the *terrazzo* where a table sits underneath a linen canopy. Mario and Marcello prepare the foods to be grilled. Torches are lit all around and Marcello turns on the music, a CD of N*apoletano* tunes he has made for me.

We share stories about life as we sip the homemade sparkling wine Marcello's family has made. It's quite delicious and intoxicating. Once again, Mario and Marcello keep refreshing our glasses.

"No, *grazie,*" we say as we hold our glasses close to us and wave them away. But they keep pouring. We giggle after each pour because the little champagne bubbles are running through our blood. As we laugh and share stories, the men barbecue chicken and shrimp. Once they have served us, they sit down and the Italian dining experience begins.

The food is delicious and naturally there is far too much. We have fruit, melon with prosciutto, then cheese and olives. The second course is chicken and shrimp, which are large and sweet. Next, the pasta that Louisa has made is placed on the table along with my salad. I picked the arugula from the garden and dressed it with gorgonzola cheese, lemon, salt and olive oil. I had this dish while in Umbria so I'm happy they like it. And finally, the gelato and sweets are served with limoncello. They continue to push more onto our plates as if it's a love ritual. The more food they offer you, the more they love you. But finally, you must say, "no, stop, *fermati. Sono piena,* I'm full."

How do they stay so lean? I feel like I could explode! Mario tries to pour limoncello for me but I wave him away and say, "no, *grazie.*" I cannot squeeze another ounce of anything into my body or I will not be able to walk home.

"Roxanna, limoncello helps you digest. It is good for you when you eat too much." Donata tries to assure me that it will help like an Alka-Seltzer. I'm skeptical but trust them and take a sip. Within minutes, my digestion has softened. I'm realizing this golden liquor has been made by the gods to cure all things.

I look around the table and realize how blessed I am to have found this beautiful family. I thank them profusely for all they have done for me since I arrived and for the meals we have shared. I also thank Mario for taking me with him through the Campania and Basilicata regions, my own personal *Festiva de San Michele.* He is pleased and proceeds to tell funny stories of our travels which Donata translates into English for me.

Soon, the night comes to an end. I'm so sleepy that I grow concerned I will not be able to find my way home in the dark. There are no streetlights on the island which means I will have to use my cell phone to light the way. Donata and Louisa offer their husbands for my safety and Mario and Marcello nod in agreement as if the two-mile-walk (one mile each way) is no big deal. I tell them I can find my way, thank you.

The hugging and kissing takes ten minutes at least and then I'm off. I'm safe since there are no coyotes or strange animals to jump out at me ... only cats and dogs and Italian men. I sway from side to side, sashaying my way down the walkway to my villa. I remember Elana and smile.

I think of Natale and wish he were here with me. I hug my pillow tightly to my breast pretending it's him and this is how I fall asleep.

The dream ... I awaken to San Michele beside me at the edge of the gardens looking out toward the bay.

"Now you know who I am, sweet woman. I have always been with you."

I begin to weep and he places his hands upon my shoulders and turns me to face him.

"Life is about noticing the signs, and you paid attention to those that brought you here to your homeland. Don't ever be frightened of anything in your life for you can change anything in a flash. Nothing is permanent. And you are never alone. We are all here. Your trip to the Basilicata region was a sacred journey and everyone you met along the way was an angel to insure you were safe—especially those two." (He's referring to Giuseppe and Mario).

"And now you have found a long-lost family once yours in another lifetime. So, welcome home. But now, it is time for you to go on another great adventure. Go to Greece. You already know where."

He kisses the top of my head and leaves me at the edge of the cliffs.

I awaken to the breeze outside my window as it rustles the grape leaves on the vines.

What shall I do today?

The dream! Greece!

I leap from the bed.

Why not? I've wanted to go for years, dreamt about it. When Capri came up, I put Greece on the back burner because I was called to come here. But Greece ... where the world began ...

I move to the bath to start my day. I'm on a mission to go to the bookstore in Capri and purchase yet another tour book.

CHAPTER 31
ATHENS, GREECE

Mythology, thought to be a collection of mythical stories, is one of the cornerstones of ancient Greek civilization. It has always been a belief that the Athenians were descendants of the gods.

Hesiod, a great poet from 700 B.C. wrote an epic poem called *The Creation of the World*. He believed that the beginning of creation started with Chaos, Gaia and Eros. Eros and Night were born from Chaos, and Ouranos and Okeanos were born from Gaia. Ouranos coupled with Gaia and they became the first gods to rule the world. They bore twelve children known as the Titans—Okeanos; Koios; Kreios; Hyperion; Iapetos; Kronos; Theia; Rhea; Themis; Mnemosyne; Phoibe; and Tethys. They also bore the three Cyclopes—Brontes; Steropes; and Arges; and the three Giants with the "hundred-hands"—Kottos; Gyges; and Breareos.

After the birth of his children, Ouranos realized he didn't want to lose his power or become dethroned when they became of age, so he made his wife hide them deep within her bowels. Gaia, his wife plotted to take away her husband's strength to achieve the goal of freeing her children, and armed her son Kronos with a sickle to cut off his father's genitals. When Ouranos's seed fell into the sea, Aphrodite was born, and when his blood was spilled onto the earth, the Fates, the Giants and the Meliai Nymphs were born.

Kronos succeeded his father and married his sister Rhea, then freed the rest of his brothers and sisters. Unfortunately, he eventually became as fearful as his father had. So, he swallowed his and Rhea's children—Hestia, Demeter, Hera, Hades and Poseidon.

Rhea fooled her husband by wrapping a stone in a cloth (instead of Zeus) to hide him from his father. She then hid Zeus by having him taken to Mount Dikte to be raised by the Nymphs. Kronos swallowed the stone without knowing her secret. Eventually, her son, Zeus grew to manhood, dethroned his father and saved the rest of his siblings.

Not everyone accepted Zeus in power. Gaia talked the Titans, the brothers of Kronos, into revolting against him. This was known as the *Battle of the Titans*. Zeus and other members of the Olympic pantheon sought refuge at Mount Olympus and finally managed to defeat the Titans."

Outraged, Gaia went to the Giants thus the *Battle of the Giants* ensued. They were savage monsters who had human bodies with serpent heads or serpent tails instead of legs. This battle changed the course of rivers and moved mountains and islands. Zeus and the other gods were finally successful but only after great damage was done.

From then on, the twelve Olympian Gods—Zeus and his brothers and sisters: Poseidon, Demeter, Apollo, Ares, Aphrodite, Dionysus, Athena, Artemis, Hera, Hestia and Hermes—ruled from Mount Olympus democratically. Mankind was then created by the gods who made them from a compound of earth and fire and then added whatever other materials they could mix together. The ancient Greeks also gave their gods human weaknesses such as jealousies, infidelities, loss, grief and love so of course there was much angst and drama among them.

Aside from the twelve who ruled, there were also many other deities who determined the fate of man. Hesiod very poetically described the solar cycle and the theory of time -

Helios the Sun, Selene the Moon, and Eos the Dawn were the children of two of the Titans—Hyperion and Theia. Every morning, Helios rises from the ocean in the east and rides his chariot pulled by his four horses through the sky to descend to the earth at night. When he completes his journey, Selene bathes in the sea, dresses herself and finally ascends into the heavens. The following day is brought by Eos and once again, Helios sets out on his journey.

Some don't believe that these stories and myths are true. If they aren't, why are there temples and buildings everywhere throughout Greece in their honor? And why was Greece one of the most powerful civilizations in ancient history? It was the seat of the world from which other countries were birthed.

The story goes that the Olympian Gods awarded the city of Athens to Athena the Goddess of Wisdom, over Poseidon. Both had fought over the city since it had become the leading metropolis in Greece, everyone wanting to own it. It was home to the likes of great philosophers—Socrates, Plato, Aristotle, and great poets such as Aeschylus, Sophocles, and Euripides.

I've arrived in Athens and hike up the great Acropolis Hill where the most famous remnants of Greek history lie. With my book as my tour guide, I approach the *Propylae,* the entrance to the Acropolis. I'm enamored with Greek history and mythology and cannot wait.

As I near the *Parthenon,* I'm awestruck by its construction. The highest structure on the site, the temple of the Virgin Athena, was erected in 500 B.C. It had survived fully intact for two thousand years until the 17th century when a European General Morosino gave the order to strike it with a mortar and detonate it with gunpowder causing much damage.

A smaller building, the *Temple of the Wingless Victory*, stands on the southern part of Acropolis Hill, built for the *Goddess Nike* or *Victory*. Although it had been demolished in 1679, Greece rebuilt her. The *Erechtheum,* is the most ancient sanctuary of the Acropolis, housing three temples—the *Temple of Athena Polias*, the *Temple of Erechtheus* and the *Temple of the Nymph* or *Maiden Pandrosus*. The southern portico to this building holds six statues of virgins used as columns to support its roof. They are still remarkable, most of their features still visible.

I roam for hours looking at each ruin from every angle. Those that I can lay my hands on, I do. How incredible that they have survived. Despite the destruction by the Persians in 480 B.C., much has been miraculously preserved. The museum holds pieces from the *Temple of Athena*, the *Frieze of Victory*, and the unique *Kourai maidens* thought to be Athena's high priestesses. A bas-relief of Athena leaning on her lance and fragments of great sculptures are on display from the *Frieze of the Parthenon*. A statue of Nike loosening her sandal is housed there along with all the other great antiquities.

As I walk toward the southern slope of the Acropolis, the *Odean of Herodes Atticus,* the great stone amphitheater comes into sight. It was built by an Athenian magistrate, Herodes Atticus, in memory of his wife. It was carved out of the rocks in 161 A.D. and was also where Yanni played in the Acropolis in 1993 as the lights from above shone down upon him.

I spend most of the day in the museum at the Acropolis walking around the complex looking down at Athens which spreads out before me as far as the eye can see. Making my way down the big hill is a challenge and it has started to rain. Luckily, there's no downpour before I reach the Plaka, the oldest district in Athens which is filled with shops, kiosks, restaurants and bars. Greek music plays in the streets as I lazily window shop and people-watch.

Each time I pass a restaurant or cafe, the waiters stand outside giving away their business cards trying to entice the passing tourists. I come upon a small boy of about eight with the most soulful black eyes and thick curly hair. I stop to watch and listen as he plays a mandolin, a big smile across his cherubic face. As soon as I give him a handful of coins, he thanks me in Greek and scoots off. I decide this is the perfect place to eat.

Inside, giant vertical rotisseries are filled with lamb and chicken. The men slice the meat from them for the patrons. I'm seated outside and soon served *souvlaki*—meat and vegetables grilled on a skewer—Greek salad, rice and olives. But as soon as the waiter comes, the skies open and waterfalls pour down from the heavens, dumping onto the awning, dropping heavily all around. These are the biggest raindrops I've ever seen. Everyone has stopped where they are as if they are frozen in time.

The waiter immediately picks up my plate and motions for me to come inside where he clears a space for me and my table in the middle of the room. He stands in the center of the room, snaps his fingers and soon a table and chair are delivered and set up. As I'm kindly seated in the center of the deli area, people wonder who I am, the only patron from the patio who has been brought inside as the others stand huddled together. I'm also wondering who they think I am to be treating me so well. I laugh at this quick change of events.

Two young women from Australia ask if they may sit and share my table, and I say yes. They've just come from the islands.

"Where will you go next?" they ask. One is petite and blonde and the other has dark hair and blue eyes. They've been traveling throughout Italy and Greece and are on their way to Turkey and Istanbul, a continuation of their month-long holiday.

"I'm going to Mykonos next and then Santorini. My friends in Italy tell me Mykonos is fun and Santorini is beautiful. So, I'll start there. Who knows after that."

"Good choices. They're both so different. Mykonos is filled with nightlife and the clubs don't come alive until midnight. People never sleep there." I can tell Rebecca loved Mykonos.

"But Santorini, you will absolutely fall in love with." Wanda, the dark-haired woman's eyes light up at the memory. "It's indescribable. We loved it there. Going to Mykonos first was a great idea." They both nod in unison and stand to leave.

"Have a wonderful time on your holiday, Roxanna. Oh, when you visit Mykonos, don't forget to go to Paradise and Super Paradise. You must see them."

"Thanks, it was nice to meet you." Now I'm excited and intrigued about Mykonos. Since I'm alone, I won't be going to any clubs but it sounds like a fun place to be.

I pay my bill and leave a tip for the waiter. There is something to be said about a woman traveling the world alone. I think she gets treated better than the other tourists. I can attest to that.

Shop owners start to pull their wares back out to the streets and others remove the tarps they had quickly covered their goods with. I wander through the Plaka looking for my hotel but I'm lost.

I should write a book titled "Lost in Paradise." I laugh out loud at my own humor.

"Excuse me, could you please tell me how to get to the Olympic Palace Hotel?" I stop at a restaurant at the edge of the Plaka to ask for directions. The young man at the entrance seems happy to help. He stands tall and smiles.

"I can help you. I am Stavros." He takes my hand and shakes it. "And you?"

"Nice to meet you, Stavros. I'm Roxanna. Is it this way to this hotel?" I pull out a business card from the hotel.

"No, it is where you came from." He begins to speak slowly so I will understand his directions.

"Follow this road all the way to the end and then you can only turn left or right. Go right. Then it will turn a few times like this." He makes a snake like motion with his hand. "You see? Then, when you get to this point (he points to the end of the snake), you go right. No problem. You will be outside the Plaka and your hotel is one street up from there."

I hope I can follow his directions ... "Thanks for your help."

"Roxanna, please come back for dinner. Here is my card." He writes his name on the back of it. "We have Greek dancing here at night and you will enjoy it. Remember the name, Mourayio's Restaurant. If you can't find us, ask. Everyone knows us. And remember me, Stavros."

"Thank you, Stavros. I will think about it." I wave goodbye and walk on. I hadn't thought that far ahead. I'm not sure I want to venture too far from my hotel in a city I am not familiar with. But within five minutes, my hotel comes into view.

I lounge in my bubble bath asking myself if I should return to the Plaka. Why not?

After asking directions from three different people, I finally arrive at Mourayio's. Stavros is outside soliciting the tourists; he sees me and smiles.

"Roxanna, I am happy you are here. Come."

He takes me to a table inside, close to the floor where the musicians are already playing.

"Do you work all day and night, Stavros?"

"When the tourists come, yes, we work very hard but I have a break before dinner. And we have a long holiday in the winter."

He pulls out a chair for me. I sit.

"The dancing will start in one hour. I will find your waiter."

The food is good and the ambience is wonderful. I'm enjoying myself. As I finish my last bite of baklava, four men dressed in traditional Greek garb start to dance. They change costumes three times in between sets and I'm amazed at their clothing that is so strange to me. Most are colorful tunic types, belted at the waist. Their shoes seem bigger than their feet with big black bumps on the tops of them.

When the musicians leave the stage, I think the show has ended but after a short break, they come back to play more music and four men come out onto the dance floor dressed in modern black pants and black dress shirts with high collars. To my surprise, one of them is Stavros. I laugh and clap as he dances in line with the others, their hands on each other's shoulders as they move their legs in unison, kicking one out in front of them, then the other.

They continue to perform dances I have not seen. In one, each of them takes a turn dancing in the center of the circle while the others clap. When it's Stavros' turn, he crosses his arms and dances slowly, inching down toward the floor with his shoulders, bending his knees further each time. Eventually, he's in a position that I would have doubted a human being could shape himself into. His back is literally one foot from the floor but he is still on his feet being supported by his upper leg muscles as he moves to the music. In between his upward and downward motion, he thumps his hands behind himself on the floor, then brings them up in front, clapping once to the music. Then the dance repeats itself and the patrons, mostly tourists, are going crazy clapping and shrieking. The Greek men are shouting "Opah!"

One of the other dancers brings a shot glass and ceremoniously, places it on Stavros' forehead. The glass is filled with ouzo, and as they clap louder cheering him on, he keeps the

208

rhythm of his movement. He claps one last time and with a final loud thump to the floor with both hands, he manages to maneuver the shot glass so that it flips in the air. When it comes down, the liquid has fallen into his mouth and he catches the glass with his teeth.

The crowd goes wild and the screams bringing people in from the streets to see what has happened. I screech with delight for I have never seen anything like this. The dancers lift Stavros over their heads and parade him around the room as if this is a ceremony for someone who has reached manhood by passing this special test.

"I can't believe you did that. How did you do it? You must be incredibly strong to put that kind of pressure on your thighs. I can't believe you can bend like that!" I gush.

He's proud. He places two glasses of ouzo on the table.

"It is nothing." He lowers his eyes shyly. "My father taught me to do it. It was a game when we were little.

"Is it a traditional Greek dance like the others?"

"No, we do it for the tourists. They think it's Greek but it is not ... only something we made up. You like?" His English is a bit broken.

"Yes, yes I do." I'm still excited and the energy in the room is electric.

"Good. Stay and watch more dancing and have more ouzo. It is good. If it is strong, put water in it."

He smiles at me and walks back to the dance floor where the other men are now gathering. The music begins and they start to pull women from the tables to dance. Stavros comes to me and tries to pull me from my chair.

"I can't dance like that." I fight him nervously, afraid to dance.

"I teach you. Don't be afraid." He has a good grip on my hand and won't let it go. "Come."

I love the way the men on this side of the world always say, "come," as if you will because they are in charge. Eventually, I relent and let him lead me to the dance floor. He holds me and walks me through the steps of one of the traditional dances and I think I've got it. In fact, I catch on so quickly that the patrons begin to whistle and clap. I'm mortified but having the time of my life. We dance until the belly dancer comes out. I leave for my seat but she comes after me and pulls me to the dance floor. Now, I'm belly dancing with a scarf around my waist and little golden bells strung through my fingers ... in Athens ... in Greece. What a life!

After drinking ouzo, I dance the night away with the confidence of Athena herself, once again in a far-off land with Stavros and the beautiful Greek belly dancer. When the dancing is finished for the night, Stavros sits with me and we talk about his life in Athens and my travels. Before I know it, the restaurant is closing and it's 3:00 a.m. Now I know how the Greeks stay up all night. They drink ouzo, dance and lose track of time!

"Come. I walk you to your hotel." I'm concerned a bit, but more concerned with becoming lost at this hour. We find my hotel quickly.

"Thank you, Stavros." I give him my hand to shake, but instead, he leans in and steals a quick kiss. I should be good at dodging them by now, but obviously, I need more practice. "No. I ... I don't know you." I move away uneasily.

"It is the Greek way." He smiles at me but moves back to a safe distance to assure me his intentions are honorable. I thank him by kissing him gently on both cheeks in the Italian way.

"Efcharistó, thank you. Good bye, Roxanna." He turns back toward the Plaka.

... just a kiss ...

Tiredly, I enter the hotel and my room and fall into bed wondering how Natale is.

CHAPTER 32
MYKONOS, GREECE

Greek mythos says Mykonos took its name from the son of Anios who was a descendant of the god Apollo and the nymph, Rio. The large stones that cover the island are believed to be the petrified giants that Hercules once defeated. It's also believed that the body of Ajax Locros was buried here after his ship sank.

In ancient times, the Egyptians, Phoenicians, Cretans, Ionians and the Romans all took their turn inhabiting the island. Long ago, Barbarossa captured and ravaged it, and the Venetians ruled it at different times for more than five hundred years. But in 1822, Mykonos finally belonged to Greece.

The island is far different than Athens, its terrain arid, the Aegean Sea lapping its shores. Whitewashed houses dot the landscape, each with a dovecote, a nesting place for pigeons (the design brought here by Venetian nobles centuries before, who raised them for their meat). Luminous white windmills line the coast like sentries guarding the island.

The houses are simple and awash with bright, white paint. Most of their doors are the bright cobalt blue color of Greece, yet one or two are proudly painted red or yellow, wanting to be seen. The buildings sit side by side on narrow spiraling alleyways of white-washed flagstones between shops, restaurants and art galleries. Flower boxes filled with vibrant plants and bougainvillea hang everywhere adorning walls and staircases. An ancient church with a blue domed-roof lies in the distance.

I check into a quaint two-story hotel in the middle of town, the Hotel Philippi. It is picture-perfect, white with blue-framed windows and doors and a patio for sunbathing.

The sun is hot, as hot as Capri on a summer day, but sans humidity. As a matter of fact, it's desert dry. I leave my room in search of mineral water and somewhere to sit and read my guide book. I choose one of the many cafes on the water's edge and enjoy my cool drink.

My guide book tells me there are 500 churches on the island, mostly Greek Orthodox. I have seen a few as I walked the winding lanes. On my flight to Athens, I read that most were built by the islanders who had been out to sea. In treacherous moments when they thought they would not survive, they found religion and promised that if they were saved, they'd build a church. So, they did. Most are extremely sparse and simple, unlike the Catholic churches throughout Italy.

Finished with my drink, I set out for adventure on this small island and come upon the *Paraportiani*, one of the most photographed churches in the world. As I move closer for a look, I realize it's five buildings melded into one. I pull out my guidebook for more details. It used to be a complex built between the 16th and 17th centuries—four churches on the ground and one on the roof. But time has eroded their structures and they seem to have fused together. The Mikonians continue the upkeep of this complex and each year, paint them with fresh, sparkling paint.

I watch the fisherman as they come in with their daily catch, their wives waiting patiently on the beach. I realize this must be the ritual—the wives waiting for the fish to sell while their men sit together over Greek coffee or ouzo and tell stories of the sea. The fishermen are listening intently to the oldest as he puffs on a cigarette and weaves his tales.

I yawn and realize my eyelids are heavy and then I remember I slept little the night before. Time for a much-needed nap.

When I awaken at 7:00 p.m., I feel Natale heavy in my chest. I miss him today as I have every day since I left him. Some days are harder but with the distractions of travel, the nagging subsides … at least for a bit.

I reminisce about how he used to sing to me at night when we were about to drift off to sleep. He'd turn to face me, stare into my eyes and rub the side of my face, all the while singing a love song in Italian.

I remember the night he said, *"Non preoccuparti io sis ono per te."* I asked him what it meant. He tried to explain. "It means you will never have to worry about anything. I will take care of you. You are my woman. I have got you."

No one has ever said that to me. Although I'm still confused as to what my next step is, I am not confused about his love for me. It all seems like a dream.

I wonder where he is tonight? I want to call him, tell him to come. But I do not and will not. I sigh and hope I know what I'm doing. I'm gambling everything, I know, but I don't have any answers yet.

What if he's not there when you are finished? What if he falls in love with another? What will you do then?

"I don't know ... I don't know," I say aloud. "I don't know what I'll do."

Maybe I made the whole thing up. My feelings for him ... this romance I think we shared ... it's because of Elana and her romantic notions! Sometimes, you need to use your brain to think out your life, don't you? I hate it when my head debates my heart!

I move from the bed and shower before leaving the room.

I've been inside my head since I awoke. As I roam the streets, I finally look up and think I'm in Venice, Italy. I realize I've actually made my way to a district in Mykonos called "Little Venice." The buildings are close together and the Aegean gently laps against their facades. Many are stone and painted Greece's brilliant white. Others are wooden and all have brightly colored porches and window frames. The restaurants and bars have cement terraces lined with tables and chairs for dining. It's breathtaking as the sun starts to lower itself in the sky.

The voice of an angel wafts through the air. Where is it coming from? I chase it up an outer stairway and enter the Veranda Bar, a lounge overlooking the sea. I step inside and realize the music is emanating from speakers. The angel is Sarah Brightman and she is singing a celestial tune. I find a cushioned bench at a small table and sit. People are laughing and drinking cocktails as they watch the sun's descent.

"May I help you?" My waiter is a handsome young man with strong Greek features.

"Do you have a drink menu?" I'm not sure what to order, but I know it won't be ouzo. After perusing the menu, I order a "Greek Passion Drink."

I'm mesmerized by the sun as it gently slips into the Aegean, the sky changing to shades of orange, pink and yellow-gold. Yanni's soul-stirring music is now playing. This and the atmosphere, the smell of the sea and the palette of color before me, gives me gooseflesh.

"Excuse me, is anyone sitting here?"

I think for a moment that Omar Sharif has joined me but I realize I'm mistaken. He speaks as though he has been schooled in America. He is pointing to the empty seat across from me.

"No, there's no one."

"I'm sorry to hear that. You shouldn't be alone on an island such as this."

I blush and turn my gaze from him. He orders a glass of champagne from the waiter. He doesn't seem Greek since he is not ordering ouzo or grappa. He reads my mind.

"Even though I'm back in my homeland, I still love the taste of good champagne. The waiter comes and he lifts his glass.

"To Helios." I lift mine to his.

"It's a miracle each day that the sun rises in the east and sets over the western sea here, each day that we breathe, each day that he is successful in his journey." This man has my attention with his eloquent and poetic speech and his mythological ideals.

"Yes, I agree. Are you from here?"

"No, no. I grew up in Kalamata where the olive trees grow on the hillsides above the sea. But I now have a home here as well. I have always loved this little village and its people."

He lifts his glass and savors a small sip.

"You cannot find a people better than those on Mykonos. Once they get to know you, they will treat you with kindness and then take you into their hearts as well as their homes. That's what happened to me and that's why I am here. They are the family I always come back to when I return from America each year."

"Where do you live in America?"

"I live in Cambridge, Massachusetts for most of the year. Every year, I come here to visit friends and family, to rest and to pay homage to the sun God, Helios." He smiles reverently. "You know the skies are usually gray in New England no matter the season."

He has kind eyes, silver streaks in his hair. When he smiles, his dimples deepen. Although his face is aged from the sun, it's warm and welcoming.

"I've never been to Boston, but I know the weather."

The conversation continues and after a time, he flags the waiter for another glass of champagne. He asks what I would like and although my stomach growls for food, I want to stay and talk with him a little longer. It's as if he is a male counterpart of Elana.

"No, please. I'll have what he's having."

"Excellent choice; it is Veuve Clicquot, a French champagne."

The waiter delivers my order and we toast again.

"To all those who came before us and created this glorious civilization; Opah."

Decadent ... the bubbles tickle my insides and I giggle.

"Thank you. It's delicious."

He extends his hand to me and introduces himself.

"My name is Christos; but you may call me Chris as everyone does in the States."

"I am Roxanna."

We politely shake hands.

"Where are you from, Roxanna?" He seems pleasant and well-bred with his beige linen suit and woven leather shoes.

"I'm from California near San Diego."

"I travel to California a few times every year. What's the name of the town?"

"Carlsbad."

"Yes, I've been through there. Are you traveling alone, Roxanna?"

I hesitate for a moment.

"Yes. A little vacation I guess you could say."

We sit and talk for an hour as we finish our champagne. I learn he has a wife, an American woman who is a professor at Boston University, and three boys who are all in college. I enjoy talking to this man with the sweet face and a wonderful outlook on life. Everything is poetry and music to him. Nothing gets by him without notice and he explains his thoughts eloquently. I ask him if he is a writer or a poet but he says he is simply a businessman.

Soon, I find myself telling him about my wild journey and how I have left my life to find myself, the music in the background and my second drink setting the scene.

"Have you found what you are looking for yet, Roxanna?"

I'm startled.

"I apologize. I did not mean to pry," he says.

"No, no. Don't apologize. I'm still on the journey, but I've realized a lot about myself on this trip."

"Excellent, then. Everyone needs to do what you are doing. Most of us get to the end of our lives with regret, realizing we didn't know what would make us happy. So, we leave this earth unfulfilled."

I never thought resigning from my career and leaving like I did was something so positive, but hearing it said out loud by Christos has made me sigh with relief.

"What's so amusing, Roxanna?"

"I'm just happy right now. And a little hungry. I haven't eaten much today and this is my second drink!"

"Then we shall feed you! You need your strength, young lady. Would you like to join me for dinner?"

He pays the bill and we leave, arm in arm, in search of a restaurant. We turn a corner in Little Venice and arrive at Nico's Tavern.

"Will this do for you, Roxanna? It has the best seafood on the island, caught fresh every day."

"Yes, this is perfect."

I've been quiet as we walk, deep in thought, as Christos talks about this shop that we have just passed, or the owner of that one, or this man's family, or the weather. I shake my head to tell him

I'm listening, but I'm not. Am I finished traveling? Is it time for me to return to Rome? Capri? America?

A man with a large white apron approaches Christos and hugs him. He seats us at a table with a view. Christos orders fresh fish for both of us and the owner takes him outside to the case filled with fish to choose our meal from the fresh catch of the day.

We are served Greek wine, *spanakorizo,* spinach and rice, *kolakothopita,* zucchini pie, the fresh grilled fish and Greek salad. As we eat, the local pelican named Petros, the island's mascot, has arrived at the front of the restaurant and is causing quite a stir. He's a big one, three feet tall, and tries to nose his way into the case of the fish. The owner is talking loudly but lovingly to him to move away, scolding him as if he were a small child. His hand is on the pelican's long beak as he steers him out into the square. Everyone laughs at this funny site, the pelican looking as if he is the one in control while the owner looks like a crazy Greek talking loudly with his hands.

"Petros is the local celebrity, you know. Everyone loves him, but he's like a two-year-old, always into everything. He has been tormenting poor Niko ever since I started coming here." He smiles and I notice the roadmap of his life etched upon his face in the candlelight. I must ask him.

"Christos, why is your wife not with you on this trip?"

"Ah, my Teresa ..." The look of a man in love washes over him. "She likes to go to the Cape, you know, Cape Cod. She's not one to travel the world like me. She prefers the sounds of the same ocean lulling her to sleep at night while I prefer to roam the world in search of many different sounds. I'm always up for an adventure." He winks at me and his dimples deepen.

"Where do you go? What are some of your favorite places?" I'm intrigued by this unique human being who sees light in all things and beauty in every breath he takes.

"I have homes in Kalamata, Mykonos, in Cambridge, Mass. and one in Falmouth on Cape Cod. I would have homes all over the world if I could, but these are my favorite places. My beautiful wife allows me to travel to Greece whenever it calls to me, as long as I return to her when I am finished feeding my soul. So, I travel the world and return to her when I'm done."

He continues.

"I fell in love with her the first moment I saw her. We were students at Northeastern University many years ago. She was blonde which we Greek men love. We fall in love with everything you know." He laughs out loud at his own joke.

"I asked her out many times but she was never interested in someone as rough-looking as me. She told me so. She's spicy, that one. She's never been afraid to tell me what she thinks."

"I was a young man in love pining away for her for many, many months before she finally did me the honor of accepting my invitation for dinner. Well you can guess that I brought her flowers and we celebrated with champagne. After that first night, she was mine. And what a prize she was. She knows I cherish her but she lets me run free."

"She's a very lucky woman, Christos. You are unique and I'm sure she is as well. Relationships like yours don't happen every day."

"Thank you for the compliment, Roxanna. And you, what is your experience with love?"

His question is unexpected. I think about my life for a moment—my past relationships and my ex-husband. Then I think of the sweet parts of my relationship with Natale.

"I found love unexpectedly in Rome, Christos. But before I go back to him, I must be sure this is what I truly want. I met him when I was searching for parts of me I had lost. So, I want to make sure I'm not just trying to fill that empty place in my heart. I want to make sure it's real."

"What is real, Roxanna? What you felt in those moments with him was real. I know because I'm much older than you. I have more experience with such matters." He laughs big, his chest rising and falling with each guffaw.

"Enough talk of life now. Let's enjoy the food and drink."

I'm relieved to change the subject for I know I spend far too much time pondering this dilemma.

The night comes to an end and Christos and I link arms and walk back to my hotel.

"Roxanna, I'm here for another day and I'm going to the island of Delos tomorrow to pay homage to Apollo. It's not far from here. Would you like to go with me? I will show you Delos like no one else can. It is a very sacred place—his and his sister's birthplace."

"Yes; what time and where shall I meet you?"

We set a time and say good night. As I ready myself for bed, I wonder if most Greeks are like Christos and have the depth he does.

CHAPTER 33
DELOS, GREECE

Christos and I have boarded a small boat and are motoring toward Delos.

"That landmass there," he points to the large landmass before us. "it's actually two separate islands connected by that narrow strait."

"This one, the smallest is Delos. It's where we are going. That one over there used to be called the Great Delos because it's three times bigger but it is actually Reneia." He continues. "History goes back to at least 400 B.C. when the Athenians ordered the purification of Delos. They thought it to be sacred because it was the birthplace of Apollo and Artemis. So, they moved all women who were about to give birth, and all those who were on the verge of death, to the island of Reneia to keep Delos pure. Have you heard the story, Roxanna?"

"No." I had read about it but want to hear his version.

"The story goes that Zeus loved beautiful women ... goddesses that is. He was married to Hera, but had a love affair with Leto, and his wife was so enraged because of his infidelities that she sent out an order that no place in the world was to receive Leto and allow her to give birth there. Zeus went to Poseidon and asked for his help. Poseidon then struck the sea and the Cyclades, a group of islands appeared. Delos was one of them ... flat, rocky, barren and treeless, with no mountains ... except for that small mount, Kynthos. It's a very sacred place."

He points to a small rise in the earth and continues.

"It is bathed in sunlight, a place that the god Helios blesses daily. They say it draws the light into itself and reflects it back to the one who is looking down upon it. That is how Zeus and Leto saw it when they chose this place."

I enjoy his tale and close my eyes as the sun bakes my skin. The air is hot and dry, but when a small sea breeze blows off the water, it cools me.

"Leto took refuge on the island and brought Apollo and Artemis into the world here. There's a museum in Athens, the national Archeological Museum. Did you visit there, Roxanna?"

"No, I'm afraid I ran out of time."

"You must go there some day. It has many mythological artifacts that you will enjoy. Anyway, there is a figure of her dated 370 B.C. She is surrounded by Athena, Aphrodite and a few others as she stands and holds onto a palm tree while giving birth." He gazes out toward Delos as he recalls the image in his mind.

"I love Greek Mythology, Christos. I really believe the Greeks were the first to inhabit the earth and from here, humanity was born."

"Yes, I do, too. The world is divided on that one, but at least the Greeks are on your side."

We step off the boat and walk along a dry, sandy path as a lizard scurries from our sight.

"Tell me more. I love to hear your stories, Christos."

He takes my arm and links it with his as old friends do when they walk together.

"So, you like my stories, eh? Let's see ... they say the island is held in place by diamond columns that no one can see but the gods. Once Apollo was birthed here, it became a very sacred place. Do you know about Apollo, Roxanna?"

"I know he's the God of Music."

"Ah, but he's so much more than that, although they say no one played the lyre as well as he did. He's also known for his skills in archery ... and medicine for he held the secrets to healing humanity. But what many don't know about him is that he was a prophet of sorts. He's the one who found the sacred site in the

Parnassus Mountains called Delphi. There, his sacred temple was built and Pythia, the priestess, communicated his prophecies to the world. You see, he wanted the world to know and understand his father Zeus, hence the oracle of Delphi and the temple."

"I read that many kings and emperors traveled far to seek answers to their questions," I say.

"Yes, you are correct. Even Alexander the Great visited the place for he thought he was the incarnation of Achilles. He traveled to Apollo's Temple and took the great bronze, tin and silver armor and the helmet with its triple crest that belonged to Achilles. The priests were holding it for safe keeping in the temple because it was considered a sacred object and when Alexander saw it, he knew it should be his. So, he took it. He was after all, a descendant and heir to Achilles. But in his mind, he was his reincarnation. Who knows; maybe he was."

"Did you hear these stories as a child?" I'm curious.

"They are our history. And yes, I loved them. My grandfather used to tell me stories of the great gods and goddesses every day of my life as we worked in the fields. These are my fondest memories of Kalamata." He looks off into the distance.

We continue to walk through the ruins, past the Avenue of the Lions who once watched over the Sacred Lake that has since dried up.

"Around 400 B.C. there was a great plague on Delos. People thought it was the wrath of Apollo which is why they decided to move all the pregnant women and the dying to Reneia. It's one of my favorite places because I'm very fond of Apollo. He is the god of light and all that is important in life."

As we walk through the ruins, Christos points out each temple, agora and house and tells their stories. I'm amazed at how many there are. There are the houses of Cleopatra, Dionysus and Trident, the House of Masks, the House of the Dolphins, the Temple of Serapis and the Temple of Apollo. Everything is built from marble with mosaic floors, many still beautifully preserved. Most of the original statues have been removed although a few are still standing. The headless statue of Cleopatra remains and there are other partial statues throughout the city. Many of the columns have been patched back together so one can envision how they looked at the beginning of time.

Below Mount Kynthos lies the Terrace of the Foreign Gods and the Temple of Hera. Everywhere I walk, the mosaics on the floors are superb, but the most memorable is in the House of Dionysus. I shoot photos with my camera and hope the blinding sun doesn't wash them out. He is dressed in robes of gold and white and sits on the back of a panther. Its head is turned upward toward his rider and his eyes are wide, his teeth bared. His huge talons are ominous as he glares at Dionysus, a spear in his hand. It is a glorious mosaic still vibrant with color.

"Roxanna, each year, I hike up to Mount Kynthos to pay homage to the gods. Would you like to join me?"

I consider it for a moment but want to sit alone amongst the ruins.

"No, thanks. I'll sit here and wait for you."

So, I sit outside Apollo's sanctuary and feel the heat of the sun upon my face and eyelids. It is said that Delos is flooded with light, and it is. As I open my eyes and study the ruins, I notice the blurriness and iridescence in the distance that comes with extreme heat and light. It appears that the earth boils there. I close my eyes again to protect them.

I sense someone's presence and immediately open them but I am mistaken for there is no one. I wait, familiar with the energy of the spirit world. I now feel the radiance of light surround me as if I am being bathed in it. I hear a voice.

"I am Helios, the God of Light and of the Sun. You have come to my sacred place to connect with the light and with Apollo. Know that he and I are one. If you study the faces on many of the statues that mankind has sculpted, you will see our resemblance. I assisted in creating this place for him for it is also a place for me. When you pay homage to Apollo, you pay homage to me. You see, the light heals all that ails humankind and Apollo knew this, but no one would listen. Did you know that when you are bathed in sunlight, it rids the body of disease?" He laughs.

He is luminescent. Although he comes to me without form, his voice is strong and powerful. I hold my breath and cannot speak.

"Do not be afraid, as I am here in love. You were meant to come here to connect with me, Roxanna for I am a friend of the one they call Mich-I-El-Rah, the Lord of Truth. Bask in the sun here and heal yourself, for once you feel me, you will yearn for me upon your body every day. That is why you love Capri, the place that worships the sun and the light."

He is gone before I can open my eyes and I'm dazed. I have always called San Michele, Mich-I-El-Rah. He loves Capri … said it was his place … Helios is connected to Apollo … okay … I understand that … but how is Michael connected to them? My mind swims in confusion. I am light-headed.

"Roxanna, are you alright?" Christos has returned from the mountain. "You have been in the sun too long, I fear."

"I need water."

"Let's walk toward the museum. I know the cafe there."

He holds my arm and we walk carefully upon the scorched earth.

"What do you know of Apollo and Helios? Are they connected in any way?" I don't want to tell him a thing.

"Ah, Helios … some believe that Apollo and Helios are one being, that Apollo is a reincarnation of Helios. They say that Helios was not content with only the power of making the sun rise and set each day and with bringing light to the earth. He also wanted to make people aware of the power of the light and its healing effects, so the only way he could do this was to be reborn as Apollo, the Great Healer. They say that even then he wasn't satisfied, thought he had not touched enough of the world so he chose to reincarnate again and again."

We have reached the concession area and I excuse myself and walk into the restroom. I need a few moments alone.

If Helios is Apollo, is he also Michael? He has always been with me in my times of darkness, holding my hand … and the times when I was ill. He is the bringer of light and truth. The bringer of light … everything is running together in my mind like melting snow.

"Yes, yes, we are one and the same."

I hear the voice clearly.

Christos is standing outside the bathroom door with a bottle of water. He hands it to me.

"Are you feeling better?"

"Yes, thank you." I have collected myself.

All the artifacts in the city have been moved to the museum so we enter. Each room is filled with ancient sculptures and bas-reliefs. Most are in good condition while others have been broken and cemented back together. There are many of Apollo, Artemis, Athena, Kouros and other Greek gods and goddesses.

After an hour, we return to the boat. It's mid-afternoon and I'm sorry to be leaving this sacred island. I promise myself I will be back.

"Roxanna, I would like to take you to a beach at the end of the island, Paradise Beach."

I nod my head, yes. I remember the Australian tourists I met on Mykonos, both telling me I needed to go there.

"Good, we will leave from the port." Christos smiles.

CHAPTER 34

Back on Mykonos, we walk to Christos's scooter. I hop on and we ride the three miles to Paradise Beach. It's quite an alluring place. The beach is lined with bars offering exotic drinks as Euro-disco music plays in the air, its gyrating beat hypnotic.

Cabanas and chairs sit at the edge of the turquoise sea. A sandbar is visible a half-mile out. A young man in a pink speedo is standing on it as the Aegean laps at his feet. I realize that most are nude.

It's a nude beach!

Christos laughs at the surprised look on my face.

"Yes, yes, they are nude. But pay no mind. It is old news. For everyone here, it's a way of life."

He takes me to the back of one of the bars called Nirvana where there is a small harem room filled with beds adorned with colorful, stuffed pillows and a small pool of water in the center. I can imagine what goes on in these more private quarters which are somewhat hidden by sheer curtains. I notice couples naked in these private rooms and some are kissing and touching each other or dancing erotically to the music. I turn away, slightly embarrassed.

Where would you like to sit, Roxanna? We can choose a room here or in chairs on the sand closer to the sea. It is up to you."

The private room seems too intimate so I opt for the sea view.

"I'd like to sit on the water if you don't mind."

We head toward the beach and find two chairs. Christos orders a bottle of champagne—Veuve Clicquot, and proceeds to remove his clothing.

"I hope you don't mind, Roxanna. This is how I enjoy the sun." He says it pragmatically, as if it's an everyday occurrence.

"Not at all."

I recline on my chaise, my clothes still on. All the men are naked and most women are topless or completely nude. Strangely enough, no one is looking at anyone else. I begin to relax a bit. I glance around and realize not all are young and beautiful. There are people of all ages with all different body types, but they aren't the least bit self-conscious. They appear rather relaxed. Most are lying on their backs with their arms behind their heads, naked for the world to see and enjoy. I start to giggle.

"What's so amusing, Roxanna?"

"I was just thinking about how self-conscious I am and how hot I am. No one else seems to mind that they are naked as the day they were born. You have to remember, I'm American. We don't sit around naked in front of just anyone."

"Yes, I know. They don't do this on Cape Cod either but you do what you need to do." He pats my leg and says, "I'm going for a swim."

I watch him walk to the water and steal a glimpse of his manhood as he turns around and waves to me. It isn't every day I get to see so many men naked ... such a wide range of flaccid sizes. I had no idea. The champagne and sun have gone to my head and I giggle ... alone in my chair ... surrounded by all this nudity.

Christos's body is well-toned. He dives into the water and I imagine what its coolness would feel like on my perspiring body. I wipe the beads of perspiration from my face and neck. Then I remember what Mich-I-el-Rah said to me before I allowed Valentino to sketch me in the nude, "Drop the puritan attitude ..."

This is silly. Well, it's now or never. I remove my shirt and bra and stand to remove my shorts and panties. *Oh, how delicious!*

The breeze ripples across my bare nipples and the rest of me. I walk as quickly as I can to the water and then into it hoping no one is looking. I dive in and feel the coolness washes over me and I shiver with ecstasy.

Mmmmm ... This is like making love.

I swim out to Christos who is floating near the sandbar, his manhood cresting the water-line.

"Ah, this is the life, eh Roxanna? I'm happy you joined the rest of us in paradise."

He closes his eyes and relaxes back into the water. I do as he does and allow my naked breasts to be revealed to Helios and Apollo and all the other gods and goddesses looking down upon us. We play in the water for quite some time before retiring to the sand where we bask in the sun like lizards.

"Thank you for this, Christos. I'm still quite shy. It's a shame some of us are so inhibited and not as free as these people. Look at what I've been missing."

"I know. I struggled with that raising my sons. Their mother had a very strict upbringing in New England and the naked body was not to be taken lightly." A smile creeps across his sweet face, "I wonder what she would think if she knew I was sunbathing naked with a beautiful woman? She wouldn't understand that it's innocent. I love her far too much to wander into the arms of another, even though you are lovely, my dear."

"You flatter me, Christos. And you're right. She probably wouldn't understand, because I wouldn't either."

When evening comes, Christos takes me to his house in the countryside not far from Paradise Beach. It's a small cubical two-story building, white washed with red door and window frames instead of the blues I have seen everywhere. The only way to the upper level is via an outer stairway which is lined with colorful potted plants. Bougainvillea has grown all around the front door and up the side of the building. Its chimney is shaped like a church spire. There is nothing fancy or opulent about it. It's simple with clean lines and brilliant white paint. Cacti and small trees sit on the property but no gardens, I am guessing, because it remains empty most of the year.

"How often does your wife come here, Christos?"

"She has been maybe five times in the last ten years. She really is a homebody and when she's not teaching in the summer, she loves the Cape house in Falmouth."

We talk as Christos makes dinner, and soon it's laid out on the table. He has prepared fresh local white fish, salad, bread, *keftedes, kopanisti*—a soft spicy cheese made from goats' milk, and *tzatziki*—a sauce made from yogurt with garlic, all of which we stopped to purchase on our way to the house.

"It is nice to have company here, Roxanna. Thank you for allowing me to make dinner for you. I will be leaving the island tomorrow and going on to Kalamata. I love the quiet there and the smell of the olive groves which brings back wonderful memories."

"What was it like growing up in Greece?" I'm interested in the culture which I know little of, aside from its mythology.

"Ah, it was wonderful," he says dreamily. "We did not have much money but I never knew it. Our olive groves were expansive, so as boys, we worked long days during harvest with my grandparents and parents. It was a way of life. The rest of the time, besides the menial chores around the house, we played in the groves on the hillside or went swimming. Life was good." He continues.

"I spent much time with my grandfather whom I loved dearly. At night, we would walk down by the sea and he would tell me stories of ancient times. I still remember his pipe. He'd stopped in the middle of a story to take a puff and let the smoke out. I was always waiting for him to finish. He'd take his time, stretching the silence. It was excruciating but it was also a game between us. He schooled me on how Greece came about—the Creation of the World with Gaia, Eros and Chaos, and the Battles of the Titans and the Giants. Then there were all the stories of the heroes— Herakles, Odysseus and Achilles."

"The story of the Fall of Troy has always been a favorite of mine," I say, hanging on his every word.

"Ah, yes, yes. Paris and the taking of Helen ... Achilles, his dear friend Antilochos, and Agamemnon, the ten-year battle ... I love all the stories as well. Roxanna, do you believe that they existed? The gods and goddesses?"

"Yes, I do." I think of telling him about my experience on Delos, but stop myself.

"You know that no one took Apollo seriously in the matters of healing. He passed these skills on to his son, Asklepios who became a great teacher of medicine."

"I had no idea. I never knew the name of his son although I assumed that he must have had children."

"Asklepios was extremely popular in his time but Zeus was offended by his talents. He wanted to have the most power and didn't want men to believe that Asklepios might be more powerful than him, so he killed him with a thunderbolt. Of course, that didn't put an end to it. There was a temple built in his honor in Epidauros in the 5th century B.C. and thousands traveled there from all over the world to be healed. It is believed that when they made it to the temple and prayed to Apollo, he would later come to them in their dreams and tell them what to do to further their treatment. I find this fascinating. Don't you?"

I'm lost in thought, thinking about that moment on Delos when Helios spoke to me about Apollo and the healing properties of the sunlight. Now, I realize my sole purpose for coming here to Mykonos was to be given this gift of knowing which is now being confirmed by Christos. He's an angel that has come into my life and bestowed his vast knowledge upon me. Nothing is as it seems ...

"I'm sorry, Roxanna. I hope I am not boring you with my foolish preoccupations."

"No! Not at all. Please don't stop. It fascinates me."

"Please, do tell me when you've had enough for I love them as well and could go on forever. Sometimes, I think I have become my grandfather!"

We both laugh as he rises to clear the table.

"Have you ever heard the story of the Sphinx?" My heart skids to a halt; I can hardly get my answer out.

"No, I haven't."

"At one point in time, there was a monster with the head of a woman and the body of a winged lion who came to Thebes and started tormenting and killing everyone who crossed her path. She said she would stop only if she could be defeated and to do so, someone had to solve her riddle."

"The riddle was -

'What being may have two feet, three feet or four feet;
is the only one of all the beings who can move on the earth,
in the air and in the sea; who can change form;
and who moves more slowly when it has three feet?'"

"If anyone came near her and had the wrong answer, she killed them. The King of Thebes at the time, I can't remember his name, proclaimed that if anyone could solve the riddle, he would make him king and he could marry his beautiful daughter, Jocasta." He continues, caught up in his own story.

"Well, at that time, Oedipus was traveling to Thebes and had just killed the king, who unbeknownst to him, was his own father. When he arrived, he came upon the Sphinx and solved the riddle—by the way, the answer was *man*—and she, the Sphinx, was so outraged that she jumped from the rocks and died. Of course, Oedipus became king and then married Jocasta who was actually his mother ... but that's another story for another time."

"Christos, I'm confused about the sphinx. So, it was actually a bad thing?" I'm curious about the one in my dreams and at the Villa San Michele.

"No, the sphinx on Capri is Egyptian and represents the sun god, Helios. It has the head of a pharaoh and the body of a lion, correct?"

"Yes."

"I am speaking of the one in Thebes who was a demon and sent by Hera. It was either Hera or Ares ... I can't seem to remember. Age must be catching up with me."

I'm put to ease knowing it's Egyptian and not Greek. But now this, the fact that it's the representation of the sun god, Helios ... Apollo ... I think of the Pharaoh Ramses who some believe to be the reincarnation of the sun god. My mind is swimming once again. I try to refocus on what Christos is saying.

"... over 4500 years old ... faces the rising sun in the east ... so with its sacred association to the sun and the sun god, and with the head of a pharaoh, it is actually a good thing. It brings luck and healing."

I'm overwhelmed and starting to short-circuit. Christos notices my blank stare.

"It's time for me to deliver you to your hotel. I see you are very tired, my dear." He smiles like a father does and takes my hand and guides me out the door and to his scooter.

We arrive at my hotel and say our goodbyes since we will probably never see each other again.

"It has been a pleasure, Roxanna. I have enjoyed our conversations and your companionship. I hope we meet again someday."

He bends to kiss my hands and my cheeks, and I realize he will be gone in a moment as if I had never met him or known him ... except for the imprint he has left.

"*Efcharistó*, Christos. You have taught me so much, and thank you for your hospitality. I have enjoyed Mykonos just by having known you. I will miss you and our conversations."

"Yes, I will miss you as well. Remember one thing ... remember that feeling of love, will you? Good luck, princess."

He winks and rides off.

I awaken on my last day on the island and lounge in bed as the mist from my dream dissipates. In it, the great sphinx on Capri is speaking to me, but it's an imaginary dream ... not like San Michele coming to me and speaking with me. This one is fabricated by my mind and last evening's stories, I am sure. I can't even remember what it was saying except that the sound of the voice was like that of a woman.

My next thought is of Christos ... such a passionate man. I realize I've only met wonderful, kind and passionate people on this journey. I smile.

Christos talks about life as if it's a sweet dessert, each bite described in detail. I admire him for the way he adores his wife and the fact that he is not uncomfortable undressing himself in front of another woman. I think of the men on Capri holding their babies in their arms as if they are trophies. I think of Marcello who told me how much his two-year-old son Luca meant to him, his chest rising with pride as he pounded it proudly with his fist. Greece is like Italy for me, always teaching me something new,

232

always showing me yet another chamber in my heart to be opened.

I roll over on my stomach and tuck my arms underneath my pillow. "God, I love my life."

CHAPTER 35
SANTORINI, GREECE

The story of the lost continent of Atlantis ... is it fact or fiction? Myth or reality?

At the airport, I purchased a book on Santorini. It says that Plato, in his *Dialogues of Plato*, wrote about Atlantis which consisted of two islands—Meizon and Elasson. From his description of these two land masses, scientists now believe they were actually Santorini and Crete. He even went so far as to say that Atlantis's city of Metropolis was the island of Strongili, now known as Santorini, and that the city of Vasiliki Politeia was Crete.

What will it feel like to be on Atlantean soil? I wonder.

It is believed that this ancient civilization of Atlantis was destroyed in 1500 B.C. by a volcanic eruption which took place on Santorini. The 210-meter tidal wave created by the eruption, was 70 meters high by the time it hit Crete, sixty miles away. The waves reached the island within an hour, devastating the entire civilization within minutes. The eruption sank the central and western parts of Santorini forming the caldera and it was buried under 30 meters of pumice stone.

Santorini has had many names. First it was known as Strongili meaning, "round." Then it was called Kalliste, "most beautiful." And at one point in history, Thera's son settled in Santorini and the name was changed to Thera.

In recent history, the name was changed to Santorini after the main church on the island, which honored St. Irene. It was also called Aghia Irini by the Greeks, and Santa Rini by foreign sailors. Today, it is mostly known as Santorini, except for the locals who call it Thera.

Phew! That's a lot of names!

I check into a "traditional house" which I'm told is a bed & breakfast of sorts. Family is the most important thing to the Greeks. It is their culture and their tradition, hence the name.

I follow the houseboy, Marko up the outer winding staircase to the top floor. I think there are six levels! The vistas are awe-inspiring and breathtaking. From this height, I recognize the caldera that has been left by the volcanic eruption centuries before; a few tiny islands dot the seascape before me.

Santorini is a crescent-shaped island that sits 564 meters (1,850 feet) above the sea. Its walls drop down into the Aegean reminding me of the Grand Canyon with its reddish brown and black colors. It also resembles the surface of the moon. The contrast of the sea and the deep blue sky against the colors of the cliffs is surreal. To my right, houses line the cliffs. They glisten like snow in the moonlight but I'm told it's the white paint that the Greeks use.

"My God ..."

"You like?" Marko is pleased.

He smiles proudly as if he has created it. He's thirty with light-colored eyes and short brown hair. He doesn't look Greek at all and has a thick accent which I don't recognize.

"There," he points to the caldera. "Is called Nea Kameni, New Burnt Island. Behind is Palea Kameni, Old Burnt Island. You see?"

I barely see it with the slight haze of cloud cover due to the altitude. I wonder about the names of the islands and Marko's interpretation of the translations. I would learn later that they were in fact exact translations, as strange as they seem.

"There, Aspronisi, White Island."

He points to a tiny island to the left of the caldera and moves closer to me so we are at the same eye level. He points out the landmass that is further back behind the caldera.

"This, Therasia. Five. Five islands make up Santorini." He holds up five fingers before picking up my bags again.

I tip Marko and hurry out onto my deck with my camera. Before I take any pictures, I bow down to the gods and mouth, "thank you." Santorini takes my breath away. I'm so high up that if there were any clouds, we'd be inside them! The cruise ships far below look like tiny matchboxes and the smaller ships are nearly invisible. I stand for quite some time thinking about Greece and the Greek gods that have been here before me.

This must have been Mount Olympus ...

In my small apartment, a bed lies in the center of a sunken alcove. The windows are covered with lace-trimmed white curtains that dance back and forth in the breeze.

A small living area holds a couch, a sofa table and a large armoire for clothing. Three steps lead me into a dressing area with a large vanity and sink. Beyond this is the marble bathroom with a shower and window above it which overlooks the sea.

I can view the caldera as I shower! This is heaven.

The rooms are painted white—the walls, the floors and the countertops. The accents pieces and the wood trim are painted Greek blue. My mouth is agape in disbelief. It's to die for.

Eventually, I pull myself away and check with Cassandra, the woman at the front desk, for the best tours of the island. She pours me a cup of Greek coffee and we talk about Thera and what to see. She also tells me that she and her husband have built their home from the ground up. Every year, they add another apartment to it. She's proud of the infinity pool on the rooftop that overlooks the sea and the caldera. For this reason, she says she will die here. I like her immediately.

She recommends two tours—a tour of the caldera this afternoon, and tomorrow, the sunset cruise to Oia.

My donkey slowly takes me down a steep road to the port often stopping along the way. My guide prods him from behind, continually scolding him in Greek. Cassandra also suggested this. I laugh at my wildness.

We finally make it to the port below and I'm led to the boat that will take us on the tour. Our guide is a cute, young blonde in her early twenties who reminds me of the actress, Kate Hudson. Her name is Alexandria or Ali for short. She's exuberant with deep dimples and white teeth. I found myself smiling through the entire tour because of her energy. Although she speaks fluent English and was schooled in the States, she tells us she has lived with her Greek father and American mother on Thera her whole life, except for a brief four years in college in the States.

The tour begins and we travel around the three inner islands—Aspronisi, Palea Kameni and Nea Kameni—that Santorini seems to wrap her arms around as if protecting them. Then we ride along the coast of Thirasia, the largest landmass, and the one that is the furthest from Santorini.

We dock in Nea Kameni and our guide leads us up to the rim of the volcanic crater. Here, she tells the story of the strong earthquake and a volcanic eruption that took place. It was so massive that it blew out a chunk of the middle of the once massive island which then filled with sea water. All that was left on top of the water was Thera, the further piece of land that is now called Thirasia, and the little island of Aspronisi. The two smaller islands which were the center of all the volcanic activity—New Burnt Island and Old Burnt Island were created by the volcano itself.

We dock at New Burnt Island or Nea Kameni. Ali jokes about how simple the Greeks are when naming their islands. She explains extensively about the history of Thera - Santorini and the ten known volcanic eruptions, the last one happening in 1950 which formed the Palea and Nea Kameni islets.

She shares with us how the Therans used to worship the twelve Olympic Gods of Ancient Greece and then the Egyptian deities who were brought to the island by the Ptolemies, Cleopatra's family. Today, most inhabitants are Greek Orthodox and Catholic. I learn that like Mykonos and Athens, Santorini had been occupied by the Ptolemies of Egypt, the Romans, the Venetians and the Byzantines. The Ottomans, led by Barbarossa a Turkish Sultan, also occupied the island for a time. He was the same pirate who also invaded and plundered southern Italy including the towns along the Amalfi coast and Capri. I think that after this tour, I will be well-schooled on Greek history.

We hike to the highest point on the island, the Georgis dome, stopping along the way at the Mikri Kameni dome, the Fouque and Reck lava domes, the Niki dome and the great Daphne crater. The walk is strenuous but the vista from the Georgios dome is well worth it. I catch sight of Palea Kameni, and to the east, a valley of gray and black lava fields known as the Liatsika, lava left behind from the eruption of 1950.

It's like being in camp with Ali as our tour guide, her telling Greek jokes and singing Greek songs. She says she can get away with them since she's Greek. Her knowledge and effervescence make the tour.

I arrive back in Thera in time for dinner and ride the *funicolare* to the top where I walk the streets until sunset. I stop to catch a glimpse of the sky and the sea. I cannot believe I'm on this crescent moon of an island with cliffs that raise up into the clouds and upward toward the heavens. I think about the Sun God Helios and picture him with a crown of sun rays above his head standing in his golden chariot with his four-winged horses pulling him across the sky. I remember the house of light that Axel Munthe built and think of San Michele. Even in Greece, I can hear him calling to me. I revel in the scene before me and then say, "Thank you, Helios." I blow a kiss to the sky, to the sun and the sea.

I come upon a doorway open to the sea, the name above it is "Sphinx." Of course, I enter and am in awe. This is clifftop dining at its finest, 1800 feet above the sea. How dizzying. I am led to a white linen-covered table with a long, tapered candle at its center, its fire dancing with the breeze.

I think of Christos and decide to have a glass of champagne, a toast to Santorini. This is what he would have done if he were here. My only regret is that the sun has already set.

The champagne bubbles light up in the candlelight and the local shellfish is sweet. I never for a moment forget that I'm sitting on the edge of the cliffs as I look out over the sea and see the lights of the tiny boats below. Another place where magic happens ... how silly, I think. Magic happens anywhere and everywhere. "It's how you look at life, my dear." I hear Elana's voice in my head.

Then Natale enters my thoughts. I promised myself I'd call him when I arrived here. The thought of hearing his voice sends butterflies from my stomach to my heart, so I pay my bill and leave for the long walk back to the Altana to call him. When I reach my room, it's almost midnight which is perfect since he finishes work then.

My hands shake as I dial his number, afraid of what he might say to me, or worse, that he might not pick up my call at all. He's probably worried about me. I didn't even send a postcard, thought it too cruel since I'm off traveling without him. The phone rings but he does not answer and it goes directly to voicemail.

"*Ciao*, Natale. It's me, Roxanna. How are you? I know it's been awhile. I wanted to say hello and hear your voice. If you're angry with me, I understand. I miss you. I'll try again. *Ciao*."

It's a lame message and I wonder if he thinks so as well. Why didn't I say anything else? Tell him where I am? Tell him I love him? The distance between us has grown. A soft breeze blows gently across my body and I shiver.

Natale has missed Roxanna's call, busy with the last few customers of the evening. When everyone has left and the restaurant is quiet, he retrieves his messages from his phone. His heart stops and his throat closes when he hears her voice. He's been thinking of her day and night. A shot of grappa is the only thing that dulls the ache in his belly and his heart.

He doesn't know how he has survived this long without her. The last few nights have been a bit easier as her memory has started to fade, slowly being erased by time. But now ...

In her message, she never told him where she was. She only says "*ciao*." He listens to it over and over, in hopes that he has missed something ... anything that might mean she is on her way back to him. Crestfallen, he decides to walk the three miles home in hopes that by the time he arrives, he will be physically exhausted. If not, he is prepared to sit up and watch the sun rise, which has become a ritual since she left.

"Damned you, Roxanna!" He kicks the curb hard and pain shoots through his ankle.

"This has to stop. I can't go on like this. No more … I am done … *Finito!*"

○

The cool breeze awakens me as it slips through the thin curtains and steals across my face. The only thoughts I have are of how the air feels and the sounds I hear at this altitude. It's quite heavenly.

Breakfast awaits me on the lower patio where Cassandra has laid out tea, fresh breads, cheeses, fruits and yogurt with honey, a Greek tradition. Marko has come by to chat and see how my stay is. I find out he is from Croatia but works in Santorini during the summer. We talk about which tour I should take today and he confirms Cassandra's recommendation, the Sunset Tour to Oia.

Before the tour, I decide to visit Oia to shop and see the sights. Oia pronounced "**E**-ah" is about ten kilometers from my hotel, its white and okra houses carved into the rocks. It's a quaint village, quieter than Thera and with fewer tourists. The streets are narrow lanes with flagstones and all the buildings and walkways are painted sparking white. Here, more so than Thera, the town is awash with color. The gates, doors, terrace floors and simple wooden patio chairs that are placed here or there, are all painted with bright colors of brick red, blue, fuchsia and yellow. Even the large decorative urns are painted brightly. Bright umbrellas and colorful flowering plants are everywhere. I spend the next three hours enjoying my time here before departing to see a few of the beaches I have read so much about. They say in Santorini, you can choose whichever color beach you prefer because there are black sands, red, brown and gold, all from past volcanic eruptions.

CHAPTER 36

I return to Thera and take the *funicular*, the cable car to the port in search of the 18th century schooner replica for my tour. I cannot seem to find anyone who speaks English. The only words I've grasped since arriving in Greece are *efcharistó* which means "thank you," and it took me about twenty-five times before I finally got it. I'm at such a loss with this language. Now I understand the expression, "It's all Greek to me."

I manage to purchase a ticket. Don't ask me how since no one at the ticket counter speaks English today. The sun and the heat have created a mirage, and the seascape before me is surreal. A massive ship, the *Bella Aurora,* is docked before me. I flip open my brochure to a picture of the ship.

This seems to be the one. There is no one I can ask and no one else is waiting for a tour. If I was in Italy, I would assume everyone was running late.

A young man in his twenties is on board sweeping the deck and I call out to him. He motions to me to board the ship.

"Excuse me. Do you speak English?"

"Ah?" was all I get. Obviously, he does not.

"Do you speak English?"

He shakes his head as if to say no then holds up his index finger signaling me to wait. He leaves and a few minutes later, another man who looks to be in his early forties, appears. They are both well-built and tanned, I imagine from a life of hard work on the ship. Again, I try.

"Do you speak English?"

He shakes his head as well. A third man approaches and he doesn't speak English either.

Mamma mia.

They try communicating in Greek, but I don't understand so I shake my head from left to right. They begin to speak louder as if this will help. I hold my ticket up to them, point to it, and then to their ship.

Finally!

The oldest of the three pulls the others aside. They walk off with my ticket and a few minutes later, return and motion me on board.

I hope someone speaks English on this tour; then I remember that the brochure states there will be an English-speaking guide. I assume they will be here later and everyone else is running late as is the case many times in this part of the world. It seems to be perfectly acceptable. Everyone is late and everyone else waits for them patiently, unlike us Americans.

Since I'm the first to board, I have my choice of seating; I move toward the back where I will have the best view. After ten minutes, the ship suddenly jerks and pulls away from the dock. I realize that besides the three men I have spoken to, I'm the only other person on board. I'm dumbfounded. Eventually, my curiosity gets the best of me and I rise and walk over to one of the men.

"Excuse me, but where is everyone else?"

He stares at me blankly. I move to the next man and he talks rapidly in Greek, all the while using his hands to express himself. He keeps moving them as if he were smoothing the wrinkles out of a blanket ... and I think that if I was in Italy, this would mean *piano, piano* ... easy, easy. He motions with his hand for me to sit. I move back to my seat and start to panic.

What's happening? I'm the only one and I'm here with three Greek men who can't speak a word of English. Where are they taking me? My imagination is working overtime as I quickly dream up different scenarios. I'm stupefied.

Then a soft mist from the sea blows up with the breeze and pulls my hair from its clip, pushing the strands in front of my eyes.

I pull them back and carelessly fastened them into place. At the same time one of the men approaches me. He motions toward the two islands in front of us.

"Nea Kameni ... Palea Kameni." He points to them as he says their names and then points to himself and to me and shakes his head as if to say, "this is where we are going." I take this to mean we are headed there, just as the guide book says. Okay, this is a bit strange. Me and the three of them ... at least they're following the tour in the guidebook. Why wouldn't they cancel the tour if only one passenger showed up?

I quietly look out to sea as the schooner slices through the water as if it were a knife cutting through an ice cream cake. I say a quiet prayer and ask if I should be alarmed and the answer that comes back to me is, "No."

Okay, I guess I'll sit back and enjoy this tour.

With closed eyes and my head tilted upward toward the sky, the sun is hot upon my face making me drowsy. I feel like a cat ready for a nap. I'm still slightly nervous about this predicament of being the only sightseer on board but I trust that all is well.

The motion of the schooner is smooth and calms my nerves as we make our way to Nea Kameni. Within forty minutes, we stop and drop anchor. Two of the men jump overboard for a swim and call to me to join them. I'm still not comfortable enough so shake my head and say, "no, thank you." Instead, I watch them as they play like little boys trying to out-dive and out-swim each other, laughing all the while. The youngest is about twenty-five and the others tease him constantly which seems to be a Greek tradition where the older men torment the youngest in the group. They wrestle and take turns dunking each other.

Once back on the ship, we pull up anchor to move on to Palea Kameni, the smaller island. Here, they drop anchor closer to shore so I can swim in the natural hot springs that have been created by the volcano. The two younger ones jump in and I follow their lead. It's warm and refreshing and I cover my body in mud as they all do. I'm enjoying myself and am entertained by their horseplay.

There's a small church on this island and they motion for me to go. I do. It's very sparse and I can tell it's no longer used. I imagine that long ago, sailors stopped in for a quick prayer to keep them safe on their long voyages to far-off places.

Once back on the ship, we head toward Thirasia, the farthest of the islands, and sail around its entire mass. The three men come to me and introduce themselves. The oldest, Apollo is about sixty and the captain of the ship. His complexion is rugged, I imagine, from being on the sea and in the sun his whole life.

Palo is the middle-aged one. As he tells me his name, he puffs out his chest and thumps it with bended thumb. The indents on his face appear to be dimples but instead, are deep crevices connected to the laugh lines on his cheeks. His hair is thick, long and black, and pulled into a ponytail reminding me of Yanni. I can tell he is the mischief-maker, always trying to pull one over on the others.

The youngest is Dino, probably short for Constantinos, a traditional Greek name from which many other names spring. His face is strong, but the expression on it is soft. He studies me with gentle curiosity as I cower in my seat. The wind whips through the curls of his shoulder-length hair, sending them flailing all about the contours of his face. In another situation, I might have thought him handsome.

They're all smiling and seem happy. I wonder if it's the work they do and their life on the sea. I try to imagine what it would be like to sleep on a ship such as this, the waves and the rocking of the ship lulling me to sleep.

These men are close friends, the kind that would probably die for one another. I see it in the way they are with each other. Even though Apollo and Palo tease Dino, Palo instigating it all, they are tight as I imagine they must be on a ship such as this where all hands and eyes have to watch one another and become one as they master the sails.

As we circle Thirasia, Palo points to different areas on the island and calls out Greek words which I assume are the names of the cities—Agrilia, Potamos, and Manolas. Occasionally, one of them will comes to me and communicates via sign language or Greek. I nod my head as if I understand, but I don't.

Palo points toward the horizon and mouths something but I don't understand. He may be trying to explain where we are headed next. The only reason I think this is because I've read the itinerary in the brochure. We are to circle Thera and then set sail to Oia to watch the sun set. Palo proudly tells me that the name of the ship is the *Bella Aurora* as he points to the floorboards and spread his hands out saying its name in English.

Dino turns the music on and it plays through speakers on the deck. It's a mix of international artists and pieces that sound like a Buddha Bar compilation. This, along with the light of the day creating millions of dazzling diamonds upon the surface of the water, soothes me. This is paradise and I'm sailing to the ends of the earth, somewhere in Greece where civilization began with the gods. I think of Helios and Apollo.

Strange that Apollo is captain's name ...

Dino and Palo have pulled their black tee-shirts off and wrapped them around their heads. Their bare suntanned chests and backs are brown and shiny in the sunlight. For a moment, they resemble modern-day pirates ... or is it my imagination? As we get closer to the northwestern tip of the big island, the dance of the raising of the sails begins.

I watch in awe as both men work in unison, an extension of each other as they move quickly from one place to another working the sails and rigging. Dino follows Palo's lead as he seizes the lines to release them. They nod their heads and speak the unspoken language of sailors that have been at sea together for a long time. When the furled linen sails are in the correct position high above them, Dino shimmies up the mast to release them, moving quickly from one area to another like a monkey. He unfastens them and they drop, filling quickly with the wind. The schooner picks up speed and its sharp prow slices through the Aegean Sea as an Arabic singer croons his song to a rhythmic beat ... so appropriate for the scene before me.

My heart is full and I'm amazed at what I have just witnessed ... the dance of the high seas, between the wind and the sea and the men who know how to harness its energy. And in this moment, Aeolus, the Greek god of the winds comes to mind.

We move quickly toward Oia where we will watch the sunset. The tour book says this is the most desirable place in Thera to view it from. Dino brings Retsina, Greek wine which I know is made from pine resin, hence the very pungent taste. He motions to me to come to the helm where Apollo is. They have laid out a spread of appetizers of *keftedes*, stuffed grape leaves, olives, breads and cheeses. We enjoy the food and wine as we move along the coastline of Thera toward its northern point where Oia lays. I'm blinded by the brilliance of the sunlight as it reflects off the white painted houses high atop the cliffs.

Dino has brought a mandolin and starts to play as Apollo and Palo sang. The wine, the wind, the music and the sounds of the ship, as it moves across the Adriatic, relax me and I close my eyes. As we approach Oia, the sun is at the edge of the horizon and the colors of the sky and the sea begin to change into orange and golden hues. Paradise. There is no place on earth that I would rather be than right here, right now.

Once again, the dance of the sails begins and both Palo and Dino take their places to lower them. Apollo must have put the music back on for a Greek singer is crooning another perfect song. I move to my seat for the ride back to Thera. The colors begin to fade as the schooner picks up speed. I quickly realize we are not moving back toward the south and Thera but continuing around Oia and to the northeastern side of the island. I jump to my feet in a panic and approach Palo.

"Palo, Thera is in that direction." I point toward the rear of the ship. "We need to go that way." I'm now officially alarmed.

"Anafi. Anafi."

"No, Thera! I need to get back to Thera!"

On hearing the commotion, Dino has gone to get Apollo.

"Thera is that way! Where are we going?" I ask Apollo as he approaches.

"Anafi. Anafi."

He pats my shoulder as if to tell me everything will be okay and heads toward the helm. I am shaken, shivering with fear.

Am I in danger? Am I being kidnapped?

CHAPTER 37
CYCLADES ISLANDS, GREECE

This isn't my tour! How stupid of me to think so and to board this ship in the first place! I reach into my bag for something warm but only find a damp towel. Palo catches sight of me shivering and brings a heavy jacket, probably his own.

Okay. I'm sleeping on the ship for the night, but what will happen in the morning? What about tomorrow? I know we're heading east away from Thera because the lights are behind us, receding in the distance.

Dino brings a bottle of ouzo and four cups; the others join us. He pours and we toast. I grimace at the taste but it warms my insides.

We sit together and they talk amongst themselves, laughing and poking at each other. Apollo sits back and lights his pipe, clearly enjoying himself. They seem kind enough ... but can I trust them?

My lids suddenly grow heavy. Apollo sees this and brings me a blanket. He motions for me to lay down and go to sleep. I take his direction gladly but try to keep one eye on them. Before I know it, I'm gone from this world.

The sounds of the sea awaken me. It's early morning and Dino is washing the deck as Palo works with the nets. Palo sees me sitting up and races off only to return with a cup of Greek coffee. I gladly sip the thick and bitter brew. I assume it would be too much to ask for sugar and how could I communicate this anyway? Apollo brings a pot of coffee and breakfast which consists of bread, cheese and some type of cold fish, which doesn't look very appetizing, but I'm starving and devour it.

Apollo tries to tell me where we are headed.

"Anafi." He points toward the helm. Then he points toward the stern and says, "Thera." I think he's telling me we will move on to Anafi before returning to Thera.

"No, Thera! Take me to Thera," I say. He smiles, puffs on his pipe and lays his hand flat out in front of him. The gesture either means *aspetta*, wait, calm down or not now. I haven't a clue.

In the distance, an island appears which I assume is Anafi. What will they do there? And what will they do with me? Maybe they really are modern-day pirates and have stolen this ship. But they're feeding me. No one has crossed the line with me or made any advances so this is a good sign. I have a knot as big as a fist in the pit of my stomach.

As we move into the bay, Apollo drops anchor and he and Dino prepare to take the dinghy to shore while I stay with Palo. Time drags as my mind runs wild.

An hour later, they return and load crates onto the ship. Are they filled with drugs? Guns? Maybe it's a smuggling operation. Is there a drug problem in Greece? I wish I had read up on their culture and their crime statistics before I came here.

We leave the port and I look back at Anafi. Only one town is visible on the island. I discern the remnants of an old castle which I assume was built by the Venetians since Anafi had been conquered by them in the past.

After we set sail, I approached Palo.

"Where are we going now?" He stares blankly at me. I point toward Anafi and say, "Anafi." Then I point to the horizon before us hoping he understands my question. He does.

"Ah, Amorgos."

He mouths something that I think means east and points

toward Thera. Then, he points toward the horizon and mouths Amorgos again, and another word I think means north. Another island ...

I sit in my usual spot and resign myself to the fact that I am powerless.

I observe Dino busily polishing the wood while Palo polishes the brass. Well, if they had stolen the schooner, they wouldn't be taking such good care of it, would they?

It's noon, the sun directly overhead. My stomach starts to groan from hunger. Then I realize with horror that I haven't brushed my teeth since yesterday morning.

God, I wish I had a toothbrush.

I'm delirious as I think of being on this ship, in the middle of the ocean, on the other side of the world with three pirates, and I'm ruminating about brushing my teeth!

I lie on the deck, bathing in the sun even though I'm covered in 30-sun block. I'm happy to have remembered it. Who knows how long I will be here.

Sitting alone with my thoughts and no one to talk to reminds me of Mio Paradiso and my little villa. There are no distractions here except for my own mind.

After the fears die down and I'm a bit more relaxed, realizing they aren't going to harm me, I'm able to enjoy this tour, if that's what you'd call it. I try to pretend that this is my own sailing vessel, and a fine one it is. It has two large rectangular masts and two smaller triangular ones. The deck and floor seem to be made of hand hewn wood that has been highly polished and the rails are made of brass that shimmer in the sunlight. I know absolutely nothing about sailing ships, but I do know this one handles well ... either that or Apollo has a gift.

Once again, they come with food. This time, we eat fresh white fish that Palo must have pulled up in the nets this morning. There is also Greek salad, bread, olives and wine. Again, they converse with one another as I strain to hear any words I might recognize. But it's all Greek to me.

Apollo points in the direction of the islands we are heading toward and says, "Amorgos." I contemplate the island and notice a monastery built into the side of the mountain covered with crosses. Another ruin, a Venetian castle, sits at the top.

This time, we dock on the island and both Dino and Palo leave, and once again I'm motioned to stay with Apollo. I watch them unload eight crates from the Bella Aurora. We are close enough to shore so that I can see them. A man in a black sea cap and an old tattered button-down work shirt hands money to Palo. What could possibly be in them? I haven't seen any signs of guns ...

Dino returns to the ship but Palo walks toward the town, only to return ten minutes later with four packages wrapped in white paper. I imagine they are filled with either cocaine or marijuana. Maybe they're moving drugs from island to island.

Palo boards the ship and the other men slap him on the back as if to acknowledge his hard work. He beams as he speaks to them in Greek, pounding his chest. I can't believe I didn't even buy a Greek-English dictionary for this trip. What was I thinking?

Stupido.

I had been so in love with Italy, wanting to learn the language, that I didn't want anything else to interfere with it or cloud my mind. Now, because of my stupidity I am out here in the middle of Greece at the mercy of hand signals and charades.

Exhaustion has taken over my mind and it's suddenly too tired to talk to me. There is nothing for me to do except watch the men as they work. I've been told via sign language that we are heading east for the island of Ios. This is promising, since Thera is also east.

Palo is teaching Dino how to tie a special knot with the rope which becomes a game. It's probably not your typical knot, but a puzzle or joke that he's playing on Dino that he can't seem to master. Each time he fails, Palo laughs and talks with his hands as if to say, "It's so simple ... watch again." After thirty minutes of this, Dino gets tired of the game and walks away, throwing his hands up in the air, leaving Palo laughing behind him.

The winds have picked up. The sky quickly changes and heavy black clouds roll in. Apollo yells for Palo and Dino to quickly lower the sails so they race to their posts. It's a matter of minutes before the job is finished and the ship rocks wildly with the power of the sea.

I remember this term from Capri used by Enzo, a young man who works on a boat in Marina Grande. I had asked for its translation in Italian and he told me it was *forza del mare*. At the time, I had tried to arrange for a boat ride around the island but there was a storm moving in the next day and the force of the sea was *quattro*, four, too high for a small craft on the water. I guess that, in this moment, the force of the sea must be a six or seven.

The winds whip the water into churning waves that rock the ship violently; all I can do is hold on to the rail and hope I don't fall overboard or vomit. My stomach is turning over and over like a washing machine. I hold my breath in hopes this might help but I realize it only makes me feel worse. A thin film of sweat has covered my clammy body. I become violently ill over the side of the boat, releasing all into the foamy sea. My hair and face are wet and I shiver uncontrollably.

Dino yells behind me but I can't move my head in fear of vomiting again. Palo runs to me, picks up my limp body and lays me down on the deck. Then he gives Dino instructions. He quickly returns with blankets and a bottle of ouzo. The ship continues to tip back and forth wildly; I wish it would stop.

Palo takes something out of a small tin that smells like camphor and rubs it under my nose. Each time I breathe in, it relaxes my stomach muscles. He speaks to me, softly, his gentle voice calming, even though I don't know what he is saying. He wets a towel and places it on my forehead. After a few minutes, he motions to Dino to pour the ouzo into a cup. Palo holds my head up and Dino makes me drink. I want to gag, but I don't. He won't remove the cup until I finish it. Then, he motions with his hands as if to say, "piano, piano … easy, rest now."

I lie on the floorboards, my eyes closed, drifting in and out of consciousness as the rain falls upon my face. I'm lost in the misery of retching, which has caused my stomach and chest great pain, and feeling comforted by the men, the camphor, the ouzo and the blankets.

Is this what it feels like to die at sea?

The thunder and lightning have raced toward the horizon taking the rain with it. The winds have died and the sea is an eerie calm. I quickly fall into sleep.

When I awaken, I'm miraculously better. Who knows how much time has passed. I only remember how ill I felt and how Palo took care of me. I pull myself from the blanket and sit, my back against the polished wood. Palo and Dino are standing on the rocking ship, their strong legs firmly planted. The motion doesn't seem to bother them. I carefully stand as they do and realize I am no longer bothered by the movement, no longer fighting the motion of the ship.

I, too am rocking with the motion of the vessel, relaxing into it … surrendering to it … becoming one with it. Palo turns toward me, smiles and winks.

On the darkened horizon, virga dances high in the sky never touching the sea. I smile for the first time today.

By late afternoon, we reach the island of Ios, a mountainous island with many coves cut into the rocks, the crystal-clear water moving in and out of each one. Its white houses and the chapels remind me of Thera.

Once anchored, the pirates motion for me to come with them. We take the dinghy into the port, disembark and walk into the town and a tavern. An older man named Dimitri comes to Apollo and kisses and hugs him. An old friend possibly. A sea cap covers most of his silver hair and he sports a large, thick mustache that spreads wide when he smiles.

Dimitri motions us to a table and food and wine are quickly brought. We feast for hours as the owner's wife brings dish after dish. I'm much better now that I'm on land so my appetite has come back to me.

Palo and Dino sit quietly as the older men talk and tell stories, none of which I understand. I wonder if I should try to escape. Would anyone on this small island speak English? Would I be better off staying with the pirates in the hopes that they might take me back to Thera?

I quickly scan the pub and realize most of the patrons are men. They seem to be kind and gentle people ... not like they're part of a smuggling operation. Then I realize they couldn't possibly be people who buy and sell drugs or weapons. I can tell by their eyes. They seem honest and kind, the type you can trust with your life. They look like people who would take you in and care for you if you needed them to do so.

I look up to see Apollo gazing at me. His eyes show the same compassion and empathy that these people do. I wink at him and he winks back. I decide that this is another wild adventure I'm on and that I must trust they will deliver me safely back to Thera. Trust ... okay. I take a deep breath, allowing myself to finally let go of all the madness in my head. Then, I hear the spirit laugh.

Is this a wild goose-chase you have sent me on? I ask him with my mind and not my mouth so no one else will hear. I furrow my brow to show him how serious I am and he laughs louder. In an instant, he disappears and I'm drawn back to the table and the men talking.

Apollo whispers to Dino and Palo. They leave and minutes later, they return with two crates. The owner smiles and claps his hand excitedly as if the trunks were filled with treasures. He quickly pries them open. Inside are jars of olives, pickled fish, cheeses wrapped in paper and bottles of wine.

Dimitri cradles Apollo's face with both his hands and kisses him hard. Then, they touch forehead-to-forehead. He thanks him for the gifts, and this time, there is no money that passes hands. After many kisses, hugs and back-slapping, we leave for the ship.

CHAPTER 38

Once on board, Palo says, "Ios," and points back to the island we just left. Then he says, "Sikinos," and points out to sea.

"No Sikinos!" I shake my head back and forth. "I want to go to Thera, Thera!"

"Sikinos," he says firmly as he makes the motion with his hands of smoothing out the wrinkles in a blanket.

"Yeah, yeah, I get it … *piano* … *piano*." I say with deep frustration.

"*Parla Italiano?*" Palo asks excitely.

"*Si, si, Io parlo un po'. Tu?*"

Great God in heaven!

"*Un poco.*" He points to his chest and nods his head up and down.

Good! Let's see how this goes.

"*Adesso*, Sikinos. *Dopo*, Thera." Palo tells me that next, they will stop in Sikinos but later they will go to Thera.

"*Quando* Thera? *Oggi?*" I ask when exactly and if it will be today.

"No, *domani* Thera." Tomorrow.

Okay … another night on the ship. This is insane! Will anyone ever believe this actually happened to me?

"Okay, *domani* … *promesso?*"

Palo laughs full and hardy with his crooked teeth, his head bobbing up and down.

"Si, promessa." He crosses his heart.

We have entered the waters surrounding the island of Sikinos. The sun is setting and its light has cast an orange glow upon the turquoise sea, an incredibly beautiful site.

The island is like the others, illusory snowcaps blanketing it. Palo tells me we will go into town in the morning to deliver *così,* things and then we will leave for Thera, arriving there late afternoon. I'm happy with this news and prepared to enjoy the rest of my captivity.

As we drink Retsina and eat the food Dimitri has given us, I relax and enjoy the stories and the conversations that Palo translates into Italian for me, and most of them I understand.

"Perché mi hai preso, why did you take me?" I ask.

Palo talks with the others, then answers. *"Per divertimento e ti posso far vedere le isole*, for fun and so I could show you the islands."

Really? Another joke, I'm sure, instigated by Palo. I teasingly punch him in the chest. He laughs and puts his hand where I hit him as if he is bruised there, and Dino and Apollo laugh at Palo as if to say the joke is now on him.

I look up into the heavens, and the stars wink at me, as if to say, "Everything is good."

Mich-I-el-Rah appears before me. We stand at the rail looking out at the night sky filled with shooting stars.

"Look, the heavens have come to offer you a wish. What do you wish for, Roxanna?"

I think for a moment.

"I wish for more escapades such as this!" I shake, even though I am still asleep.

"And so you shall. Not everyone has your courage."

"It's easy when you have angels and spirits surrounding you."

"Ah, but everyone does … silly humans. You only need to ask for help."

We stand quietly looking outward. I feel the moist air in my lungs and the undulation of the ship. I also feel his hand on my shoulder. He is the first to speak.

So, sweet woman, you finally got it. This time, it was about trust and surrender." He smiles at me lovingly.

"Why didn't you come to me sooner and tell me I would be safe?"

"It was your final lesson ... it is not about this voyage. It's about your life. Surrender and trust. Haven't I always walked with you and kept you safe?"

"Yes."

"Haven't you always felt me near?"

"Yes."

"Then all is as it should be." He smiles lovingly with his penetrating electric blue eyes.

"It is about surrendering to every moment in life and letting it take you like a lover. It's only good if you allow it to be. Now go and surrender to the rest of your life. Go and make love to it! And remember, if you need me, just call my name."

"Thank you for everything." I'm filled with gratitude, my tears now flowing.

"No need to thank me. I will always walk with you as you learn to walk with a foot in both worlds." He kisses my forehead and then dissipates into the mists of the sea.

I awaken electrified. Every word he has spoken comes back to me; I will never forget them. I realize for the first time, I've actually had a conversation with him and have been able to ask a question and receive an answer before he has disappeared. Our encounters and relationship have moved to a new level. This whole adventure—being kidnapped by modern-day pirates, is about trust and surrendering to life.

I cannot sleep, so I lie awake for hours gazing up at the stars.

After our morning delivery to Sikinos, we have breakfast together before Dino and Palo are off to doing their daily chores while I'm left alone to contemplate my time on the ship. I'm going to miss this life on the high seas. It was quite an adventure having my own private schooner and crew to take me to far-flung places.

When we reach the port in Thera, none of us wants the journey to end. Palo throws Dino overboard, Dino mouthing Greek words of protest all the way down until they are muffled by the water. Then, Palo proceeds to chase me around the deck until he catches me and throws me overboard, too. I pretend to act annoyed and protest in Italian. He then jumps in after us as Apollo watches from the rail of the ship, all the while, belly-laughing at our horseplay.

The water refreshes me and cleanses my body of the remnants of my life of no baths for these past few days. I swim to Palo and pound his chest in protest as I had done before, but he's too fast a swimmer for me.

Eventually, it's time to say our goodbyes. It isn't easy to part. I hug them all and Palo takes my hand and carefully helps me off the ship, in his sweet and gentle way, as he did when I was seasick. I'm going to miss my new friends, the Pirates of the Cyclades.

Onboard my flight to Napoli, I remember how concerned Cassandra was with my absence for the past few days. When I eventually returned, she was curious and thought I'd met someone, fallen in love and had been whisked away to another island. She wondered if I would ever return to fetch my things from the room and she was quite curious, asking lots of questions. But all I would tell her was that I had found a wonderful adventure, and didn't divulge any more than that.

God, if she only knew, what would she think? I feel as if I've been gone forever.

CHAPTER 39
CAPRI, ITALY

Sleep comes easily once I'm settled at *Mio Paradiso*. It stays with me for the next twelve hours in my soft bed with Italian linens, much softer than the floorboards on the ship. So many scenes of my time in Greece weave together in my dreams. When I awaken, I realize that once again, I am wrapped up in the magic of Capri. I have come home, and this time, I will stay for a while.

I don't leave the villa for three days. I lounge on the property staring at the Mediterranean as if I am waiting for something to rise up out of it. I sit and watch the hydrofoils cross the bay to Napoli, Ischia, Sorrento and Amalfi. I watch the lizards and the cats as they lazily bask in the warm sunlight. And when I'm tired of sitting, I walk from one end of the property to the other, stopping at each flower, each bush and each grapevine to see them all and to note what new babies have bloomed or how much they have grown since I've last seen them.

I am elated to be home.

Yes, this is my home.

My last adventure was quite different than all the others in that I had no control over my surroundings, the events that took place or the people I was with. I had to learn to surrender, to give up control and allow life to carry me. Once I was finally able to, I realized I could do it in any situation.

God, how I've grown ... I promise from this day forth, I will be open, flexible and trusting, no matter what comes my way.

My breath catches because I know myself and I know it's easier said than done. Not having the control lever in my hand sends chills through me. But then I remember San Michele, Mich-I-el-Rah and know he will always be with me, never too far away should I need him.

The flame of a candle flickers a golden glow across the room as I sit in my little kitchen enjoying my dinner. Italian music emanates from my laptop as a slideshow of my Greek journey plays before me—Athens, the Acropolis and the Plaka, dancing with Stavros, Mykonos, Cristos, Delos, Paradise Beach, Santorini ... I mean Thera, the sunset over Oia, the brightly colored buildings atop the caldera and my adventures on the high seas with modern-day pirates.

I have numerous pictures of my time on the ship with my new friends—Apollo, Dino and Palo. I have captured their mischievousness and their smiles, and at the same time, their hard work as they raise and lower the sails and care for the ship. I see the deep lines in Palo's face as he grins at Dino the day they were playing with the knot. I captured Dino's lean and muscular body as he walks the mast above my head to raise the sails. I had photographed Apollo in the tavern on Ios, the pride on his face, as his old friends, the owner and his wife, praised him for his gifts. Now, I realize how much I miss them and will probably never see them again. Ah, the memories ...

I love my life.

I smile at the pots and pans hanging on the wall and at my computer screen. Then, I stand and dance to the music, twirling and whirling around my tiny kitchen. I feel free and happy having roamed throughout Italy and Greece. And this day, this night, this meal is my crowning glory, for I have finally found freedom—the freedom of learning to surrender to whatever came next. I'm intoxicated, without even a sip of wine, and soon take myself to bed. I hope my dreams are of my journey on the ship.

And they are. This night, I am sleeping on the schooner with my pirates. My bed rocks as if I am on the sea. I laugh into the wind with Palo, Apollo and Dino and then I'm on the isle of Ios eating in the pub as we had done. I walk through my dream as if I'm still there, just as I did with Capri when I was in California. Somehow, Greece has changed me. I'm no longer the same woman. All my pieces have finally come back to me.

Natale's face awakens me in the middle of the night. It's as if he's in the room with me. But then, he's gone. I feel guilty because I did not think of him once when I was on the ship. Is this odd? I feel a heaviness as I realize that somehow, we are fading from each other. Sleep is now elusive so I walk outside and watch the light as it changes the night sky into dawn.

As I walk into town, my mind is on Natale. I am not paying attention and as I turn the corner I literally bump into Nunzio. He almost knocks me over.

"Roxanna! Are you okay?" We both laugh.

"Yes, I'm fine." I straighten myself and he kisses my cheeks.

"Where have you been? It has been a long time since I have seen you."

"I have been to Greece—to Mykonos, Delos, Athens and Santorini. It was wonderful, Nunzio."

"I have also visited Santorini. The view is beautiful, is it not?"

"*Si, si.* It reminded me of Anacapri a bit because it's so high in altitude."

"Hmmmm ... not me. It's very different, but it's okay. You know they say pirates still roam in these waters. I hope you were careful."

I laugh.

"You have no idea how careful I was, Nunzio! I need to shop for food now. It's good to see you. *Ciao.*"

"Welcome back, Roxanna. *Ciao, ciao.*"

He waves goodbye to me and I turn toward the *piazza* and walk down the small street to Federico's studio.

"Ah, *bella, come va*? Where have you been? I have missed your smiling face." More hugs and kisses.

"*Bene, bene.* I have been to Greece traveling around a bit and now I'm back."

"Please, come sit with me and tell me all about it."

He takes my arm and walks me into his studio to the little couch. The tourists have not arrived on the first bus of the day so we have time to talk about my holiday before he must tell them the story of each painting.

"Can I get you something to drink, *bella?*"

"No, *grazie.* I'm okay. It was nice traveling but I missed Capri."

"Yes, she does that to you. It's intoxicating, like the scent of love. Once it grabs your heart and invades your senses, you are captivated and can never leave."

"Said like a true *artista.*" He laughs at my Italian accent. I tell my tales of Greece but leave out my capture and journey throughout the Cyclades.

"Sounds like a wonderful trip. Where will you go next, Roxanna?"

"Federico, I'm staying put for a while. I miss my home here. All this traveling ..." I pinch myself at the thought for I am one lucky girl.

He turns to me and takes my hands; he looks deeply into my eyes.

"*Amore mio,* have you started to paint yet?"

"No, not yet. Soon, though."

I fidget nervously. He immediately releases my hands from his, rises from the couch and starts to pace as he rubs his forehead.

""*Mamma mia, Mamma mia* ... what in God's name are you waiting for, Roxanna? If you don't use this gift, it will be taken away from you. You are doing a disservice to yourself and to all of *Italia* if you do not paint."

I feel scolded.

"Okay *domani*, tomorrow. I will come and paint with you. I promise."

He sits and takes my hands again. One by one, he kisses my fingers, talking in between each kiss.

"You ... will come ... at 10:00 o'clock ... and I will have ... a canvas for you ... and we will sit ... until you are comfortable ... and no longer fear … the paint brush …" He smiles at his silly joke and I start to laugh.

"I'm afraid, I guess."

"But what are you afraid of, *amore mio*?" His eyes are filled with compassion.

"I'm afraid I have forgotten how … and maybe won't be as good as I used to be." My laughter quickly leaves me and tears fill my eyes.

"Oh, *bella, non finisce mai*, it is never-ending. Once you have the gift, you will always have it. You only need to work the muscles of your creativity that you have abandoned for so long. It will all come back to you." He wipes my cheek with his thumb. "You will be okay, *bella*. You wait and see, *domani*. I will be with you holding your hand. We great painters have to stick together, you know."

"*Grazie*, Federico. I will be back tomorrow at ten o'clock." I hug him and kiss his cheeks. "I have to go now. *Ciao*."

"*Ciao, ciao … domani*."

As I walk the street toward the San Michele Villa, I think of his sweetness. Since I came to the island, he has counseled me, guided me and been a dear friend. If I'm going to dive into the abyss of painting again, who better to hold my hand than Federico. And I could not be in a better place than on this island.

I am let into the San Michele Villa *gratis*, free of charge since I visit so often. The tourists have not yet arrived today so I'm alone as if it's my own private residence. I meander through the gardens, breathing in as I go. I gaze out over the *Mediterraneo* with my hand upon the back of the great sphinx and realize I have no wishes, so instead, I tell him all that I am grateful for. I try to state them all but am sure I have forgotten a few.

The sea is calm, the sky melted into it … so peaceful, so quiet. I only hear the beating of my heart and the sound of a distant scooter on the winding road below.

Soon, the silence is interrupted by a large group of tourists who have arrived on the first bus of the day. I decide that it's time to leave for Capri to purchase paint supplies and to stop and say hello to Raffaello. It has been a very long time.

When I arrive at the Hotel Quisisana, I search the restaurant for him but he's not there. I ask the man at the front desk. He makes a call and tells me Raffaello will be down in a few minutes.

I think of Natale and wonder if I will feel differently about Raffaello when I see him. My mind wants to move to chaos and confusion about my feelings for two men. But there is no time. Raffaello suddenly appears.

"Roxanna, this is a surprise."

He's happy to see me and my heart responds reminding me of this crazy love for him. We embrace each other and kiss each other's cheeks, slowly ... as slow as we possibly can without giving ourselves away. Neither of us wants to part, but we know we must.

"Raffaello, I've been traveling and just returned to the island yesterday. I was in Capri and wanted to come to say hello."

"I'm happy to see you. Would you like me to take you to the dining room?" His hair has grown a little longer and bits of silver frame his face. The salt and pepper look serve him well.

"No, thank you. It's too early for lunch." He looks disappointed.

"Come, let's walk." He takes my arm and guides me out into the gardens. The aroma of the blooms mixed with the salty air are intoxicating.

"I have been thinking about you since the first time I met you, Roxanna."

"I think about you too, Raffaello," I say shyly.

"It's nice to know that we have met again after all this time."

We both laugh at our private joke. We are still arm in arm, his hand placed over mine for safe-keeping.

"I thought you had left to go back to America."

"I would have come to say goodbye first; I'm staying through the summer."

"I'm pleased to hear this," he says with a broad smile.

I love the lines in his face. I want to touch them but know he is a married man and this is too intimate a gesture. To take my finger and caress this line, this crease that runs along his mouth, would be like making love to someone's face ... a secret touch that would arouse the senses, both his and mine. He seems to feel my thoughts for he shudders.

"Roxanna, I miss you." He whispers now. "I have a room here where sometimes I rest in between my shifts. Please come with me." I can tell it is not easy for him to ask.

"Raffaello, I can't." I pull away from him and walk a bit to put space between us so I may speak the truth.

"I met someone in Rome. I'm in love with him and I can't complicate things ... and you are complicated because you are married to someone else. And I, too am complicated now because I am in love."

"It does not matter. I have two wives—her and you." He smiles.

"Yes, but life has taken us down different paths this time. Do you understand?"

I notice the hurt in his eyes. Although he is married, I think he dreams we might be together someday. He walks toward me and takes my arm and squeezes my hand, letting me know he cares. Although it is simply a touch between two hands, it's like a soft kiss.

"*Capisco.* But I am still yours and will be here for you. For now, we can stay like this."

We walk through the garden that faces the sea and the Bay of Napoli.

"It is a good life here, Roxanna. There is no other place like this. I hope you stay forever and never leave. Maybe someday ..."

"Who knows where life will take us next. Every time I think I know, it turns out I don't." I pause for a few moments.

"I must go now."

I pull away to face him and take both his hands in mine, raising them to my lips to kiss them. We are at the edge of the garden and there is a tree blocking us from the hotel. He pulls me close. Softly and sweetly, he kisses my lips. It's a quick and gentle, caring kiss ... the deepest of its kind and I let him do so. It seems that it's a forever moment, although I'm sure it is only a few seconds.

"Please come soon and I will feed you and take care of you, *amore mio.*"

"*Ciao,* Raffaello." I smile at him and his eyes grow wet.

My soul is all turned up like whipped crème, soft and filled with air. I release his hand and walk away. Then, I turn to look back. His shoulders are bent, his eyes cast downward. This may be the last time I come to see him. Walking away is not easy.

As I roam the streets, I think of Raffaello and our special connection. Then, I think of Natale and my heart opens wide. I walk by two lovers feeding each other gelato and wonder what he is doing.

CHAPTER 40

The sign above the store reads *L'arte Fornisce*, art supplies. Once inside, I choose the things I left in Rome—two soft-haired sable brushes, a palette, a knife and an array of oil paints. I'm sure if I have forgotten anything, Federico will provide it.

Once back at the villa, I fret for hours about painting Natale. I'm nervous and believe that if I do so, I will be breathing life back into our lost relationship. I have grown to love who I have become since leaving Rome. I am confident and unafraid. I am self-assured. It's as if the pieces of my life have all come together nicely. I was only in Rome with Natale for six weeks ... But there was so much love between us in that short time. As a matter of fact, it was more intimate than my relationship with Ed. Trembling, I open my sketchbook.

You can do this, Roxanna. My own words settle me. *Maybe this will be my parting gift to him.*

This night, I fall into a deep sleep but am suddenly awakened by a woman's screams. I hold my breath and listen intently but there is only silence. Must have been a dream. Bits and pieces come to me ... fire ... people running. My heart pounds with fear. I rise and walk out into the night where the stars shine brightly and the quiet envelops me. Lights still burn brightly across the bay.

It was just a dream. Nothing more.

My mind relaxes and the unsettling memories of the woman's screams fade.

The heat and humidity of the day has started, so I'm up early. The weather is already intense but I made a promise that I would paint today. I leave in time to get to the studio at 10:00 a.m. The humidity is so high that the short walk to the gate of the villa leaves me dripping with perspiration. Ah, *paradiso* in summer.

I contemplate the fact that this will be the first time I have held a brush since my life … correction … since Deborah Allen's life blew apart. Will I remember how? Do I have any talent? What if I can't paint and only thought I could because I was in love with Ed?

Get hold of yourself, Roxanna!

And for my first piece, I choose to paint Natale. I must be insane! But if I can do this, maybe … somehow, I will know what to do next.

"Roxanna, you have come." Federico jumps up from his chair and kisses me; he gently pulls me into his studio. I'm quiet and move to the canvas he has prepared. I set up my paints and remove my brushes from the sack. He immediately senses what I'm going through and gives me a few moments.

"*Pronto*, are you ready?"

"*Si*, I am ready."

My hands shake as I quickly sketch Natale's image on the canvas from my sketchpad. After twenty minutes, he gazes back at me with those soulful eyes. I take a deep breath and pray.

I call forth Apollo, the God of Healing, so he will soothe my soul. I call forth San Michele, the God of Truth, so that I'm honest with myself in all of this. I call forth Santa Maria so she will watch over me and guide me with her love and compassion. I call forth Athena, Goddess of the Art, and then I call forth San Francesco because he loves me so. I don't stop there … I call forth my father Vesuvio and my mother *Mediterraneo*, and my brother the sphinx to be with me—to give me power and strength.

I don't want to do this alone. This is not simply about painting a portrait. It's so much more. It's my destiny, closure for my old life and the beginning of my new one ... With sable brush in hand, I dab sienna paint onto the canvas. Then, I am lost in ecstasy. I never hear Federico as he guides me ... never see what I am painting.

At times, I don't even see the colors I choose. I just know as if the old Italian masters are guiding me. I paint and paint and do not stop for hours. Federico quietly watching me. He has put his glasses on and moves closer. He studies the canvas, mystified.

It's as if the spirit of Capri and the sea are feeding me. I don't even have to think about what I'm painting or my technique. It just comes to me. It's as if my soul is the one painting and I'm merely the vehicle that holds the brush.

Two hours pass before I come to my senses. Federico is sitting on the sofa, bug-eyed. He's speechless but jumps up quickly to take my arm and guide me to the couch. I can see in his eyes that he recognizes the state I have been in, a place he is familiar with. He moves quickly and returns to me, a glass of water in hand.

"Drink."

Once he's sure I have hold of the glass, he rushes off and returns with a plate of grapes and cheeses. I recover, although I'm still dazed. I look up and see Natale's face. My heart skids to a stop. It takes me a few moments to realize the magnitude of what I have accomplished in such a short time.

"*Santa Maria* ... look at what you have done. You did not tell me you could paint like this. This is *magnifico ... il milione cronometra grande ... molto bello* ..." Then he's quiet as if he were in church taking a moment for silence.

I still cannot speak which is good because if I do, I think I shall weep. Instead, I sit with a blank stare. I drink only the wine and play with a few grapes. He waits with me. Thankfully, no tourists have come into the studio. They only linger at the paintings lining the outer walls.

After a while, I stand and kiss Federico's cheeks.

"I will keep this for you. Return whenever you like and we will finish it."

I have lost this day. I don't remember any of it, except that I have brought Natale back to life and feel my love for him again. I lounge on the terrace, quiet with no thoughts. I forget to eat and do not remember what time I go to bed.

"Poppeus, where are you? Claudius ..."

The woman chokes in between her anguished cries. She's running through old Roman streets as ash and large pumice stones drop from the sky. The angry mountain above the city is rumbling and liquid fire spews from its peak. People are running for their lives dodging all that is raining down upon them. A small boy is hit by a stone and falls to the ground. His mother cries out to the fire god.

"Please, not my child! Take me!" She searches the crowd trying to find someone to help but to no avail.

As the screams grow louder, I awaken with a start and wipe the perspiration from my face. I jump from the bed and pace the floor. My heart beats wildly and I nervously wring my hands. Why is the woman familiar to me? God, it's only a dream ... it seems so real ... as if I'm there with her. I start to remember bits of it. A volcano has erupted and people are trying to escape the chaos and devastation. Is it Mount Vesuvius? Pompeii? I cannot see any buildings, only people running.

I stand outside and scan the bay and Vesuvius. The sky is still dark, only the lights along its base visible, possibly from the cities of the new Pompeii and Ercolano. I shiver as a breeze brushes across my arms.

I contemplate what it would be like to die in a volcanic eruption. Would it be by poisonous gas or extreme heat that melts the body? Would I be buried alive by ash or pumice? I shudder and try to shake off these thoughts, to forget the dream; but all I can think of is the distressed woman with the long dark cloak.

It's 5:00 a.m. and I'm so unsettled that I can't go back to bed. Instead, I sit at the little table on the *terrazzo* and watch the colors of the night melt away and turn into daylight. My eyes never leave Vesuvio; if I wait long enough, maybe it will tell me its story. I eventually finish my tea and my anxiety and the dream fade.

The day passes as any other. I walk to town and chat with my friends. I choose not to walk down to Federico's studio to paint for fear he will ask me what is wrong and I'll have to tell him. I cannot talk about this with anyone. It's too real ... too haunting ... too close to me for some reason.

I try to follow my normal routine. I ride the *seggiovia* to the top of *Monte Solaro* and walk along the cliffs. I watch the tourists. I have a sparkling water in a cafe and read my book. Eventually, I find the quiet inside me.

Then, as night falls, I visit the Caesar Augustus Hotel and my friend Massimo Pappini. He is a thin man with big spectacles and a perfect Roman accent. The first night I visited the hotel, I had dinner on the veranda. He waited on me and we became friends. I stop by each week and he helps me with my Italian. He also fills me in on the events taking place on the island and in the hotel. He likes to talk and I enjoy his stories and his Roman accent. This night, they put me at ease and I forget about the dream.

On the way back to my villa, I pray my sleep is without dreams.

Lying in bed, I think of Natale and how much I miss him. My emptiness is deep.

CHAPTER 41
POMPEII & ERCOLANO, ITALY

◯

"**H**elp me ... please help me."

The woman looks like a ghost as she runs through the streets. Her cloak is singed and blackened, her face and hair covered with ash. Her hands are clasped together as if in prayer. No one helps her because they are all trying to save themselves. It's eerie ... she seems to be speaking directly to me.

Suddenly, the earth rumbles followed by an explosion. The ground shakes and the woman falls. As she struggles to rise from the ash, what seems like an avalanche of pumice stone starts to rain down upon the city. It's heavy and the stones, large. One hits her and she stumbles again.

◯

I'm fully awake and jump from the bed.

What can I do?

I pace back and forth and walk outside to study the volcano across the bay as if it will tell me its secrets.

"Damn you!" With clenched fists, I scream at my father, Vesuvius. "How could you do this!"

I cannot get her face out of my mind. I realize I must go to Pompeii and at least be there ... stand on the soil ... see if I can help. Maybe if she knew I had come, she'd be comforted somehow. How silly of me. But I don't know what else to do. How can I help this stranger? She must be real or it wouldn't be a repeating dream.

I await daylight. When it comes, I ready myself for the trip. The 6:00 a.m. ferry will have me in Sorrento in one hour. Then I'll go straight to the train station for the one-hour ride to Pompeii.

On the train, I read the stops on the overhead neon sign—S. Agnello, Piano, Meta, Seiano, Vico Equense. If I walk the city, maybe I can connect with the woman.

Then what? How could I possibly help her? She's in 79 A.D.

Scraio, Pozzano, C.mare Terme, C.mare Stabia. We move closer. Maybe if I meditated on Pompeian soil ... Maybe I could make a connection with her. My mind races. Maybe in one of the temples I have read about ... the Temple of Isis or Apollo ... the Temple of Venus. I'll know when I get there.

I must help her, or I'll never be able to sleep again.

V.Nocera, Pioppaino, Ponte Persica, Moregine ... Pompeii Scavi ...

At last ...

I bolt from the train and make it to the entrance, but it's only 8:30 a.m. and the sign says the park doesn't open until 10:00 a.m. Maybe I can scale the fence, find a way in. But there isn't. For now, I order *espresso* from a stand on the corner and wait until 10:00 a.m. which seems to take forever.

Once inside, I walk aimlessly about, looking for a sign ... anything. I move through the Porta Marina, the main entrance from the west. If I could close my eyes and follow my heart blindly, I would do so but the uneven Roman stones in the street are too dangerous. Each stone is bigger than my foot and each set with a six to eight-inch gap in between it and the next one. I know this is from over two thousand years of erosion. If I should lose my footing, I could sprain or break an ankle so I must walk consciously and carefully.

I stop to read the map at each intersection in this large city.

The Porta Marina, also known as the Sea Gate, faces the sea and was the gate to the Forum Plaza which was the nucleus of Pompeii at one time. From here, I move onto Via della Marina; the Temple of Apollo comes into view.

This is where I need to be.

I move into the center of the temple, across the grass which used to be a marble floor, and then up the stairs to the altar. The columns, the roof and the statue of Apollo are gone and only broken pieces of the flooring remain. I sit down and close my eyes in the hopes that I will receive a message. Nothing comes. I linger for almost an hour, trying desperately to connect. My legs are cramped and my spirit dampened.

"I thought this would be easy!" I shout angrily. I'm alone, my words falling upon deaf ears, both in this world and the next.

I move about the temple area and then back out to the street. Next is the Temple of Jove, the city's main sacred site. Here, I sit and try again. Nothing. I move from one sacred site to the next as I try to connect with the woman or receive guidance about where she might be.

I spend the day walking the streets in hopes of a sign. After the temples, I move to the smaller Forum Baths, and on to the larger Stabian Baths. I roam throughout the insides of the buildings and the grounds. All day, I move quickly, from the temples and public buildings to the gardens and the Grand Theater. I never stop to study the frescoes. I have no time for that. I'm here for the woman. My head is spinning and I feel lost.

It's late afternoon when I stumble upon the Temple of Isis. It's a small temple that sits upon a high podium with four marble columns and two niches where the statues of Anubis and Harpocrates stood two thousand years before. Now, only two of the four columns remain and the statues are gone. All that's left is the stone platform that was once the altar and the stairs that led up to it.

I sit with my head in my hands, tired and hungry. A whisper, "Go to Herculaneum."

"Why? What will I find there?"

No answer. I pull my *Circumvesuviana Autolinee* map from my pocket and try to find its location. There. It lies beneath the new city that was built over it—Ercolano, and it is eleven stops from Pompeii to its north. God, it's already 3:00 p.m. will I make it before they close for the day?

I head back out the gate and board the train. As we move north toward Napoli, I think about the dream, the woman and her surroundings. I hope to find her in Herculaneum. There were three cities that were destroyed by the volcano in those three days that August in 79 A.D.—Pompeii, Herculaneum and Stabia. Waiting for my stop, I read the guide on the three cities.

Stabia had been a vacation spot for many with large villas scattered throughout. Herculaneum, a seaside resort was where the wealthy had homes. Pompeii on the other hand, was a flourishing coastal city and residential center inhabited by nobles.

When the mountain blew its top spewing tons of molten ash, pumice and sulfuric gas miles into the atmosphere, all three cities were buried. A ground-hugging avalanche of hot ash, pumice, rock fragments and volcanic gas called a pyroclastic flow rushed down the side of the volcano at an estimated 100 kilometers per hour. The temperature was said to be greater than 500°. Those who survived the poisonous vapors were soon engulfed by molten debris or suffocated by the blasting heat wave. I shudder at thoughts of what those mortal souls went through.

Within forty-five minutes, we arrive. I jump from the train in search of the now lost city of Herculaneum which lies at the foot of Mount Vesuvio. I walk up a long, narrow road the distance of a mile before I arrive inside the city. I reach the main entrance and step inside. I'm exhausted from my long day and all the walking I've done, but I keep moving, haunted by the woman.

I roam the streets and am amazed at the size of the villas, some covering entire blocks. I try to tune in to wherever I'm supposed to be ... to whatever is calling to me ... but nothing. I pass the House of the Inn and the House of the Wooden Partition. I walk by the House of Neptune and Amphitrite and then the House of the Beautiful Courtyard.

After this, I stop to rest at the Forum Baths. I enter the

women's section where the floors are mosaic tile with octopuses, morays and Triton with dolphins. It has survived well.

"Where are you? How can I help?" I ask out loud. I'm frustrated and with exhaustion setting in, I'm losing my patience.

I must be insane. What the hell am I doing chasing a stupid dream?

I'm too tired and dejected to move, so I sit for a time and rest before I leave.

Eventually, I make my way to the north end of the inner city and a broad plaza with a wide brick arch at one end. It appears to be the old city's public area. I move on to the Sacred Area, a compound that encloses two places of worship—The Temple of Venus and the Temple of Four Divinities.

The sun hangs low in the sky. I know I need to leave but I cannot find my way out of the city. I come upon the Villa of the Papyrus to the west. It's an expansive complex with many large rooms and a magnificent view. I walk through them in awe of what remains of the tiled floors and frescoed walls and ceilings. It's grand. There's a large garden with replicas of statues, the originals long ago moved to museums. I mindlessly roam through an area where a swimming pool used to be and a rotunda-shaped belvedere. I am drawn here and cannot pull myself away. I rest my aching back against a column on the belvedere.

The vision comes—a woman in a long white dress with a green sleeveless over-coat draped over one shoulder and clasped at her waist. Her sandals are brown leather with straps laced up her calves and a golden band is woven through her hair. She's about twenty and is standing inside her home at the edge of a pond where a swan lazily floats through the water in between the lily pads. Two boys play a game of stones on the tiled floor at the feet of someone who I assume to be her husband, their father. He, too is dressed in a white pleated caftan with an overcoat that's green in color.

I hear them speak in an unfamiliar foreign language and I hear the children's laughter as they toss the stones into the circle. The father, a tall handsome man, is giving them instruction on how to play as the woman watches them. The scene changes and the husband and wife walk across the belvedere. They stop and the husband fastens a red hibiscus in his wife's hair.

The couple hold hands and walks to the edge of the rotunda. They stop and kiss. And at this moment, I realize this is their home. They must have been wealthy people for the villa is large and was once lavish. I see the woman's face and hear her husband call her by name, Corelia Pthengis, as he speaks of his love to her. This I know to be true, because of the way he holds her face before he kisses her ... and it's then that I realize she's the woman in my dream.

It's her. I have found her!

And they lived in this house, the Villa of the Papyrus. Just as I try to comprehend it all, the scene changes and I see the husband and his two young sons on the belvedere looking east toward the volcano as it shoots fire and smoke into the sky. As quickly as the vison has come, it fades.

I'm desperate to know more, but my stomach is growling so loudly, I cannot think. I realize I have eaten nothing today. I find my way out of the site and into the outlying area of Ercolano where I check into a small hotel. There's no way I can make the trip back to the island tonight. I have missed the last boat and am in desperate need of sleep.

CHAPTER 42

At 8:30 p.m. I find a restaurant one block from my hotel and am seated on the patio. I wonder if anyone who lives here feels what I do or dream the dreams I have of those buried beneath my feet. Do they feel any connection at all?

While eating, I review the facts and piece together a timeline in my mind. There was a seventeen-hour span between the first and second eruptions so why didn't more people escape?

"Something else, *Signora*?" The waiter removes my empty plate from the table. He's tall, his dark curls framing his face.

Lost in thought, I say, "No, *grazie*, just the check."

A few moments later, he returns with a small fluted glass of limoncello and places it on the table. He lingers. I sense he has something he wants to say.

"When I was a child, I used to have bad dreams. I dreamed of fire falling from the sky and people running for their lives. I could hear children screaming and crying and I would awaken in the night crying for my mama."

"Do you still dream these dreams?" I ask.

"No, but I have never forgotten the sounds of their voices. It is sometimes not easy living on top of Herculaneum, everyone buried underneath your feet. I know there are so many more down there that have never been found."

"Yes, I can only imagine what it would be like. Do you know anything about that time?" The restaurant is almost empty so the young waiter has time to talk.

"I have been to the site many times. I played there when I was a boy and pretended it was where I lived. I remember how they dressed and the game I played with the stones. The houses were big and everything was beautiful. I remember a painting on the wall of an old building, with Hercules at Mount Olympus. I always stopped and looked at that painting. It was my favorite."

"It sounds like you might have lived there during that time."

"Yes, I think so." He smiles shyly and walks away.

I reach for my guide book and leaf through the section on Herculaneum but there is no new information that I haven't already read. I'm curious to know more about this family and the house I have just seen in my vision.

"*Scusi*, what is your name?"

The young man has returned to check on me.

"Crescenzo, after my father." He smiles.

"Nice to meet you, Crescenzo; I am Roxanna. Do you know anything about the House of the Papyrus and the people who lived there?"

He stops clearing my table. His eyes are bright green against his bronzed skin.

"*Si.* When I was in school, I learned that the House of Papyrus was Herculaneum's most famous house." He has taken a seat across from me and continues. "The villa was built by Emperor Nero's family. Nero's first wife Poppeae had a brother named Claudius Drusus. He built the house for his wife, Corelia Pthengis."

I have gone pale.

"Their main home was in Pompeii and this was where they came to spend the summers. Have you been to the villa, Roxanna?"

"Yes, today."

"Then you have seen the library."

I remember entering a large room but didn't realize it was the library. I nod.

"When the ruins were excavated three hundred years ago, they found thousands of scrolls that were charred, many covered with hard ash. They are still trying to find a better way to open them without damaging them and losing a lot of the text. Most are philosophical texts written in Greek. They believe that since

Claudius Drusus was related to Nero through his sister, there was a hidden room under the library where valuable scrolls were still buried. Our people have been looking for Caesar's "Civil War" and believe that the only copy is in that house. But it has never been found."

"Why haven't they excavated further?"

"I don't know. There's so much to uncover. Maybe they will start again soon. The smallest thing takes a long time in Italy."

"Did you ever learn in school if they had any warning signs that Vesuvio was about to erupt?"

"There was a half-day in between the first and second eruption. Maybe, most thought it would be as small as the first and that they would survive. Many left, but many stayed behind. I learned that it came down in layers—first light pumice, then heavier pumice. I'm sorry. I have to go back to work now. More limoncello, *Signora*?"

"No, *grazie*. Thank you for everything."

He smiles and bows politely. I rise from the table. I'm exhausted and overwhelmed with so much information that my brain cannot make sense of it.

A violent eruption rocks the earth. I am running through the narrow streets along with others, the ground shaking beneath my feet. I lose my footing on the stone road and fall to the ground. Quickly, I pick myself up in fear of being trampled. I'm running beside a woman who is crying loudly, and even though the language is not English or Italian, I understand her. She's crying out for her husband and sons, calling them by name.

"Claudius! Drusus!! Corvinus! Where are you?" She grabs my arm. "Please, save them. Help me find them."

We are running side by side and she reaches for my hand. In the dream, I'm consciously aware that I'm back in time with her and have the sense and the presence of mind to know that I'm not there at all. Does this make sense? In this state, I recall everything the waiter has told me. Inside this strange dream, I speak in her tongue.

"How can I help you? Where are they?"

"They traveled to Herculaneum on an errand for Nero," she says. "He is very angry. I am afraid they will not make it back. Where shall I go? What shall I do? My babies ..." She's distraught and confused.

I try to think. Fire rains down and singes our coats. We pat them madly but never stop running.

Suddenly, the dream changes and the woman is gone. I find myself in a large and cold room with three others. A loud explosion moves the earth. One of the boys cries out.

"Papa!"

When I turn, Claudius and his sons are before me.

"Sshhh, it is all right."

He tries to calm them as they cling to him. A lit torch hangs on the wall next to them and a lantern on a table. Then he sees me.

"Blessed Isis. You have come to save us."

"I am not Isis. I'm like you." I do not know what to say to calm the man for I'm as filled with fear as they are.

"Where is this room?" I hope I don't frighten him with this question.

"It's underneath the library, a hidden room. This is where we store the sacred scrolls. No one knows it's down here. Where did you come from?"

"I came through the door," I lie. "Where is your wife?"

"She is in Pompeii. I pray to the gods that she is safe." His face is filled with sorrow and pain. "My love, my sweet Corelia."

He weeps and it causes the boys to cry. I feel helpless but know somehow, I must ease their pain.

"It will be all right. She is safe. Pompeii is safe." I lie again. "I can't explain to you how I know this or where I came from but it is the truth for I just saw her."

"Ah, I knew you were sent by the gods."

He starts to prostrate himself before me.

"Please, protect us and save my Corelia. I will be lost without her. She is my life, my love." He lowers himself to the ground and cries softly, his face in his hands. I kneel before him.

"As you wish."

At once, he relaxes and the children stop crying. They come and sit in my lap as if I am their guardian and protector. They ask me where I have come from and if I've been sent by the gods to protect them. I say yes and tell them of Mount Olympus. Their father has moved closer and the older son goes to him. It isn't long before they close their eyes and listen to my fabricated stories, the stories I have made up to calm them. Then, in an instant they take their last breath. It's a quick and painless death as the suffocating blast of the heat wave hits us. I'm the only one who survives and I know why I have been saved.

In an instance, I'm transported back to Pompeii and running through the streets with the woman. We are hand in hand as we rush through the square past the marble statue of Augustus and the public fountain.

"We need to go back to your home now. Take me there!" I know that soon it will be the end and the safest and most comfortable place to die will be inside. I pray that Corelia's death will be as peaceful and painless as that of her husband and children.

"This way."

We are gray as ghosts and cough from the sulfur and the thick gray ash. We try to run, but the pumice rocks that have fallen cover the streets and are almost up to our knees making it difficult to wade through them. Our progress is slow as we trudge down *Via della Fullonica* and toward *Vicolo del Fauno*. The sky grows darker, a huge black cloud covering the city.

We walk past the Dancing Faun with its arms raised and a smile on his face. The ash and pumice have covered the pool of water he stands in. Turning now onto *Vicolo di Mercurio,* we arrive at the House of the Vetti where the woman lives. As we approach the outer atrium and slowly make our way through the rock, a large explosion hits and the sky lights up. Dirt and fire rain down from the heavens and our cloaks catch fire again. But this time, we must remove them or die. We quickly do so and enter the archway into the inner portico—the place from my vision where the pond lies.

"Is there a lower room in the house? It will be the safest place."

"Yes, the storeroom for the food."

We run to the back of the house and down a passageway to a darkened room. Corelia lights two lanterns and places them in the corner. We both sit on the floor. She throws her arms around me and starts to weep, and I realize she is a young girl.

"Claudius ... Drusus ... Corvinus ... I love you. I pray to Isis and to the gods that they keep you safe."

"Where are they?" I try to bring her back from her grief.

"Nero was here and requested my husband go to the other villa in Herculaneum, find the scrolls and deliver them to him. He said they belonged to him and he must have them immediately. There was an argument between them. Nero is brutal and killed my husband's sister by beating her to death when she was with child. Since then, there has never been peace between Claudius and him. I'm surprised Nero didn't kill him, too."

Now, her mind has moved from her loved ones and is focused on Nero.

"Where are your sons?"

She begins to weep again.

"My babies; they need me. They are probably so afraid right now. They begged to accompany their father. It was a trip that would only take a few days and although I said they were too young, he insisted. He told me they would be well and he would take care of them. He said they were big boys now." She continues to weep.

"I'm sure they're all right. The winds are blowing the debris from the volcano southwest toward Pompeii. That means that Herculaneum will be saved." It's another lie, but I want to put her mind at ease. I know the outcome of this and it will be the same as my experience with the father and two sons.

"Do you really think so?"

"Yes, I do." I touch Corelia's arm and she smiles a little.

"How ironic that yesterday was a holiday ... *Vulcanalia*."

I had read that August 23, 79 A.D. was the day before the eruption and a holy day, a day when the people threw live fish into bonfires as a sacrifice to appease the Fire God, Vulcan.

"Why is he angry with us?" She starts to cry again.

"It will be all right, Corelia. You will be with your family soon enough. All will be well." I hug her. And at this moment, a blast of heat sucks the breath out of our lungs ...

I bolt upright in my hotel room bed gasping for air. My body is drenched in sweat and my sheets wet. I jump up, run to the window and hang my head out to catch a breath of the night air. I have felt death twice tonight ... heard it ... breathed it ... too much for a human. I'm relieved to know that it wasn't a painful death after all. It happened so fast. Now that they are together in the next world, maybe this is all I was meant to do.

I'm still sitting at the window when the sun begins to rise, and how glorious it is. I have gained deep respect for Vesuvio, that which has the power to change the course of a life and a civilization in a flash. I think about my own life and my age. I realize we have such a short span of time on this earth for each lifetime and that it's wise to know what one wants so that one might go after it and attain it.

On the train, back to Napoli, I hear the voices of two people, a man and a woman. As the sound of the rickety car scrapes along the steel tracks, I hear children's laughter and then, a faint whisper, "Thank you." Maybe it's my imagination but it soothes me, nonetheless.

This is all I need to hear. I know they are together and all is well. The memories of Corelia's and Claudius' love for each other makes me realize how lonely I am for Natale. I weep quietly. Although it has been months since I left Rome, it seems like it was only yesterday. I think about his soft touch upon my cheek and the way his hand holds the base of my back as he gazes into my eyes. I close my eyes and feel his lips touch mine. Although it's just a memory, it feels so real.

What do I want from this life of mine? Have I found the answers yet? Then I hear the voice.

"Once you no longer ask the questions, you will know."

We have arrived in Sorrento.

CHAPTER 43

I stand on the outer deck of the hydrofoil to Capri, close my eyes and smell the sea air. Rough waves toss the boat around and I lose my balance falling backward into a stranger's arms.

"*Scusami.* I'm so sorry."

"No problem. It got rough."

He's an American, about forty, with dark hair and eyes. He grips the rail tightly as another swell tosses the boat. ITALIA in gold lettering is emblazoned across his sleeveless tee-shirt.

"There's a storm coming in. It'll be here this evening. My name's Joseph, or as they say in Italian, Giuseppe." He laughs into the sea air, extends his hand and I take it.

"I'm Roxanna. Nice to meet you, Joseph. How long are you on the island for?"

"A month; I have a villa in Anacapri."

"That's where I'm staying." We both smile and I forget about my latest adventure.

"I come every summer for a few months but this year I've been so busy that unfortunately I can't stay as long. How about you?"

"I came in April and never left. I've been traveling throughout Italy and Greece a bit, but I always come back to Capri. It's my favorite place in the world."

"I know how you feel. I fell in love with it fifteen years ago and dreamt of living here. Seven years ago, I was finally able to purchase a small villa. Now my dream has come true. You'll have to come for dinner, Roxanna. I have friends joining me tomorrow and you're invited. We're calling it a 'Welcome Home Party for Joseph.'" He laughs. "Will you come?"

"I'd love to."

"Wonderful; I'll give you my number so you can call for directions. Everyone is arriving around 8:00 p.m. Oh, are you traveling alone?"

"Yes." I don't mention Natale, but Joseph notes the change in my face and I become embarrassed.

"I'm sorry."

"I understand. Love is not for everyone. I, too miss someone but in my situation, it's a little different. Gay relationships are a bit more complicated than heterosexual ones." He sighs and takes a heavy breath.

"We have something in common," I say. "I would love to come to your dinner party tomorrow."

"Good. You can be my date then. We'll set tongues wagging all night. They'll wonder if I've gone straight." We both laugh. The heavy swells are unwavering so we move to the inside cabin to find a seat.

I learn that Joseph lives in Malibu and is a screenplay writer. He names some of the movies he has written and I tell him which ones I've seen. His ex-lover is a married man, a well-known heterosexual actor in Hollywood, who has decided to stay in his marriage because of his career. The relationship lasted two years and the break-up is only a few months old so Joseph's wounds are still fresh. Although he's very masculine and a definite head turner, I feel his soft heart and instantly want to befriend him.

He's handsome and of Italian descent, one of the reasons he loves Italy so much. His relatives are from Milan but he has fallen in love with Capri. He has this bright smile that is accentuated by his great tan. If he hadn't told me, I would never have guessed him to be gay.

As we sit and chat for the remainder of the ride, I find myself laughing hysterically at the way he speaks about things. His sense of humor is as infectious as his smile as he tells me about Richard, his ex-lover.

"And Roxanna, he's gorgeous. The first time I laid eyes on him … oh baby … I thought I'd died and gone to heaven. I almost dropped my drink in my lap! He has the face of a god and the body to match. I tell you, I was twisted in knots for weeks before I got up the guts to ask him for coffee." He's still talking as we dock and disembark.

We exchange phone numbers and I promise to call him for directions.

"How silly of me; do you want to share a taxi, Roxanna? My treat."

"I'd love to." It will give me a chance to spend more time with my new friend who I'm immediately smitten with. As we maneuver a corner on the winding road to Anacapri, Joseph gasps.

"I'm always amazed by this view. For the fifteen years I've been coming here, I never tire of it. It's as if I'm seeing it for the first time all over again."

"I know what you mean. I feel the same way."

Joseph sparkles when he talks. He sees and feels things as I do. We are kindred spirits. Because of him, the memories of the last few days have faded, thank goodness. We've reached the *Piazza Vittoria* and our taxi driver unloads Joseph's luggage.

"Tomorrow evening, Roxanna. I'll see you then."

We hug and kiss.

"I'm looking forward to it. I'll call you tomorrow afternoon."

"If you have trouble getting through, leave a message. You know how it is on the island with cell phones."

We both nod in agreement. The service is very trying here. My feeling is that the volcanic rock beneath us is saying, "No, you are not supposed to be on your cell phones but engaging in life instead."

I decide to walk home, clean up and go directly to Federico's. I want to finish Natale's painting. I feel as if I'm running out of time.

I hear my name.

"Rossana, is that you?" I turn and see Bruno. He catches up to me and we embrace. I've missed him.

"It's good to see you, Rossana. I miss seeing you."

"It's good to see you, too, Bruno. Where have you been?" We continue to embrace each other.

"Something happened to me after we were together. The next day when I woke up, I smiled and I was happy again. I had forgotten what it felt like to be happy."

"I know what you mean. It changed me, too."

He kisses my cheek again.

"Thank you, Rosanna." We are quiet for a moment, just looking in each other's eyes.

"I decided to visit Ilaria's brother. We drank wine and cried all night. We celebrated her life. We both loved her. So now, we are like brothers. Last week, we opened a restaurant together in Sorrento."

"Bruno, that's wonderful!"

"I know. I have a new girl, too. We are in love. It's all because of the magic of our time together. You are an angel." He squeezes my hands.

"It wasn't me. It was you." My tears begin to fall. "I'm in love, too. Someone I met in Rome."

"I'm so happy for you. For both of us."

"Me too, Bruno. Thank you for helping me find myself and for holding my hand all the way. I will never forget you." Now the tears have come and he too is crying.

"I wish you *buona fortuna*, good fortune in love."

"You too, Bruno."

We hug and kiss each other on the lips. Then we part. It's a blessing that we walked through the minefields of our hearts together and made it to the other side, healed. I'm grateful for him.

It's 1:00 p.m. when I arrive at Federico's studio. He's sitting on a stool outside his shop and immediately jumps to his feet when he sees me. His face lights up and he smiles wide.

"*Amore mio, come va*? I'm happy to see you. Are you ready to finish your masterpiece?"

He turns, waves to the woman he was sitting with and takes me inside. Although it's been two days since I last saw the unfinished painting, it surprises me and I'm stirred up again.

"I'm ready," I whisper.

We don't speak but get right to work. I choose the finer brush for the details and am a little more conscious than I was the first time. But after an hour or so, I am once again lost until it is done. When I step back, I'm amazed that I am the one who painted it.

"*Molto bello ... perfetto ... magnifico ... mamma mia* ... you are a master, Roxanna. He kisses my cheek and stands behind me, his arms around my waist. "You are *incredible*, unbelievable. Have you always painted like this?"

He moves closer to Natale.

"Here, the eyes. The windows into his soul. The nose, *perfetto* ... the dimples in his cheeks ... are they truly like this?"

"Yes, yes they are." I realize how precise it is and love what I have painted.

"This is the man you are in love with. I can tell. No one paints like this if they do not truly love who or what they are painting for the art is their expressed *passionne.*"

I nod in agreement, not able to speak. I'm thinking about how I will get this to Natale. How long will I have to wait for it to dry? Two months? Three? Maybe I'll write to him and tell him I've finished but the paint has not dried yet. He should have it, not me. I can paint another. Yes, I think it more important that he have it.

"Something to celebrate." Federico brings two glasses and a bottle of Moet & Chandon champagne. "I've been saving this for something special and this is it." He pops the cork and pours each of us a glass which we raise to the painting and to each other.

"To you, Roxanna. Welcome back. You are a great Italian master now, as good as the rest of us."

The golden bubbles tickle my insides and I smile. I have found myself ... another piece of me ... a substantial piece. Suddenly, I realize Vittorio is singing "*Tu Sei,*" on the CD player. I weep with joy. And at that moment, Federico takes me in his arms and we dance to the music. All the while, he hums the song and I sing "la-da-da-da-da." It's a memory I will always cherish. Again, I remember Elana.

"*Amore mio ...*" He takes me by the hand and leads me back to the couch. As he pours more champagne into my glass, he says, "To find a great love, you first have to fall in love with yourself. I have seen you become more alive and happier every day since you have arrived on Capri. Do you know what this means, Roxanna?" He takes a sip.

I shake my head, no.

"This means that this is your home, for it feeds your soul and you cannot live somewhere that does not feed your soul." He kisses my forehead.

"Thank you, Federico. You have been such a good friend and confidant."

"*Ti amo*," *he says.*

"I love you, too."

We hug, then sit quietly and finish our champagne.

"Roxanna, I am going for a swim at the *Grotta Azzurra* later. After the tour boats leave for the day, we can go inside and swim. Would you like to come with me? It would be the perfect ending to our celebration."

I think for a moment that it will be like an island baptism for me in the sacred cave and its waters, my mother there for the ceremony.

"Yes. I'll go for my swimsuit and meet you in the *piazza*."

"I will be there at 18:00. *Ciao, bella.*"

"*Ciao.*"

We meet at 6:00 p.m. and ride his scooter through Linaro and La Selva, the little pockets of Anacapri, until we reach the cliffs above the Blue Grotto.

"Be very careful, Roxanna."

We climb down the jagged steps built into the cliffside, him holding my hand as if I am his little girl. I look out over the water and see a rowboat sitting amidst the jewels that have spilled down from the sun. Federico whistles to the man on the boat and he quickly comes to us. He takes my hand as I step into the boat and Federico follows.

We enter the cavern through the small opening, a rope hanging across the entrance. As we lie on our backs, we hold onto the rope and the boatman pulls us inside. The color of the cave is an opalescent electric blue, if you can imagine this. Because the mouth of the cave is low and narrow, it doesn't allow light to enter so the sunlight penetrates the sea water and reflects upward into the cave against its walls creating this electric color. As the light reflects off the white sandy bottom, it creates an opalescent hue. This, along with the blue color coats everything in the grotto so it appears to be dripping in silvery light. The inner walls are covered in it as silver raindrops drip from the blue rocks.

The boatman begins to sing and the rock walls echo his song back to him. Federico slips over the side of the boat and swims slowly to the cave wall. I, on the other hand, am still in the boat looking out to sea through the mouth of the cave. It's like being at the North Pole, the water a shade of blue that is uncommon to the rest of the world and the air as different as the water is.

I feel like a sea nymph who has just found her home. I want to stay here and sleep in this opalescence that is edged with shimmering light. I imagine that if you make a wish here, it will come true for I feel it to be so.

I whisper to myself, "I wish to know intimately what I have been searching for. I wish to know all the secrets so I can be finished with all this and settle into my life as it is, never going backwards but only enjoying where I am right now."

There. I said it.

"Come in, come in, *bella*."

I'm roused out of my musing by Federico so I slip over the side of the boat as the oarsman holds it steady. The water is cool and my body tingles.

"It's sublime ... luxurious ... sacred ... It's like a dream." I giggle and giggle.

"Ah, *bambina*, little girl ... you are happy, no?"

He's happy that I'm happy and I'm happy that I am here in this place inside the *Grotta Azzurra* and inside this new life.

"Yes!"

I swim from one side to the other, from one end to the other, all the while listening to the oarsman's song. After thirty minutes, Federico says it's time to go so we leave and are dropped off at the stone steps for the climb back to Anacapri.

"Thank you for joining me, Roxanna. A perfect day in *paradiso.*"

"Thank you, Federico. You have no idea how much I enjoyed this."

This night, back at *Mio Paradiso*, I choose vegetables from the garden for my dinner and listen to Vittorio on my laptop as I prepare my meal in my little Italian kitchen. When I'm finished and the sun is setting over Ischia, I twirl and twirl on the terrace.

And as I tuck myself in between my sheets for the night, I declare out loud, to all those in the ethers who might be listening, "So this is what it feels like to have peace in your heart."

CHAPTER 44

Christos had told me Delos was filled with brilliant light and blessed by Helios. It was. Capri is also luminous and blessed by San Michelle which is why Axel Munthe wrote,

> *"... like a temple to the Sun,*
> *where I would seek knowledge and light*
> *from the radiant God whom I had worshipped all my life ...*
> *light, light everywhere."*

Yes, Capri is similar to Delos with its light and energy. Why else would I be here, or Munthe, or San Michele who is actually Apollo ... who is actually Helios ... I smile as my mind tries to make sense of all this enchantment. I stop my daydreaming and realize I have much to do before the party tonight. I want to call my boys, mail the letter to Natale and pick up flowers and a great bottle of *vino* for Joseph.

The letter to Natale is short. I write that I'm back in Capri for the rest of the summer and that I have finished his painting. I also say that, hopefully it will dry soon so I can get it to him. I do not say that I will mail it to him or that I will deliver it to him myself because I don't know what I will do. I'm not ready to make that decision yet and after hearing my sons' voices this morning, I miss them and think I should go home. I can always come back ...

As I approach Joseph's villa, I hear music in the air. I walk through the gate and realize how large a place it is. It's quite impressive with its balconies and a long portico that runs the length of the house. People are milling about everywhere.

"Roxanna." Joseph greets me.

He kisses me, happy that I've come. He's dressed in white linen slacks and a white linen shirt that hugs his body; his shoes look as if they have been hand-woven by the *Caprese* shoemaker in the village.

"Joseph, your home is incredible." I hand him the big bouquet of flowers from the island's only florist and a bottle of Castello di Querceto Chianti Classico.

"*Grazie,* they're beautiful." He smells the bouquet. "And thank you for the *vino.* Come, I want you to meet my friends."

He leads me into the house and hands me a glass of prosecco. Then, he introduces me to a crowd of people. A few Americans from the movie industry who I don't recognize are standing around and many Italians are talking with each other.

Joseph introduces me to Alberto and his wife Francesca. I know I have seen him before in the port. He's dressed in a gorgeous custom white linen shirt, emblazoned with his insignia, and white linen slacks. He is also wearing woven loafers like Joseph's.

"A pleasure, Roxanna," says Alberto.

Josephs interrupts.

"He is the most sought-after designer in the world right now, Roxanna. You must buy a pair of his jeans. They're all the rage. Remember his name, Alberto Bruno."

Since being in Capri, I've seen his jeans and scarves on many of the women throughout Italy, and I recognize his label from fashion magazines.

"I know your work, Alberto, pleasure to meet you." We kiss Italian style.

"And it's nice to meet you too," I say to his wife Francesca."

She's beautiful. Her hair is thick and dark, tightly pulled back and piled upon her head. Her clothes are Italian-designed, classic yet sexy, and her sandals are high-heeled and bejeweled, her toes painted a shimmering white. The only jewelry she wears is a massive aquamarine stone hanging from a string of pearls.

"*Piacere*, pleasure to meet you, Rosanna."

"*Molto grazie,* Francesca."

I realize that this is a very "in" party with "in" people. I grin wide because I'm excited.

I spend most of the night mingling and talking with everyone. The guests include an American playwright and an actress who comes to the island for a few weeks every summer. A gay couple has arrived and Joseph tells me they will be staying with him for a few weeks. I'm also introduced to Michael who is Richard's best friend ... Joseph's ex, Richard.

Joseph has taken me by the arm to meet everyone. I can tell by the looks on everyone's face that they are wondering if we're having relations. He, in the meantime is loving it, setting tongues wagging. He was right when he said they would wonder if he had gone straight. We both giggle each time we dance together, enjoying our secret.

Alberto and Francesco are telling Joseph and I that they will be taking their boat down the Amalfi Coast for a few days. Alberto is begging Joseph to join them.

"You must come. It will only be a few days. Please, Joseph."

"I can't. I've got work to do."

But you must! You are the life of the party. It won't be the same without you."

And he is. You want to be near him because you know you'll have a good time. It's not so much that he's a partier, but that he has this effervescence about him. He's honest and real, something you don't often find. And he isn't pretentious by any means. Everyone loves him. I feel sorry for Richard for breaking up with him. He must be missing him.

Joseph isn't changing his mind.

"Joseph, if you come, I promise to take you to Africana," pleads Alberto. At this, Joseph's face lights up.

"I'm there! What time tomorrow?" he says excitedly.

"Be at the dock at noon ... you know my boat, yes." He turns to his wife, "Come *amore mio;* we are sleeping in tomorrow!"

We say *arrivederci,* and as he kisses my cheeks, he says, "Oh, and please bring Roxanna."

He turns to me, "You must join us, Roxanna. *Arrivederci a domani.*"

"Thank you. I'll think about it."

"Roxanna, don't be fooled by him," Joseph whispers. "This is no small boat ride down the coast. Pack for four days! You will need dress attire as well as casual clothes. These two know how to live it up and this will be a four-day long party."

"This isn't my thing, Joseph. I'm a simple girl."

I think of the peace and quiet I have not had for months now, running here and there all over Italy and Greece …

"I won't take "no" for an answer. If I must go then you must come as my date! I need you, *bella.* Please, for me? You know I'm recovering from a broken heart and I won't be able to do it without you."

I laugh because he's on his knees with pouty lips and puppy-dog eyes.

"All right, but I don't have a thing to wear."

Then we'll have to go shopping in Positano and Amalfi, doll."

I'm giddy. Another adventure.

"What have I gotten myself into? Okay, but I must go to bed now or I won't be awake in time. *Ciao, bello.*"

"*Ciao*, gorgeous."

I leave to find my way home, just in time to fall into bed and into the arms of sleep for the next six hours.

CHAPTER 45
AMALFI COAST, ITALY

I leave early to shop in the village since I need a few things for the cruise.

I purchase a white linen skirt and blouse, a pair of dressy sandals and a bright blue pashmina. These will have to do until Joseph and I go shopping. I quickly hurry to the *piazza* to meet him.

"Roxanna, here," he waves to me. A taxi is waiting to take us to the port.

"You look well rested this morning, darling."

We slide into the back seat. The cab is open with a bright yellow canopy shielding us for the sun.

"I barely slept, I was so excited about our getaway," I say.

"Roxy, wait until you see Africana. I've always wanted to go there."

"What is it? Is it a restaurant?"

"No, a nightclub. It's hidden in an obscure place on the Amalfi Coast. Once you're inside, it's like being in an underwater cave that's the color of the Blue Grotto. The only way to enter is in through the mouth of the cave from the sea. I'm so excited, I can't stop pinching myself!"

Now I'm intrigued.

"And it's only open from June through August, so timing and the sea is everything. That's why it's taken me so long to get there."

"Maybe you'll meet someone there, Joseph." He elbows me.

"Wouldn't that be a dream?"

We arrive at the harbor and I scan it for Alberto's yacht but cannot locate it. Joseph can't wipe the smile off his face.

"What's up with you?" I ask.

"Nothing." He smiles wider.

We walk through the port toward the far end where the private boats and yachts are docked.

"Here we are."

Joseph stops and points to a massive ship anchored in the bay, *Mia Francesca* painted on its side. This can't be it. Joseph flags the tender, the small boat that will take us to the ship. It motors toward us.

"Wait, is this really their yacht? It looks as if it belongs to a king."

"Actually, it's a superyacht—300 feet long, holds up to 38 passengers and has 20 staterooms. It has a health and fitness center and a world-class spa with saunas; steam rooms and Jacuzzis; cold plunge pools; a massage parlor; beauty salon; a gymnasium ... do you want me to go on? Oh, I forgot ... there's a boutique where you can shop. Alberto and Francesca purchase all the goods for sale and all monies received go to charity. Roxy, you can close your mouth now." Joseph elbows me.

"Oh, did I mention the two speed boats for water skiing, diving equipment, jet skis ... I'm exhausted just talking about it! But you wait, doll; you're going to love it."

As soon as we step on board, Alberto is there to greet us.

"Ciao, ciao. Benvenuto."

"This is amazing, Alberto."

"Grazie, Roxanna. I named it after my wife ... only the best for her. She is my life, you know."

Francesca has come up behind him, hears his compliment and slips her arms around his waist.

"Ah, darling, there you go again, always flattering me. That's why I love you so." She turns to us. "Good to see you both. Come, and I will show you to your rooms."

We walk the ship, through a bar and lounge area with plush

297

chairs, a grand piano and a fountain; the walls are decorated with mirrors. Then we walk through a theatre room with a wall-to-wall flat screen and a stocked bar. Next is a formal dining room that seats forty-eight and is decorated in gold, white and pale blue.

We are shown more lovely rooms including another dining area. The tables are dressed in white linen and large candles adorn them. The floors are a golden-toned movingui wood from the Ivory Coast in Nigeria. Long white couches with blue and gold pillows create a lounge area off to the side. I'm in awe. Francesca smiles proudly.

"Would you like to see the spa before I show you to your rooms? We want you to enjoy yourself while you are here."

I nod, yes. Francesca leads us to the elevator which takes us to the lower level. A golden door opens and we enter a round marble room with windowed walls to the sea. It's breath-taking. A waterfall sits in the center of the room where one can sit and relax while waiting for a massage or treatment. My senses are on overload. You could live here forever and never want for anything.

"Come this way," says Francesca.

We enter a room; an enormous round bed lies in its center, an overhang of ostrich feathers above it. Everything is white and gold with golden drapery.

"Roxanna, this is your room. I hope you like it."

"It's fabulous, Francesca. *Molto grazie,* thank you." I stay behind and fall backward onto my bed as Joseph follows Francesca down the hall in search of his room.

I am Cleopatra.

I'm giddy as I roll around on the silk bedcovering. I'm grateful Joseph talked me into coming. If I had known that it would be like this, I wouldn't have hesitated for a moment.

A few hours later, Joseph and I meet up to explore the ship. We find the library on the upper deck and I am overjoyed once I step inside.

"Joseph, look! Look at these books."

"I know. I've been here before."

I start pulling tomes from their shelves and pile them on the floor. I have found first editions in Greek, Italian, and English. I can't read the ones written in Greek, but I can hold them in my hands and flip through the pages.

I find books on Michelangelo: *The Sculptures of Michelangelo;* and *The Drawings of Michelangelo.* I find two on the works of Raphael and a copy of *Dante's Inferno.* There are books on the Roman Empire; *The Plato Dialogues;* and *Plato - the Man and His Works.* I pull a tome from the shelf titled *Dionysios Solomos* and then the *Complete Works of Aristotle.*

"Joseph, I could die here!" I'm sitting on the floor leafing through as many as I can.

"What are you going to do with all these, doll? You can't possibly read them all. Dinner's in a few hours!"

"I know. I will never have time to read any of them! You go. I'm going to stay for a bit. Is that okay?"

"Anything for you, doll. Oh, but first, we need to hit the boutique on the upper deck. I saw this gorgeous midnight blue gown that would look stunning on you! What do you say?"

"Okay. I'll look, but it depends on the price tag. I'm out of work, you know."

"Don't worry 'bout a thing. I'll buy it for you. After all, you are my date. Whatever the cost, it's yours. Consider it a gift."

"I can't let you do that. But let's go look."

I leave the piles on the floor and we move to the upper deck where the shops are.

"Roxanna, it's made for you. It fits you like a glove and your breasts ..."

"Stop." I'm embarrassed and hide my face in my hands. I shyly steal another glance. I must say, olive oil is my new best friend and has done my body good. I do look amazing. I've never been in such good shape.

"Joseph, it's 2100€. Too rich for my blood."

"*Un regalo,* a gift and you cannot say no. Last week, I sold a screenplay for big money and I have no one to lavish gifts on."

He gives me the puppy-dog look again. I'm laughing so hard I can't argue with him. Instead, I cry and kiss him hard on the lips.

"Aw, Roxy. That was sweet. It's been twenty years since I kissed a girl."

I playfully smack his arm.

"Someone is going to fall in love with you in that dress. Seriously."

"That's not something I need or want in my life right now. But you, Giuseppe, you will have a gorgeous Italian lover soon. I can feel it."

We both laugh, but his eyes tell me he's still hurting inside.

We've dropped anchor off the coast of Salerno, the southernmost part of the Amalfi Coast. Alberto has given word that we will dine on the ship tonight and visit the mainland tomorrow. Dinner is formal. It's on the outer deck so I dress in my midnight blue sequined dress. My black strappy heeled sandals are the perfect accessory. Joseph knocks promptly at 17:55 p.m. and when I open the door, he's awestruck.

"If I were a straight man, you wouldn't be leaving this room tonight."

"Oh, stop ..." But I'm flattered by his remarks.

When we arrive on deck, there are thirty of Alberto and Francesca's closest friends enjoying cocktails. I remember a few of the faces from the party the night before but most are Italians I've not met.

"*Molto bella*. I knew that dress would be perfect for someone. You look fabulous. I chose it myself in Milano, Roxanna."

"Thank you, Francesca. I adore it." She's wearing a clingy black gown with spaghetti straps that hugs her body down to her hemline. From there, it fans outward. An opulent, radiant cut diamond hangs from her neck and her beautiful Italian hair is piled high on top of her head.

We join the others and are seated for what seems like a ten-course meal. I lose track after the sixth. I cannot take another bite or the seams on this beautiful dress will burst.

The food is excellent and the wine, superb—a 1995 Giacomo Conterno, Barolo Reserva, a Monfortino Red from the Piedmont region of Italy.

"Superb wine, Roxy. It's made from Nebbiolo grapes and each bottle is well over $700."

"Really ..." I sip it slowly, my seams staying strong.

Over the course of our four-hour dining experience, we listen to Alberto tell stories about the pirates that raided the towns up and down the Amalfi Coast in the 16th century.

"... and between 1510 and 1555, Amalfi's population dropped considerably due to the pirate attacks. Everyone along the coast here and even Capri, Roxanna," he turns to me as he says this, "knows who Barbarossa was—a Muslim born in Greece and a lieutenant general in the Ottoman Navy who led fleets up to 135 galleys through these waters with his three brothers. Their only mission throughout their entire lives was to fight against the Knights of St. John, the Maltese Knights, the Papacy in Spain, the Holy Roman Empire, the Republic of Venus and every other Christian led fleet who had inflicted serious damage against the Ottoman Empire or the Turks back then."

He sips his wine.

"He and his brothers were ruthless, calling themselves the Barbary Corsairs ... you know pirates from the Barbary Coast of Africa. Although he and his Corsairs raided Sicily, Spain, France and Greece, he particularly loved ravaging, plundering and ransacking every port town along the coast here, including the islands of Procida, Ischia and Capri."

He turns to me and Joseph again.

"Have either of you been to the Barbarossa Castle in Capri?"

"No," Joseph and I say in unison.

"He built a great castle there above Anacapri; you have probably seen all the forts that are still on the island that were built around that time. I imagine he loved Capri because of its cliffs, not an easy place to surprise someone in the middle of the night."

"Of course, the Christians everywhere hated him for stealing all the sacred artifacts from the churches. The Corsairs despised the Christians so much that most times, they pillaged just to throw everything into a pile and set it afire. They were ruthless."

Alberto stops for a breath. It is obvious this is a subject dear to his heart.

"You know they carried razor-sharp rapiers ... the two-edged swords with sharp points. And they wore metal helmets and breastplates, which was common battle dress back then ..."

Everyone is silently looking out toward the lights of Salerno probably wondering if pirates are hiding somewhere out there. Will we be safe tonight sleeping on the ship? I had heard stories of pirates stealing onto the cruise ships around Greece recently. The country and the cruise lines tried to keep it quiet so the tourists would still come.

Alberto continues to weave his story.

"Did you know that Barbarossa was never his real name? It was Yakupoglu Hizir meaning Hizir, Son of Yakup. Barbarossa was his brother Oruc's name and he was killed in battle. To honor him, Hizir dyed his beard red, took his brother's name, Barbarossa and took command of his fleet."

Alberto is shaking his head in disbelief.

"This stunning coastline ... pillaged and plundered for almost an entire century ...   You know he wrote his memoirs—five volumes called *Memoirs of Hayreddin Pasha*. But then they were fictionalized and retitled, *The Mediterranean Was Ours*. They truly believed it was theirs for the taking."

He is still passionately going on about them when Francesca interrupts him.

"Darling, enough about Barbarossa; maybe our guests would like to dance." Francesca reaches over and kisses her husband on his cheek.

"You're right, *amore mio.* Those Greeks ... you have to watch them every minute ..."

Everyone laughs and I think of my Greek pirates.

We dance until 3:00 a.m. When I fall into bed, I immediately fall into a deep sleep as the ocean cradles me in her arms ... my mother, *Mediterraneo* ...

Late morning has come and we are in Vietri sul Mare which lies north of Salerno. We are looking for the hand-crafted painted ceramics that the locals have created and sell out of their garages in these thousand-year-old Etruscan-style buildings. Each place of business or residence has a ceramic plaque at its entrance noting the family or shop inside. A large ceramic sign of a vineyard scene, a man stomping on grapes and bottles of *vino* painted along the edges hangs outside the wine shop. The flower shop has a hand-painted tile depicting a woman picking flowers in a field.

We roam about and most of us purchase platters, cups and dinnerware from the locals. Alberto and Francesca commission a 90-year-old gentleman to create a very large urn to be painted white with yellow trim and the big plump lemons that the Campania region is known for. Before we leave the town, we visit the *Chiesa di San Giovanni Battista,* the Church of Saint John the Baptist and find a café to sit in for a bit. I make a note to myself to come back to this picturesque place.

Back on the ship, we travel north toward Ravello, a small 19th century town in the hills high above Amalfi. Once we arrive, we are driven up the mountain and Alberto takes us on his favorite tour first to the Palazzo Sasso and then to the Villa Rufolo built for and by an aristocratic medieval family in the 1200s.

From there, we move on to the cathedral, its beautiful carved bronze doors created by Barisano da Tani. Next, we move to a place I fall in love with, the Villa Cimbrone. It was originally a cloister but is now a small hotel. The grounds are expansive with lovely gardens. This is one of the most beautiful villas I've ever seen with its belvedere looking out over the Mediterranean. Alberto tells us that this estate and its vineyards and gardens have been sold continually over the centuries, until in 1940 Lord Ernest William Beckett purchased it.

On the property, there are many structures besides the villa—a *palazzo*, a castle; a tower; the cloister; a crypt; and a tiny villa for a small child which is actually a playhouse. Busts of famous men line the cupola, the belvedere which offers a spectacular view of the sea below. From there, we move into the gardens where there are terraces and numerous marble statues. The *Belvedere of Mercury*, the *Grotto of Eve* and the *Temple of Bacchus* are partially hidden, the foliage and shrubbery grown up around them.

Francesca and I walk arm-in-arm like women friends do.

"Francesca, I love this place. I want to come back here and stay."

"Yes, it is beautiful," she says. "This is our favorite town along the Amalfi coast and we usually stay right here at the Villa Cimbrone. Greta Garbo once lived here, you know. The story is that she had a secret lover at that time and they used to meet here. The Italians still talk about it. Come; we must go to our favorite jeweler in all of Italy."

We reach the main *piazza* and walk into a jewelry shop. Francesca tells me how her husband always surprises her with a gift when they come here which they do quite frequently. As we enter, a tall man swoops down upon her, gathers her up in his embrace and starts to kiss her face all over as he speaks to her in Italian.

"Oh, Giovanni, it's good to see you, too, *bello*."

She introduces me to Giovanni and tells me he is a fourth-generation coral carver and jeweler and has created many things for the Vatican. He's dressed in an expensive suit and shuffles over to me with his cane, a slight hump on his back. He kisses my hand and leads me through a doorway into the back of the shop as Francesca leaves to find her husband who was trailing behind us with the others.

Once inside, Giovanni shows me his family's creations and collection. In both Italian and English, he takes out the cases that are lining the walls and explains that his family has made carved crucifixes and other sacred objects for the *Vaticano* for generations. He shows me an 18-kt gold crucifix encased in glass, a papal seal on it, which was recently returned to them after the last Pope's death.

Before I'm finished admiring it, he takes my hand and we move the length of the room to another doorway. As we enter, I realize this room is as big as a warehouse. There are cabinets, tables, cases and boxes everywhere. There must be thousands of religious artifacts—all made of gold, silver, bone or coral. He opens a drawer in a large cabinet and shows me its contents. There are jeweled necklaces, rings and bracelets, and statues of saints including Antonio and Francesco.

He tells me the history of each work of art, who it was made for and which family member made it. I linger before a statue of San Francesco. Giovanni sees me and moves to another case. He pulls open a drawer and carefully picks out a small case with a papal seal on it. Inside is a piece of the cloak San Francesco wore along with one of his teeth. I touch the outside of the bag and my eyes well up with tears as if he is right here beside me. I'm speechless as Giovanni moves me from one drawer to another showing me similar packages. I am overwhelmed because this one belongs to Francesco or because I feel as if I'm in the Vatican. It has been a sacred gift to be able to view these pieces.

Once we return to the front of the store, Alberto pays for a set of 18K gold and lapis earrings for Francesca. They are lovely, made of rows of little round lapis balls laced onto long golden strings. I take control of my emotions and tell her they are beautiful.

"*Buona sera, bella,*" the jeweler says to me as he kisses my cheeks and squeezes my hands. It's as if we have become intimate, our hearts coming together in a sacred way. I know he felt my love for Francesco and I am grateful that he allowed me privacy to weep openly.

"*Molto grazie.* I am honored by you." I thank him and bow slightly, although I don't know why, only that I want to. I walk quietly with the group as I contemplate this place. Is all of Italy blessed with the saints and every religious being who ever walked? Were they all born here?

Joseph interrupts my thoughts.

"Are you sad, doll?"

"No, just a religious experience I guess you could say."

He takes my arm in his and kisses my face, and we walk in silence as if he knows it's something I'm yearning for in this moment. After a time, he speaks.

"That's what I love about you, Roxanna. You're not afraid to be who you are or express your emotions."

I have no response so I squeeze his hand instead. What another great gift to come all the way to Italy to find Joseph. I feel as if we've been friends forever and that I can tell him anything. I make a note to myself that I want to talk with him about Natale ... if we ever have the time.

We stop and mail postcards before going back to the ship for the night. I mail one to Elana and my boys, but not to Natale. My letter to him should have arrived by now. I wonder how it was received.

It's mid-week in Rome and Natale has picked up his mail. He's on his way to work so he tosses it carelessly into the bag on the back of his scooter without even looking at the envelopes. With only a quick thought, he decides to open them tonight when he returns from work.

Once he finishes his shift, he sits at the restaurant until 2:00 a.m. sharing drinks and conversation with his friends. After all, there is no one waiting for him. He has once again settled into his life now that his heart has finished with Rosanna.

When he arrives home, he parks the scooter and takes his bag into the house. Then he retires to the *terrazzo* with a shot of grappa and a cigarette. He sees her letter and is shocked that she has written. Nervously, he fumbles to open it, wild thoughts in his head. Has she gone back to America? Met someone else? He tries to swallow as he opens the fine paper. It is brief, only two short paragraphs.

He doesn't sleep this night.

CHAPTER 46

Our yacht is anchored between Amalfi and Positano. Before us lies the little town of Praiano which is sprawled out over the base of Monte Sant'Angelo. Alberto points toward land.

"Left is Vettica Maggiore and to the right is Praiano." He is dreamy-eyed as if he has fond memories. Francesca squeezes his hand and kisses him.

"*Chi vuol vivere sano, la mane a Vettica, la sera a Praiano.* Do you know what this means, Roxanna?"

Of course, I don't.

"It means that for a healthy life, morning hours must be spent in Vettica and evenings in Praiano." He laughs. "It's how the Italians explain a happy life. I used to come here in the early 1970s. This was the 'in place' to be then. Film stars came here to be seen. And more importantly, this is where I took my darling Francesca when we were very young. We try to come back here whenever the Africana is open, which is only three months out of the year."

"Yes, except last year. We missed coming here because we were away for most of the summer. It's good to be back," Francesca adds with a smile.

A small boat carries us to the cave that leads us into Africana. Joseph is beside me squeezing my hand, as excited as a boy of fifteen anticipating his first kiss. We step inside and it's as if I'm in an aquarium surrounded by walls of water. The nightclub consists of two caves—one for the DJ and the other for the main bar and dance floor. Even the floor beneath our feet is a window to the sea, fish swimming below us! The scene and the music are otherworldly.

The lighting in the nightclub is an opalescent electric blue reminding me of the Blue Grotto on Capri. This, along with the rock walls, the sea and how we have arrived has left me breathless. How much more can a heart take? I have had so many extraordinary adventures since I've arrived in Italy.

The mix of Buddha Bar and electronic dance music draws me back. I'm not sure I remember how to dance but my body wants to move. I pull Joseph to the floor and he is a willing partner. After thirty minutes, I pull Joseph to a table and remove my sandals.

"Oh, my feet."

"I could never understand how women dance in those shoes. They have a martini called the Africana made with Amarula. It's sort of a chocolate martini made with this liquor from Africa that you can't buy in the States. Want one?"

"Yes, please."

I watch young couples on the dance floor. I don't remember ever dancing with Ed, except at our wedding. He was always the guy who sat at the table watching everyone else, said he had two left feet. Joseph returns and interrupts my thoughts. He places two oversized martini glasses on the table. We toast and taste the sweet, chocolaty drink and both agree it's decadent and delicious.

Soon, I'm asked to dance by an Italian man so I do. We share a few dances and then I sit with Alberto and Francesca. I sigh and think that my age is finally catching up with me and my feet.

Around 3:00 a.m. the dancers stop and three local fishermen enter the nightclub and dredge a sinkhole in the middle of the floor. They proceed to pull in the nets filled with fish. Alberto explains that this is a tradition at the Africana and the fish will go to the local restaurants for the day's menu. I'm amazed and have been giggling for hours, giddy with delight and disbelief.

Joseph introduces me to Luciano, a beautiful young man. His

thick, dark hair, strong nose and a sculpted face make me think he's of Italian and Greek descent. They dance all night and he asks Luciano to come back to the ship with us.

At 6:00 a.m. we board the tender. Joseph tells Luciano about all the amenities, preparing him for what to expect while Francesca and Alberto laugh.

Too tired to wash my face or brush my teeth, I fall into bed and quickly into a deep sleep, only to be awakened by a knock on my door. It seems like only minutes have passed but it's late-morning.

"Roxanna, we're leaving for Positano in thirty minutes. Come up for breakfast," Joseph calls to me from the other side of my door.

"Go away. I need more sleep."

I'm exhausted from this lifestyle!

"It's already noon. Time to rise, Roxy. We'll meet you on the upper deck," says Joseph, Luciano laughing beside him.

I am reminded of how short our cruise is and don't want to miss a thing. Who knows if I will ever again have an experience such as this. I pull myself from the bed and quickly shower and dress.

"*Buon giorno*, Roxanna. Did you sleep well?" Francesca is glowing in her yellow caftan and matching sandals. She doesn't seem a bit tired. She must have a secret.

"It was not enough," I moan. I turn to the waiter, "*Espresso*, please." I sound like a princess, but tell myself it's acceptable behavior for a woman on a superyacht who is being waited on as if she were someone important.

"We will return to the ship in time for a nap today. Don't worry. It was fun, no?" Alberto asks affectionately.

"Yes, it was amazing. Thank you so much for inviting me on this cruise." I gush and can't thank him and Francesca enough.

"It is our pleasure. You are welcome anytime. I enjoy your company and I know Alberto does too." Francesca continues. "Roxanna, you are sincere and authentic people are hard to find in our circle. We have lots of money as most of our friends do and for some, the money overshadows everything. These are the ones who don't like themselves enough so they try to find an image they want to project to others."

How insightful, I think.

"Francesca, you're the one who is unpretentious and real but thank you for the compliment."

Joseph and Luciano arrive at the table and interrupt our conversation.

"We had to buy Luciano something to wear today since he's coming with us." Luciano smiles at his good fortune.

"Where do you live, Luciano?" I ask.

"I live in Napoli in the winter and in the summers I live in Amalfi where I work at a *Ristorante Eolo*."

We continue to talk through our meal and I decide I like him. I can tell he has a heart like Joseph's; I can see it in his eyes. And they are enamored with each other. This might be serious.

We motor toward Positano which is awash with color. The brightly-hued villas are set into the mountain. Fruit trees, vineyards and gardens cover the properties. The beach is filled with rows of green umbrellas that shade the orange beach chairs beneath them. On the water, rows of little boats sit, rocking on the sea.

We visit the *Chiesa di Santa Maria Assunta* with its Mallorca-tiled dome of yellow and green. Then we browse the shops and walk through the alleyways and paths that lead us through a maze of stone passageways and ancient buildings. I feel as if I'm back in time, a thousand years ago, in this medieval village. Soon, we board the tender and travel along the coast for a short distance. We come upon three islets and cruise in between them where the sea water is aqua.

"You know of the sirens, Roxanna?" Alberto asks.

"Yes, I do. The Rock of the Sirens sits in Marina Piccola in Capri."

"Yes, the legend is particularly strong throughout this area. Look there." He points toward the peninsula. "That shrine was dedicated to these winged sea deities. And here," he points to three little islands, "are the *Sirenuse* and are believed to hold the three bodies of the sirens—Ligeia, Leucosia and Parthenope. Do you know the story, *The Odyssey?*"

We say yes, but he tells it anyway and I don't mind one bit because he is a master storyteller.

"Men who died in these waters through the centuries were believed to have been hypnotized by these creatures with their mystical powers. I think they were probably tired, drunk or mesmerized by the beautiful Italian women here." He laughs hardily at his own joke.

"*La Grotta dello Smeraldo,* the Emerald Grotto." Alberto points to a cave in the distance as we motor south. He tells us that the green color is created by the reflection of the sunlight, the water and the cave. His description is more scientific than mine but I am seduced by its color and his voice has melted away.

We arrive off the coast of Amalfi which is as colorful as Positano. On the sand, numerous cabanas rest dressed in white and green. In the water, rows of boats are lined up covered with bright blue tarps.

Once on land, we walk past the Amalfi pier and into the square which holds a monument of Flavio Gioia, inventor of the compass. We stroll down the main street and come to *Piazza Duomo,* a fountain of Saint Andrew, a patron saint of the Amalfi Coast and saint of fisherman sitting in its center.

We don't stop because Alberto is on a mission to show us the great church before us. We make the trek up the fifty-seven steps which lead to the atrium. I will not go into the entire history of this place but if you are thinking of visiting Amalfi, its story will interest you. Today, it's known as the Cathedral of Amalfi dedicated to Saint Andrew. Originally, it was called the Church of Assunta and was dedicated to the Blessed Mother.

The initial structure, built in in 987 by Duca Mansone I, was constructed in Arab-Norman Romanesque architectural style. Over the last two millennia, it has been expanded and remodeled using Byzantine, Gothic and Baroque architectural styles. In my opinion, it is one of Italy's most resplendent architectural wonders.

My breath leaves me yet again. It is massive and magnificent. The main door is a grand work of art—bronze that was cast in Constantinople in 1060. The atrium is designed in a unique pattern of Moorish arches that sit upon marble columns.

I study the sacred artistic works before me—paintings, sculptures, frescoes and bas reliefs—some created in the 4th century, and others in the 13th through 18th centuries. The ceilings and walls are colored in gold and white tones. In every time-period, something was bestowed upon the church.

We come upon a 17th century bust of Saint Andrew in gold-plated copper. It's so life-like; it's as if he had been dropped into a vat of liquid gold. There is so much to see and of course, I must sit for a bit to settle the beating of my heart.

I move from one place to another, not wanting to miss a thing. I follow a passageway and move through doorways until I come to the Paradise Cloister. Originally used as a burial ground for noble families in Amalfi, it's a four-sided portico with an arched roof and covered by cross-vaults. Delicately designed ogival arches sit atop small marble columns along the outer wall. In the center is a beautiful garden. I move away from the crowds so I have space to enjoy its tranquility.

After some time, we leave to find a cafe and have a light bite. Everyone is exceptionally quiet, I am sure because they are overwhelmed and feel as blessed as I do. Soon, we pile into the tender and motor our way back up the coast toward Positano and the yacht.

Dinner is a quiet event and afterwards, I choose to retire and watch the sea. Tomorrow morning, we will head back to Capri and I have much to do when I return. I have been away far too long.

In the quietness, I realize I have not yet shared my story of Natale with Joseph. Where has the time gone? I will do so when we see each other again. Let him enjoy his time with Luciano.

My last thoughts before I drift off to sleep are of my boys and of Natale.

CHAPTER 47
CAPRI, ITALY

Our superyacht has anchored in Marina Grande. There is quite a commotion as we all stand on deck hugging and kissing each other goodbye. A few couples who are close friends with Alberto and Francesco have decided to stay on and will travel to Monaco with them.

"Francesca, thank you so much for opening your home ... I mean your yacht to me. I cannot thank you enough for your kindness and generosity." I hug her tightly and kiss her cheeks.

"Roxanna, thank you for sharing your effervescence with us. It wouldn't have been the same without you. We will do this again."

Alberto grabs me and pulls me in for a bear hug.

"Ah, *bella donna*, thank you for coming."

"Thank you for having me. This trip has been wonderful. And you are a great storyteller. *Molto grazie*, thank you for everything."

"Yes, he can tell stories, this one." Francesca kisses his face.

"Ah, and I enjoy telling them," he responds. "We will see each other again soon, Roxanna."

"Hey, doll. Are you going to leave without saying goodbye?" I grab him for a big hug.

"Joseph, thank you so much. And I'm so happy for you both. I knew it would happen."

"It was magical for sure ... as if he was dropped from the sky."

Luciano grins and gently moves Joseph to the side so he can embrace me.

"Roxanna, it was nice to meet you." He kisses me.

"Are you two going back to the villa?" I ask.

"We've decided to go on to Monaco with Alberto and Francesca. Why not?" Their eyes meet and lock.

"Good for you. Enjoy yourselves. Call me when you get back to the island. Love you."

"Love you, too, doll."

I say goodbye to the others I have met and disembark. My heart is full.

Before I board the *autobus* to Anacapri, there is something I need to do.

I ride the *funicular* from the port to Capri and walk out into the *Piazza Umberto*. Only a few tourists are milling about since it's time for lunch. I sit on the bench and drop my things beside me. The sun spills its light onto the Mediterranean, a sight I will never tire of. The heat of the day lulls me into a quiet place and I close my eyes.

"You have come." Francesco is sitting next to me.

"Yes, I've come to thank you," I say.

"For what, my child? It was you, not me who chose your next steps. I was only there to remind you that you could."

I have no response. Pure joy has filled my being. We continue to sit together and enjoy each other's company.

"Roxanna, you have found inner peace. You haven't had that for a very long time. You have picked up all the pieces of yourself that you dropped along the way. Now you are who you are and you are complete. There is nothing more you need to search for. Follow your heart. Don't think about how to do it or what it will look like. In every moment, stay present and forgive your innocence. And as you go through life, forgive everyone else's innocence as well. We are all doing the best we can."

Ancient tears spill down my face as I laugh and cry at the same time.

"And by the way, you're not crazy. You are more conscious

than you think. And give yourself some credit. It's not easy being human." He looks at me with his soulful eyes.

"Thank you, Francesco. I love you."

"I love you more than you know, Roxanna. Go and finish creating your life!" He melts away before my eyes.

As I walk the distance to my villa, my midnight blue dress draped across my arm, I review these last few days. Seems like a dream.

I walk past the man who has been building a new rock wall around his property and notice it's now finished. He exits his gate with a wheelbarrow full of tree branches and weeds and smiles at me. And for the first time, he says, "*Journo.*"

"*Journo.*" I smile.

Interesting coincidence that we are both complete—he with his rock wall and me with my search to find out who I am. What now? I have unfinished business with Natale. Once I get to the villa, I will have uninterrupted time to listen to my heart and let it guide me.

My mind flashes back to the woman I was when I arrived on Capri. She no longer exists. I laugh out loud for the 100th time since I became Roxanna ... or Rosanna. I remember crossing the Mediterranean on the little boat with those two crazy guys ... the song of the sirens ... and mouth-to-mouth with Peter. I think of Antonio, that silly young boy ... Then my heart skips a beat as I think of Raffaello. I say a word of thanks to Enrico for giving me the villa that I love so much, and I think of Mario and Louisa, Marcello and Donata, and baby Luca. I also think of Federico, Nuncio and my other friends.

Then I smile as I remember Bruno and our tortured souls that were healed on the mount at the *fortino*. I shall never forget him ... or Valentino ... or Elana, Alberto and Francesca, Joseph and Luciano, Christos ... or my pirates. I bend over and belly laugh; a man stops on the path, a concerned look on his face. I collect myself and smile at him.

I remember my encounters with Helios and San Francesco and Apollo. They all lead to San Michele, Mich-I-el-Rah. I breathe in deeply and happy tears begin to flow.

I walk through the gate of *Mio Paridiso* and drop my bag and my dress. I hum the tune of Vittorio's "Tu Sei" and twirl and twirl, heart wide open, giving thanks to all that is. Then I blow kisses to *Monte* Vesuvio and the *Mediterraneo*, my father and mother.

"Thank you," I say as I look out to sea.

"Mom!" I stop.

"Mom!"

My boys ... my, how they've grown these last few months. Josh, now seventeen, has sprouted up to the height of his father. He could be a hologram of him. Devon, on the other hand, at sixteen resembles me. I have missed them. I run to them as if they were still small.

"Are you really here? How did you get here?" I hug them fiercely.

Ed enters the gate behind them.

"Deborah ... I mean Roxanna." He laughs nervously.

Ed seems older than I remember, his hair now laced with silver. He has let himself go, no longer lean and muscular. He was always fanatical about his weight.

"You look good. Actually, you look great." He ogles me from head to toe.

"Thanks. I'm so happy to see you all, but I'm confused. Why are you here?"

Ed comes to me, grabs me in a bear hug and plants a big kiss on my lips.

In the next instant, Natale rushes toward us from the villa, fists curled ready to fight Ed. They stand toe-to-toe, sizing each other up. The boys and I move away and wonder what will unfold.

"She's mine! Get away from her!" Natale says angrily.

"Who the hell are you? She's my wife!"

Ed raises his hands in front of his face like a fighter. He moves toward Natale. They both start throwing punches and Natale hits Ed in the nose, which is now bleeding. Ed falls to the ground and grabs his face and the boys run to their father. Natale comes to me and puts his arms around me, holding me tightly.

"I come as soon as I receive your letter," he says nervously. "I sleep here outside in the chair for two nights. I wait for you to return." Natale points toward the *portico* and the lounge chairs.

I pull myself from him and kneel to tend to Ed.

"Ed, I'm sorry. This is Natale. Are you okay?"

Stunned, he tries to collect himself.

"Where's Cynthia?" I'm puzzled by all this.

Ed starts crying like a baby.

"She had an affair with my business partner. I caught them having sex at work." He starts to wail.

"God, Ed! In front of the boys? They didn't need to hear that." Josh and Devon are wide-eyed, their mouths agape.

"I came to tell you how sorry I am for hurting you. I was so stupid. You were the best thing that ever happened to me. I love you, Cookie. Will you marry me?"

Natale rushes to my side and grabs my waist.

"Rosanna, I came to tell you I will move to America for you and the boys. Or I will move here with you. I will go where you go. I love you. Will you marry me?" He's down on one knee before me.

Ed jumps up forgetting his pain. He rushes toward Natale and pushes him. Both start rolling around on the ground and Josh and Devon are frozen in place.

"STOP! Both of you! For the love of God, act like grown men!" I push them apart.

"I am sorry, Rosanna." Natale lowers his head.

"I'm sorry, Cookie."

"I'm not your damned Cookie anymore. Don't ever call me that again!"

"I ... I'm sorry." Ed lowers his head and smooths out his shirt.

I turn toward the boys.

"Come, you two. Let's see if we can find you something to eat. Are you hungry?"

I stop for a moment, turn back and address Natale and Ed.

"You two stay here and apologize to each other. You need to cool off. Do not come into the house until I say you can."

I turn to the boys and point across the bay.

"Boys, look. That's Mount Vesuvius over there. Would you like to climb it with me?

"Yeah, mom, that'd be cool."

My sons pick fresh vegetables from the garden and I prepare

dinner. By 6:00 p.m. pasta primavera and a salad are ready.

Enrico stops by to welcome me home with two bottles of wine from his own private stock. I introduce him to everyone and he leaves us to enjoy our meal. Devon sets the table outside and Josh goes to fetch Ed and Natale.

I have so much to think about ...

Everyone seats themselves at the table on the *terrazzo*.

"I have an announcement to make," I say with confidence.

Natale's and Ed's eyes are fixed upon me.

"Ed, I am not coming back to you. How could you even ask after all you put me through? Our marriage has been over for a long time. You hurt me so badly; you never gave me a second thought. Then, you married her. Then you come here expecting that everything with us could go back to normal after she did to you what you did to me. Sounds crazy, doesn't it?"

He lowers his head.

"And after all of it, I still forgave you. But I will not start up another relationship with you. We will co-parent these boys as we have for the last few years. End of discussion."

Ed bursts into tears and starts sobbing loudly.

"Ed, for God's sake. Get hold of yourself!"

Natale pats him on the back, offering support.

"I'm, I'm sorry ... must be jetlag." He continues to wail, gulping in between. Natale hands him his napkin and Ed blows his nose.

I turn to Natale.

"Natale, we will have a private discussion later." He is bewildered but stays quiet.

"But I'm happy you came," I say with a smile.

At this, his dimples open wide for me. My breath catches and for a moment, I realize how much I have missed him.

We raise our glasses.

"Saluté, to life!"

THE END

EPILOGUE

Ah, yes, you are probably wondering what happened between Rosanna and Natale -

After dinner that night, Ed and the boys checked into a hotel. Natale listened as Roxanna told him how, over the last few months, she had gathered all those pieces of herself that she had lost before she met him. She told him she loved him but that their time together was far too short to make the decision of a lifetime so soon, especially since their lives were on two separate continents. When he tried to speak, she asked him not to interrupt her until she was finished. *She's a feisty one. Oh, how she has grown.*

She told him she had decided to stay on the island of Capri indefinitely and that Enrico was willing to rent her the villa long-term. She also said she would be happy to travel back and forth to Rome to spend time with him and explore their relationship further. *It only took a few months before they tired of being apart.*

He moved into the villa with Roxanna. Enrico recommended him for a job as a waiter at the Caesar Augustus Hotel. The world had open up for her. Anything she wished for in her reality, she manifested. *Yes, she was a good student ...*

Federico offered her space in his studio so she could paint and sell her masterpieces to the tourists. Art lovers came from everywhere to view her paintings. Alberto hired her to design a line of women's eveningwear for his company and it was such a success that she continues to design for him.

For the first year, Ed accompanied the boys to the island for their winter and spring holidays. They stayed at the villa with their mother and Natale while Ed rented a room in town. Eventually, he fell in love with Maria. You remember ... she owned the pizzeria in town and wanted to fall in love with an America man believing they made the best husbands. We will see how that goes as they recently got engaged. *Ah, yes, the magical isle weaves a spell on everyone who arrives on its shores ...*

Josh and Devon thought Natale was cool. He taught them Italian and schooled them on how to date girls with Italian mothers. They climbed Mount Vesuvius together and visited the ruins of Pompeii.

After a year together, Roxanna asked Natale to marry her. *The woman is unstoppable.* He was so surprised and so happy, he wept like a baby. *Ah, Italian men ... they have the hearts of women ...*

Joseph asked Luciano to move into his villa on Capri to take care of the place while he traveled to America on business, and of course live with him full-time. When Joseph heard that Roxanna and Natale were engaged, he called Alberto and Francesca to tell them the news. Together, they planned a surprise engagement party at Joseph's villa. Elana, needing a holiday from her life in Venezia, decided to surprise Roxanna on Capri. As luck would have it, she arrived in Anacapri the day of their party! It didn't take long for the island to seduce her and break the spell she had been living under. She met Massimo and fell in love. Now you will find her singing at the Caesar Augustus Hotel.

After becoming engaged, Natale and Roxanna traveled to Torino to visit his parents. His mother fell in love with her future daughter-in-law and cried nonstop with happiness which made Natale cry. *Now we know where he gets it from.*

The wedding was a huge four-day event off the Amalfi Coast on Alberto's and Francesca's superyacht. By the way, Alberto designed her gown and Natale's suit. Both were stunning. Josh and Devon gave their mother away as Natale wept like any healthy Italian male. *It was comical watching him wail with joy like a newborn baby. My, he was smitten.*

Ed and Maria, and a group of giggling American female friends from the States came. You know the ones ... they had been living vicariously through Roxanna's emails. Of course, most of them were scouting out the men, expecting to find their own Italian fairytale.

Bruno came with his new wife, the girl he had met after his time with Roxanna at the fort. Natale's parents came and were enchanted by the island as they had honeymooned there fifty years ago.

Donata, Marcello, Mario, Louisa and Luca all helped with the planning so Roxanna's mother and father only had to show up. Naturally, Luca entertained the guests with his cherubic face and *Napoletano* gestures.

Ah, and Valentino ... he sent a letter to Roxanna telling her he had finished the sculpture. She called when she received it and told him she was getting married so he invited her and Natale to Florence to stay in the castle for their honeymoon.

But it didn't stop there. After the wedding party and many, many glasses of Krug 2000 Clos du Mesnil—France's finest Blanc de Blancs style champagne supplied by the Brunos, Roxanna shared her story of being kidnapped by modern-day pirates.

Natale, outraged screamed, "*Damned Greci pirati! Sono malvagi!* Damned those Greek pirates! I will find them! Bad! They are very bad!" After everyone calmed down, Alberto excitedly offered to take them on a cruise to the Cyclades in search of them.

And the painting of Natale? It is his prized possession and hangs in the villa. When she gave it to him, of course, he wept.

Roxanna, welcome to your new life. You deserve it. You had the courage to face all those dark parts of your psyche and heal them. Not everyone is strong enough or brave enough. But you were. Remember, you can have anything you want in this life. You only need to ask for it and do a little work. I will always watch over you, my Beloved.

I knew your name would change you forever!

I Am Eternally Yours –

Mich-I-EL-Rah

ABOUT THE AUTHOR

Gail Michael has been writing since she was a child. She has written fiction and non-fiction, poetry, articles and travel blogs. In 1998, her poetry was published by Noble House and the Amherst Society. Gail wrote and published her first non-fiction book in 2002, *I Am a Thousand Winds That Blow,* the story of her mother's death and how their last year together healed their tempestuous relationship.

In 2005, after living in Italy for half a year, Gail released *The Passions of Roxanna* (now out of print). *Unveiling Rosanna* is a rewrite and revision of that book.

Her desire has always been to inspire and entertain her readers with her thought-provoking written works. In her spare time, Gail loves to travel, sculpt and write.

Connect with the author at
www.gailmichael.com

Proof

Made in the USA
Columbia, SC
03 October 2017